TERRORISM

Understanding the New Security Challenges

TERRORISM
Understanding the New Security Challenges

Niranjan Dass

MD PUBLICATIONS PVT LTD
NEW DELHI
www.mdppl.com

Published by :

MD Publications Pvt Ltd
"MD House", 11, Darya Ganj,
New Delhi - 110 002
Phone : +91-11-45355555
E-mail : contact@mdppl.com
Website: www.mdppl.com

ISBN : 978-81-7533-365-9

Published and Printed by Mr. Pranav Gupta on behalf of **MD Publications Pvt Ltd** at Mohit Enterprises, Delhi.

PREFACE

There is no universally accepted definition of terrorism and even when people agree on a definition of terrorism, they sometimes disagree about whether or not the definition fits a particular incident. In order to understand terrorism, one must assess different views of what exactly constitutes terrorism. Reaching a general conclusion on the definition of terrorism has generated much debate in the social sciences and internationally, no single definition seems to satisfy the wide interpretation of what specifically is terrorism. Most of the formal definitions of terrorism have some common characteristics: a fundamental motive to make political/ societal changes; the use of violence or illegal force; attacks on civilian targets by "non-state"/"Sub-national actors"; and the goal of affecting society.

Terrorism is an anxiety-inspiring method of repeated violent action, employed by (semi-)clandestine individual, group, or state actors, for idiosyncratic, criminal, or political reasons, whereby in contrast to assassination the direct targets of violence are not the main targets. The immediate human victims of violence are generally chosen randomly or selectively (representative or symbolic targets) from a target population and serve as message generators. Threat and violence-based communication processes between terrorist organization, imperiled victims, and main targets are used to manipulate the main target (audience), turning it into a target of terror, a target of demands, or a target of attention, depending on whether intimidation, coercion, or propaganda is primarily sought.

Terrorism is illegal violence or threatened violence directed against human or nonhuman objects, provided that it: (1) was undertaken or ordered with a view to altering or maintaining at least one putative norm in at least one particular territorial unit or population: (2) had secretive, furtive, and/or clandestine features that were expected by the participants to conceal their personal identity and/or their future location; (3) was not undertaken or ordered to further the permanent defense of some area; (4) was not conventional warfare and because of their concealed personal identity, concealment of their future location, their threats, and/or their spatial mobility, the participants perceived themselves as less vulnerable to conventional military action; and (5) was perceived by the participants as contributing to the normative goal previously described (supra) by inculcating fear of violence in persons (perhaps an indefinite category of them) other than the immediate target of the actual or threatened violence and/or by publicizing some cause.

We may therefore now attempt to define terrorism as the deliberate creation and exploitation of fear through violence or the threat of violence in the pursuit of political change. All terrorist acts involve violence or the threat of violence. Terrorism is specifically designed to have far-reaching psychological effects beyond the immediate victims or object of the terrorist attack. It is meant to instil fear within, and thereby intimidate, a wider 'target audience' that might include a rival ethnic or religious group, an entire country, a national government or political party or public opinion in general. Terrorism is designed to create power where there is none or to consolidate power where there is very little. Through the publicity generated by their violence, terrorists seek to obtain the leverage, influence and power they otherwise lack to effect political change on either a local or an international scale.

I am very grateful to Mr. Pranav Gupta, Director of MD Publications Pvt. Ltd., New Delhi, for his kind cooperation and support for this book.

Niranjan Dass

Contents

1

Understanding Terrorism: Challenges and Issues

Introduction

The definition of terrorism has proved controversial. Various legal systems and government agencies use different definitions of "terrorism". Moreover, the International community has been slow to formulate a universally agreed, legally binding definition of this crime. These difficulties arise from the fact that the term "terrorism" is politically and emotionally charged.

Angus Martyn in a briefing paper for the Australian Parliament has stated that "The international community has never succeeded in developing an accepted comprehensive definition of terrorism. During the 1970s and 1980s, the United Nations attempts to define the term foundered mainly due to differences of opinion between various members about the use of violence in the context of conflicts over national liberation and self-determination." These divergences have made it impossible to conclude a Comprehensive Convention on International Terrorism that incorporates a single, all-encompassing, legally binding, criminal law definition of terrorism.

In the meantime, the international community adopted a series of sectoral conventions that define and criminalize various types of terrorist activities. In addition, since 1994, the United Nations General Assembly has condemned terrorist acts using the following political description of terrorism: "Criminal acts intended or calculated to provoke a state of terror in the general public, a group of persons or particular persons for political purposes are in any circumstance unjustifiable, whatever the considerations of a political, philosophical, ideological, racial, ethnic, religious or any other nature that may be invoked to justify them."

A 2003 study by Jeffrey Record for the US Army quoted a source (Schmid and Jongman 1988) that counted 109 definitions of terrorism that covered a total of 22 different definitional elements. Record continued "Terrorism expert Walter Laqueur also has counted over 100 definitions and concludes that the 'only general characteristic generally agreed upon is that terrorism involves violence and the threat of violence.' Yet terrorism is hardly the only enterprise involving violence and the threat of violence. So does war, coercive diplomacy, and bar room brawls".

As Bruce Hoffman has noted: "terrorism is a pejorative term. It is a word with intrinsically negative connotations that is generally applied to one's enemies and opponents, or to those with whom one disagrees and would otherwise prefer to ignore. Hence the decision to call someone or label some organization 'terrorist' becomes almost unavoidably subjective, depending largely on whether one sympathizes with or opposes the person/group/cause concerned. If one identifies with the victim of the violence, for example, then the act is terrorism. If, however, one identifies with the perpetrator, the violent act is regarded in a more sympathetic, if not positive (or, at the worst, an ambivalent) light; and it is not terrorism." For this and for political reasons, many news sources avoid using this term, opting instead for less accusatory words like "bombers", "militants", etc.

In many countries, acts of terrorism are legally distinguished from criminal acts done for other purposes.

The term "terrorism" comes from French *terrorisme*, from Latin: 'terror', "great fcar", "drcad", related to the Latin verb *terrere*, "to frighten". The *terror cimbricus* was a panic and state of emergency in Rome in response to the approach of warriors of the Cimbri tribe in 105BC. The French National Convention declared in September, 1793 that "terror is the order of the day". The period 1793–94 is referred to as *La Terreur* (Reign of Terror). Maximilien Robespierre, a leader in the French revolution proclaimed in 1794 that "Terror is nothing other than justice, prompt, severe, inflexible."

The Committee of Public Safety agents that enforced the policies of "The Terror" were referred to as "Terrorists". The word "terrorism" was first recorded in English-language dictionaries in 1798 as meaning "systematic use of terror as a policy".

Although the Reign of Terror was imposed by the French government, in modern times "terrorism" usually refers to the killing of innocents by a private group in such a way as to create a media spectacle. This meaning originated with Russian radicals in the 1870s. Sergey Nechayev, who founded People's Retribution in 1869, described himself as a "terrorist". German anarchist writer Johann Most helped popularize the modern sense of the word by dispensing "advice for terrorists" in the 1880s.

International Law

Need to define Terrorism in International Criminal Law: Ben Saul has noted that a "A combination of pragmatic and principled arguments supports the case for defining terrorism in international law", including the need to condemn violations to Human rights, to protect the state and deliberative politics, to differentiate public and private Violence, and to ensure International Peace and Security.

Carlos Diaz-Paniagua, who coordinated the negotiations of the proposed United Nations Comprehensive Convention on International Terrorism, noted, on his part, the need to provide a precise definition of terrorist activities in international law: "Criminal law has three purposes: to declare that a conduct is forbidden, to prevent it, and to express society's condemnation for the wrongful acts. The symbolic, normative role of criminalization is of particular importance in the case of terrorism. The criminalization of terrorist acts expresses society's repugnance at them, invokes social censure and shame, and stigmatizes those who commit them. Moreover, by creating and reaffirming values, criminalization may serve, in the long run, as a deterrent to terrorism, as those values are internalized." Thus, international criminal law treaties that seek to prevent, condemn and punish terrorist activities, require precise definitions:

"The definition of the offence in criminal law treaty plays several roles. First and foremost, it has the symbolic, normative role of expressing society's condemnation of the forbidden acts. Second, it facilitates agreement. Since states tend to be reluctant to undertake stringent obligations in matters related to the exercise of their domestic jurisdiction, a precise definition of the crime, which restricts the scope of those obligations, makes agreement less costly. Third, it provides an inter-subjective basis for the homogeneous application of the treaty's obligations on judicial and police cooperation. This function is of particular importance in extradition treaties because, to grant an extradition, most legal systems require that the crime be punishable both in the requesting state and the requested state. Fourth, it helps states to enact domestic legislation to criminalize and punish the wrongful acts defined in the treaty in conformity with their human rights' obligations. The principle of *nullum crimen sine lege* requires, in particular, that states define precisely which acts are prohibited before anyone can be prosecuted or punished for committing those same acts."

Saul noted in this sense that, missing a generally agreed, all-encompasing, definition of the term:

> *'Terrorism` currently lacks the precision, objectivity and certainty demanded by legal discourse. Criminal law strives to avoid emotive terms to prevent prejudice to an accused, and shuns ambiguous or subjective terms as incompatible with the principle of non-retroactivity. If the law is to admit the term, advance definition is essential on grounds of fairness, and it is not sufficient to leave definition to the unilateral interpretations of States. Legal definition could plausibly retrieve terrorism from the ideological quagmire, by severing an agreed legal meaning from the remainder of the elastic, political concept. Ultimately it must do so without criminalizing legitimate violent resistance to oppressive regimes and becoming complicit in that oppression.*

Obstacles to a Comprehensive Definition

Diaz-Paniagua has noted that, in order to "create an effective legal regime against terrorism, it would be necessary to formulate a comprehensive definition of that crime that, on the one hand, provides the strongest moral condemnation to terrorist activities while, on the other hand, has enough precision to permit the prosecution of criminal activities without condemning acts that should be deemed to be legitimate. Nonetheless, due to major divergences at the international level on the question of the legitimacy of the use of violence for political purposes, either by states or by self-determination and revolutionary groups, this has not yet been possible." In this sense, Bassiouni notes:

> *"to define "terrorism" in a way that is both all-inclusive and unambiguous is very difficult, if not impossible. One of the principal difficulties lies in the fundamental values at stake in the acceptance or rejection of terror-inspiring violence as means of accomplishing a given goal. The obvious and well-known range of views on these issues are what makes an internationally accepted specific definition of what is loosely called "terrorism," a largely impossible*

undertaking. That is why the search for and internationally agreed upon definition may well be a futile and unnecessary effort."

Sami Zeidan, a Lebanese diplomat and scholar, explained the political reasons underlying the current difficulties to define terrorism as follows:

> *"There is no general consensus on the definition of terrorism. The difficulty of defining terrorism lies in the risk it entails of taking positions. The political value of the term currently prevails over its legal one. Left to its political meaning, terrorism easily falls prey to change that suits the interests of particular states at particular times. The Taliban and Osama bin Laden were once called freedom fighters and backed by the CIA when they were resisting the Soviet occupation of Afghanistan. Now they are on top of the international terrorist lists. Today, the United Nations views Palestinians as freedom fighters, struggling against the unlawful occupation of their land by Israel, and engaged in a long-established legitimate resistance, yet Israel regards them as terrorists. Israel also brands the Hizbullah of Lebanon as a terrorist group, whereas most of the international community regards it as a legitimate resistance group, fighting Israel`s occupation of Southern Lebanon. In fact, the successful ousting of Israeli forces from most of the South by the Hizbollah in 2000 made Lebanon the only Arab country to actually defeat the Israeli army. The repercussion of the current preponderance of the political over the legal value of terrorism is costly, leaving the war against terrorism selective, incomplete and ineffective."*

In the same vein, Jason Burke, an expert in radical Islamist activity, said:

> *There are multiple ways of defining terrorism, and all are subjective. Most define terrorism as "the use or threat of serious violence" to advance some kind of "cause". Some state clearly the kinds of group ("sub-national", "non-state") or cause (political, ideological, religious) to which they refer. Others merely rely on the instinct of most people when confronted with innocent civilians being killed or maimed by men armed with explosives, firearms or other weapons. None is satisfactory, and grave problems with the use of the term persist. Terrorism is after all, a tactic. The term "war on terrorism" is thus effectively non-sensical. As there is no space*

here to explore this involved and difficult debate, my preference is, on the whole, for the less loaded term "Militancy". This is not an attempt to condone such actions, merely to analyse them in a clearer way.

The political and emotional conotation of the term "terrorism" make difficult its use in legal discourse. In this sense, Saul notes that:

"Despite the shifting and contested meaning of "terrorism" over time, the peculiar semantic power of the term, beyond its literal signification, is its capacity to stigmatize, delegitimize, denigrate, and dehumanize those at whom it is directed, including political opponents. The term is ideologically and politically loaded; pejorative; implies moral, social, and value judgment; and is "slippery and much-abused." In the absence of a definition of terrorism, the struggle over the representation of a violent act is a struggle over its legitimacy. The more confused a concept, the more it lends itself to opportunistic appropriation."

More recently the 1977 Protocol Additional to the Geneva Conventions of 12 August, 1949, and relating to the Protection of Victims of International Armed Conflicts, which applies in situations Article 1. Paragraph 4 "... in which peoples are fighting against colonial domination and alien occupation and against racist regimes...", contains many ambiguities that cloud the issue of who is or is not a legitimate combatant. Hence depending on the perspective of the state a resistance movements may or may not be labelled terrorist group based on whether the members of a resistance movement are considered lawful or unlawful combatants and their right to resist occupation is recognized. These difficulties have led Pamala Griset to conclude that: "the meaning of terrorism is embeded in a person's or nation's philosophy. Thus, the determination of the "right" definition of terrorism is subjective."

The Sectoral Approach

In order to elaborate an effective legal regime to prevent and punish international terrorism, rather than only working on a single, all-encompassing, comprehensive definition of terrorism, the international community has also adopted a ""sectoral" approach aimed at identifying offences seen as belonging to the activities of terrorists and working out treaties in order to deal with specific categories thereof". The treaties that follow this approach focus on the wrongful nature of terrorist activities rather than on their intent:

On the whole, therefore, the "sectoral" conventions confirm the assumption that some offences can be considered *in themselves* as offences of international concern, irrespective of any "terrorist" intent or purpose. Indeed, the principal merit of the "sectoral approach" is that it avoids the need to define "terrorism" of "terrorist acts" (...) So long as the "sectoral" approach is followed, there is no need to define terrorism; a definition would only be necessary if the punishment of the relevant offences were made conditional on the existence of a specific "terrorist" intent; but this would be counter-productive, inasmuch as it would result in unduly restricting their suppression.

Following this approach, the international community has adopted the following sectoral counter-terrorism conventions, open to the ratification of all states:

- The 1963 Convention on Offences and Certain Other Acts Committed On Board Aircraft
- The 1970 Convention for the Suppression of Unlawful Seizure of Aircraft
- The 1971 Convention for the Suppression of Unlawful Acts Against the Safety of Civil Aviation
- The 1979 Convention on the Physical Protection of Nuclear Material
- The 1988 Protocol for the Suppression of Unlawful Acts of Violence at Airports Serving International Civil Aviation
- The 1988 Convention for the Suppression of Unlawful Acts Against the Safety of Maritime Navigation

- The 1988 Protocol for the Suppression of Unlawful Acts Against the Safety of Fixed Platforms Located on the Continental Shelf
- The 1991 Convention on the Marking of Plastic Explosives for the Purpose of Identification
- The 1997 International Convention for the Suppression of Terrorist Bombings.
- The 1999 International Convention for the Suppression of the Financing of Terrorism
- The 2005 International Convention for the Suppression of Acts of Nuclear Terrorism

Analyzing these treaties, Andrew Byrnes observed that:

> *These conventions, all of which are described by the United Nations as part of its panoply of anti-terrorist measures, share three principal characteristics:*
>
> *(a) they all adopted an "operational definition" of a specific type of terrorist act that was defined without reference to the underlying political or ideological purpose or motivation of the perpetrator of the act this reflected a consensus that there were some acts that were such a serious threat to the interests of all that they could not be justified by reference to such motives;*
>
> *(b) they all focused on actions by non-State actors (individuals and organisations) and the State was seen as an active ally in the struggle against terrorism the question of the State itself as terrorist actor was left largely to one side; and*
>
> *(c) they all adopted a criminal law enforcement model to address the problem, under which States would cooperate in the apprehension and prosecution of those alleged to have committed these crimes.*

Byrnes notes that "this act-specific approach to addressing problems of terrorism in binding international treaties has continued up until relatively recently. Although political denunciation of terrorism in all its forms had continued apace, there had been no successful attempt to define "terrorism" as such in a broad sense that was satisfactory for legal purposes. There was also some scepticism as to the necessity, desirability and feasibility of producing an agreed and workable general definition." Nonetheless, since 2000, the United Nations General Assembly has been working on a proposed Comprehensive Convention on International Terrorism.

Comprehensive Conventions

The international community has worked on two comprehensive counter-terrorism treaties, the League of Nations' 1937 Convention for the prevention and punishment of terrorism, that never entered into force, and the proposed Comprehensive Convention on International Terrorism, that has not been finalized yet.

League of Nations

In the late 1930s, the International community made a first attempt at defining terrorism. Article 1.1 of the League of Nations' 1937 Convention for the prevention and punishment of Terrorism, which never entered into force, defined "acts of terrorism" as "criminal acts directed against a State and intended or calculated to create a state of terror in the minds of particular persons or a group of persons or the general public". Article 2 included as terrorist acts, if they were directed against another state and if they constituted acts of terrorism within the meaning of the definition contained in article 1, the following :

> *"1. Any willful act causing death or grievous bodily harm or loss of liberty to:*
>
> *a) Heads of State, persons exercising the prerogatives of the head of the State, their hereditary or designated successors;*
>
> *b) The wives or husbands or the above-mentioned persons;*
>
> *c) Persons charged with public functions or holding public positions when the act is directed against them in their public capacity.*
>
> *2. Willful destruction of, or damage to, public property or property devoted to a public purpose belonging to or subject to the authority of another High Contracting Party.*

3. Any willful act calculated to endanger the lives of members of the public.

4. Any attempt to commit an offence falling within the foregoing provisions of the present article.

5. The manufacture, obtaining, possession, or supplying of arms, ammunition, explosives or harmful substances with the view to the commission in any country whatsoever of an offence falling within the present article."

Proposed Comprehensive Convention on International Terrorism

Since 2000, the United Nations General Assembly has been negotiating a Comprehensive Convention on International Terrorism. The definition of the crime of terrorism, which has been on the negotiating table since 2002 reads as follows:

"1. Any person commits an offence within the meaning of this Convention if that person, by any means, unlawfully and intentionally, causes:

(a) Death or serious bodily injury to any person; or

(b) Serious damage to public or private property, including a place of public use, a State or government facility, a public transportation system, an infrastructure facility or the environment; or

(c) Damage to property, places, facilities, or systems referred to in paragraph 1 (b) of this article, resulting or likely to result in major economic loss, when the purpose of the conduct, by its nature or context, is to intimidate a population, or to compel a Government or an international organization to do or abstain from doing any act."

That definition is not controversial in itself; the deadlock in the negotiations arises instead from the opposing views on whether such a definition would be applicable to the armed forces of a state and to Self-determination movements. Thalif Deen described the situation as follows: "The key sticking points in the draft treaty revolve around several controversial yet basic issues, including the definition of ´terrorism´. For example, what distinguishes a "terrorist organisation" from a "liberation movement"? And do you exclude activities of national armed forces, even if they are perceived to commit acts of terrorism? If not, how much of this constitutes "state terrorism"?" The coordinator of the negotiations, supported by most western delegations, proposed the following exceptions to address those issues:

> *"1. Nothing in this Convention shall affect other rights, obligations and responsibilities of States, peoples and individuals under international law, in particular the purposes and principles of the Charter of the United Nations, and international humanitarian law.*
>
> *2. The activities of armed forces during an armed conflict, as those terms are understood under international humanitarian law, which are governed by that law, are not governed by this Convention.*
>
> *3. The activities undertaken by the military forces of a State in the exercise of their official duties, in as much as they are governed by other rules of international law, are not governed by this Convention.*
>
> *4. Nothing in this article condones or makes lawful otherwise unlawful acts, nor precludes prosecution under other laws."*

The state members of the Organisation of the Islamic Conference proposed instead the following exceptions:

> *"2. The activities of the parties during an armed conflict, including in situations of foreign occupation, as those terms are understood under international humanitarian law, which are governed by that law, are not governed by this Convention.*
>
> *3. The activities undertaken by the military forces of a State in the exercise of their official duties, inasmuch as they are in conformity with international law, are not governed by this Convention."*

Sectoral Conventions

The various sectoral counter-terrorism conventions define and criminalized particular categories of terrorist activities.

Terrorist Bombings Convention

Article 2.1 of the 1997 International Convention for the Suppression of Terrorist Bombings defines the offence of terrorist bombing as follows:

> *"Any person commits an offence within the meaning of this Convention if that person unlawfully and intentionally delivers, places, discharges or detonates an explosive or other lethal device in, into or against a place or public use, a State or government facility, a public transportation system or an infrastructure facility:*
>
> *a) With the intent to cause death or serious bodily injury; or*
>
> *b) With the intent to cause extensive destruction of such a place, facility or system, where such a destruction results in or is likely to result in major economic loss.*

Article 19 expressly excluded from the scope of the convention certain activities of state armed forces and of self-determination movements as follows:

> *"1. Nothing in this Convention shall affect other rights, obligations and responsibilities of States, and individuals under international law, in particular the purposes and principles of the Charter of the United Nations, and international humanitarian law.*
>
> *2. The activities of armed forces during an armed conflict, as those terms are understood under international humanitarian law, which are governed by that law, are not governed by this Convention, and the activities undertaken by the military forces of a State in the exercise of their official duties, inasmuch as they are governed by other rules of international law, are not governed by this Convention.*

Terrorist Financing Convention

Article 2.1 of the 1999 sectoral United Nations International Convention for the Suppression of the Financing of Terrorism (Terrorist Financing Convention) defines the crime of terrorist financing as the offence committed by "any person" who "by any means, directly or indirectly, unlawfully and willfully, provides or collects funds with the intention that they should be used or in the knowledge that they are to be used, in full or in part, in order to carry out" an act "intended to cause death or serious bodily injury to a civilian, or to any other person not taking an active part in the hostilities in a situation of armed conflict, when the purpose of such act, by its nature or context, is to intimidate a population, or to compel a government or an international organization to do or to abstain from doing any act."

Nuclear Terrorism Convention

The 2005 United Nations International Convention for the Suppression of Acts of Nuclear Terrorism defines the crime of nuclear terrorism as follows :

Article 2

1. Any person commits an offence within the meaning of this Convention if that person unlawfully and intentionally:

(a) Possesses radioactive material or makes or possesses a device:

  (i) With the intent to cause death or serious bodily injury; or

  (ii) With the intent to cause substantial damage to property or to the environment;

(b) Uses in any way radioactive material or a device, or uses or damages a nuclear facility in a manner which releases or risks the release of radioactive material:

  (i) With the intent to cause death or serious bodily injury; or

  (ii) With the intent to cause substantial damage to property or to the environment; or

  (iii) With the intent to compel a natural or legal person, an international organization or a State to do or refrain from doing an act.

Article 4 of the convention expressly excluded from the application of the convention the use of nuclear weapons during armed conflicts without, though, recognizing the legality of the use of those weapons:

1. Nothing in this Convention shall affect other rights, obligations and responsibilities of States and individuals under international law, in particular the purposes and principles of the Charter of the United Nations and international humanitarian law.
2. The activities of armed forces during an armed conflict, as those terms are understood under international humanitarian law, which are governed by that law are not governed by this Convention, and the activities undertaken by military forces of a State in the exercise of their official duties, inasmuch as they are governed by other rules of international law, are not governed by this Convention.
3. The provisions of paragraph 2 of the present article shall not be interpreted as condoning or making lawful otherwise unlawful acts, or precluding prosecution under other laws.
4. This Convention does not address, nor can it be interpreted as addressing, in any way, the issue of the legality of the use or threat of use of nuclear weapons by States.

Definitions of Terrorism in other UN Decisions

In parallel with the criminal law codification efforts, some United Nations organs have put forward some broad political definitions of terrorism.

UN General Assembly Resolutions

On December 17, 1996, the non-binding United Nations Declaration to Supplement the 1994 Declaration on Measures to Eliminate International Terrorism, annexed to the UN General Assembly Resolution 51/210, condemned terrorist activities in the following terms:

> *"1. The States Members of the United Nations solemnly reaffirm their unequivocal condemnation of all acts, methods and practices of terrorism as criminal and unjustifiable, wherever and by whomsoever committed, including those that jeopardize friendly relations among States and peoples and threaten the territorial integrity and security of States;*
>
> *2. The States Members of the United Nations reaffirm that acts, methods and practices of terrorism are contrary to the purposes and principles of the United Nations; they declare that knowingly financing, planning and inciting terrorist acts are also contrary to the purposes and principles of the United Nations;*
>
> *3. Criminal acts intended or calculated to provoke a state of terror in the general public, a group of persons or particular persons for political purposes are in any circumstance unjustifiable, whatever the considerations of a political, philosophical, ideological, racial, ethnic, religious or any other nature that may be invoked to justify them."*

Antonio Cassese has argued that the language contained in these declarations "sets out an acceptable definition of terrorism."

UN Security Council

In 2004, United Nations Security Council Resolution 1566 condemned terrorist acts as:

> *"criminal acts, including against civilians, committed with the intent to cause death or serious bodily injury, or taking of hostages, with the purpose to provoke a state of terror in the general public or in a group of persons or particular persons, intimidate a population or compel a government or an international organization to do or to abstain from doing any act, which constitute offences within the scope of and as defined in the international conventions and protocols relating to terrorism, are under no circumstances justifiable by considerations of a political, philosophical, ideological, racial, ethnic, religious or other similar nature,"*

The High-Level Panel on Threats, Challenges and Change and The Secretary General

Also in 2004, a High-Level Panel on Threats, Challenges and Change composed of independent experts and convened by the Secretary-General of the United Nations called states to set aside their differences and to adopt, in the text of a proposed Comprehensive Convention on International Terrorism, the following political "description of terrorism":

> *"any action, in addition to actions already specified by the existing conventions on aspects of terrorism, the Geneva Conventions and Security Council resolution 1566 (2004), that is intended to cause death or serious bodily harm to civilians or non-combatants, when the purpose of such an act, by its nature or context, is to intimidate a population, or to compel a Government or an international organization to do or to abstain from doing any act."*

The following year, the then Secretary-General of the United Nations Kofi Annan endorsed the High Level Panel's definition of terrorism and asked states to set aside their differences and to adopt that definition within the proposed comprehensive terrorism convention before the end of that year. He said:

> *"It is time to set aside debates on so-called "State terrorism". The use of force by states is already thoroughly regulated under international law. And the right to resist occupation must be understood in its true meaning. It cannot include the right to deliberately kill or maim civilians. I endorse fully the High-level Panel's call for a definition of terrorism, which would make it clear that, in addition to actions already proscribed by existing conventions, any action constitutes terrorism if it is intended to cause death or serious bodily harm to civilians or non-combatants with the purpose of intimidating a population or compelling a Government or an international organization to do or abstain from doing any act. I believe this proposal has clear moral force, and I strongly urge world leaders to unite behind it and to conclude a comprehensive convention on terrorism before the end of the sixtieth session of the General Assembly"*

The suggestion of incorporating such a political definition of terrorism into the comprehensive convention was rejected. United Nations' member states noted that a political definition such as the one proposed by the High-Level Panel on Threats, Challenges and Change, and endorsed by the Secretary General, lacked the necessary requirements to be incorporated in a criminal law instrument. Carlos Diaz-Paniagua, who coordinated the negotiations of the proposed Comprehensive Convention on International Terrorism, stated that a comprehensive definition of terrorism to be included in a criminal law treaty must have "legal precision, certainty, and fair-labelling of the criminal conduct all of which emanate from the basic human rights obligation to observe due process."

European Union

The European Union defines terrorism for legal/official purposes in Art. 1 of the *Framework Decision on Combating Terrorism.* This provides that terrorist offences are certain criminal offences set out in a list consisting largely of serious offences against persons and property that;

> *...given their nature or context, may seriously damage a country or an international organisation where committed with the aim of: seriously intimidating a population; or unduly compelling a Government or international organisation to perform or abstain from performing any act; or seriously destabilising or destroying the fundamental political, constitutional, economic or social structures of a country or an international organisation.*

In National Law

India: The Supreme Court of India adopted Alex P. Schmid's definition of terrorism in a 2003 ruling (Madan Singh vs. State of Bihar), "defining acts of terrorism veritably as "peacetime equivalents of war crimes.""

Syria: In relation to the United States attack on Abu Kamal the Syrian Foreign Minister Walid Muallem defined terrorism as "Killing civilians in international law means a terrorist aggression."

United Kingdom: The United Kingdom's Terrorism Act 2000 defined terrorism as follows:

(1) In this Act "terrorism" means the use or threat of action where:
   (a) the action falls within subsection (2);
   (b) the use or threat is designed to influence the government or to intimidate the public or a section of the public; and
   (c) the use or threat is made for the purpose of advancing a political, religious or ideological cause.

(2) Action falls within this sub-section if it:
   (a) involves serious violence against a person,
   (b) involves serious damage to property,
   (c) endangers a person's life, other than that of the person committing the action,
   (d) creates a serious risk to the health or safety of the public or a section of the public or
   (e) is designed seriously to interfere with or seriously to disrupt an electronic system.

The Terrorism Act 2000 defines terrorism so as to include not only violent offences against persons and physical damage to property, but also acts "designed seriously to interfere with or to seriously disrupt an electronic system" if those acts are (a) designed to influence the government or to intimidate the public or a section of the public, and (b) be done for the purpose of advancing a political, religious or ideological cause.

Section 34 of the Terrorism Act, 2006 amended sections 1(1)(b) and 113(1)(c) of Terrorism Act, 2000 to include "international governmental organisations" in addition to "government".

United States: United States Law Code the law that governs the entire country contains a definition of terrorism in its requirement that Annual Country reports on Terrorism be submitted by the Secretary of State to Congress every year. It reads:

> *"(d) Definitions (...)*
>
> *(2) the term "terrorism" means premeditated, politically motivated violence perpetrated against non-combatant targets by sub-national groups or clandestine agents;"*

US Federal Criminal Code

The United States has defined terrorism under the Federal criminal code. 18 U.S.C. §2331 defines terrorism as:

> *...activities that involve violent... or life-threatening acts... that are a violation of the criminal laws of the United States or of any State and... appear to be intended (i) to intimidate or coerce a civilian population; (ii) to influence the policy of a government by intimidation or coercion; or (iii) to affect the conduct of a government by mass destruction, assassination, or kidnapping...."*

US Code of Federal Regulations

The US Code of Federal Regulations defines terrorism as "...the unlawful use of force and violence against persons or property to intimidate or coerce a government, the civilian population, or any segment thereof, in furtherance of political or social objectives" (28 C.F.R. Section 0.85).

US National Security Strategy

The current US national security strategy defines terrorism as "premeditated, politically motivated violence against innocents."

United States Department of Defense

The United States Department of Defense defines terrorism as:

> *Premeditated, politically motivated violence perpetrated against non-combatant targets by sub-national groups or clandestine agents, usually intended to influence an audience.*
>
> *–Title 22 of the United States Code Section 2656f(d).*

A definition qualifies and explains the Department of Defense's understanding of this legal definition:

> *For the purposes of this definition, the term "non-combatant" is interpreted to include, in addition to civilians, military personnel who at the time of the incident are unarmed and/or not on duty. We also consider as acts of terrorism attacks on military installations or on armed personnel when a state of military hostilities does not exist at the site, such as bombings against US bases in Europe, the Philippines or elsewhere.*

USA PATRIOT Act

The USA PATRIOT Act defines terrorism activities as "activities that (A) involve acts dangerous to human life that are a violation of the criminal laws of the U.S. or of any state, that (B) appear to be intended (i) to intimidate or coerce a civilian population, (ii) to influence the policy of a government by intimidation or coercion, or (iii) to affect the conduct of a government by mass destruction, assassination, or kidnapping, and (C) occur primarily within the territorial jurisdiction of the U.S."

US National Counter Terrorism Center

The US National Counter Terrorism Center (NCTC) described a terrorist act as: "...premeditated; perpetrated by a sub-national or clandestine agent; politically motivated, potentially including religious, philosophical, or culturally symbolic motivations; violent; and perpetrated against a non-combatant target."

The controversy over support for the U.S. proxy army reflects these priorities. "Contra leaders and their backers in Washington," the media explain, "are acutely aware that the future of the entire project could turn on how much military success the contras can have" before the next congressional vote on aid. They understand very well that the purpose of U.S. aid "is to permit people who are fighting on our side to use more violence," in the words of Assistant Secretary of State Elliott Abrams. Accordingly, the contra leadership does not approach Congress with the plea that they can win popular support through the appeal of their political program and organizing achievements in Nicaragua; rather they insist that with U.S. military aid and CIA direction they can kill enough people and cause enough destruction to "soft targets" to make a difference. In adopting this public stance, they register their understanding that the debate within elite circles is largely tactical, and that in a terrorist cultural climate, nothing counts except the success of violence.

This perception is well-supported in editorial and other commentary, which regularly stays within this framework of assumptions, warning to select a typical example that the contras "have some distance to go before convincing the American people that they are capable either of forcing the Sandinistas to the bargaining table or of scoring a military victory," and "may well be deprived" of further funding "unless Congress becomes convinced that they are up to the job." In the light of the inconvenient hence irrelevant diplomatic record to which we return, we may dismiss the reference to "forcing the Sandinistas to the bargaining table" as mere parroting of state propaganda, designed to cover up the real issue: "scoring a military victory." Syndicated columnist Smith Hempstone fears that "it will be difficult for Reagan to wangle a two-year financial commitment for the contras," though "a major contra military victory" before the next funding request "would help enormously." Such commentary, virtually exception less, amounts to an acknowledgement that the contra leadership comprehends the mentality of U.S. elites quite well in these circles, the overriding criterion is the success of violence. If it succeeds only after reaching the level of Pol Pot-style atrocities as in El Salvador and Guatemala, that is a proof of our heartfelt commitment to democracy and human rights; if it appears that violence may fail, as in Nicaragua, that shows that Nicaragua may be "beyond the reach of our good intentions."

In accordance with the guiding principle of "change of course," it is permissible to concede that events of the past reflected more unsavory features of our "national purpose," but now everything has changed, though in reality nothing has changed and our traditional victims will relive past horrors, suffering as well the burden of our uplifting rhetoric and self-congratulatory posturing as we keep them in their proper place. It is doubtful that any crime, however grotesque, might fail to be absorbed with equanimity into this remarkable system of intellectual self-defense.

Similar concerns over the effectiveness of violence were voiced internally during the Vietnam war. Thus William Bundy urged in June 1965 that "our air actions against the South should be carried on a maximum effective rate," including B-52 bombardment, though there was one and only one—problem: "we look silly and arouse criticism if these [B-52 raids] do not show significant results." Meanwhile, B-52 raids in the densely populated Mekong Delta were showing "significant results" in demolishing the civilian society, presumably relieving these doubts.

We therefore should feel no surprise when we learn that the U.S. command is proud of its success in directing its terrorist proxy forces to attack "soft targets" such as the "precise military targets" identified by the *New York Times*. Other "soft targets" include the health centers, medical workers and schools "targeted" by the contra forces with some success as noted, and civilian farms, which, as contra leader Adolfo Calero has explained, are legitimate targets. State Department spokesman Charles Redman, at a July 1, 1986 press briefing, confirmed U.S. support for this strategy, explaining that cooperative farms "often have a dual military-economic purpose" and their inhabitants "are armed and receive regular military training." Citing Redman's statement, Americas Watch observes that it would do credit to George Orwell's Ministry of Truth. It would be interesting to know, however, whether [the State Department] considers how its theory that a cooperative has a "dual military-economic purpose" and, therefore, is a legitimate target for attack, might be applied, for example, to an unfortified Israeli kibbutz where attackers kill and injure children, burn houses and kidnap civilians. Is it now U.S. policy that such an attack would be legitimate?

More important for assessing the nature of a terrorist culture is that the principles expressed by the State Department are generally accepted, even by critics of government policy. The media derisively dismiss atrocity mongering by Sandinista apologists who ignore the possibility that civilians assassinated by the contras might have been armed or accompanied by armed militia; the murder of agricultural workers in Israeli collectives, armed for self-defense, or rocket attacks on these defended outposts, is treated somewhat differently. *New Republic* editor Michael Kinsley , a liberal dove by the standards of American discourse, writes that the State Department defense of "bloody contra attacks on government-sponsored farm cooperatives" has merit, because "In a Marxist society geared up for war, there are no clear lines separating officials, soldiers and civilians" a justification that could be offered with ease by Abu Nidal. The attacks on other "soft targets" are also appropriate as a means "to undermine morale and confidence in the government," Kinsley continues, "a perfectly legitimate goal if you believe in the cause" as he does, in essentials—"but impossible to achieve without vast civilian suffering." A "sensible policy," then, must "meet the test of cost-benefit analysis," an analysis of "the amount of blood and misery that will be poured in, and the likelihood that democracy will emerge at the other end." In El Salvador and Guatemala, "cost-benefit analysis" apparently reveals that the policies were sensible: 150,000 corpses, well over 1 million refugees, unknown numbers tortured, raped and starved "poured in," and "at the other end," the kind of "democracy" that passes muster by the standards of liberal American opinion.

Kinsley's colleague, *New Republic* editor Morton Kondracke, offers his basis for cost-benefit analysis with refreshing clarity. "The *contra* movement seems to have done its part to earn refunding," he concludes, because, according to Reagan administration officials, the contras "have overrun several garrisons and cooperatives," which "contra leaders claim are not civilian and agricultural" but rather "militarized" as are Israeli kibbutzim. The success of violence is the crucial factor, and since it is adequate by his standards, the contras merit further support, particularly because contra military commander Enrique Bermudez assures him of the popular support for his forces within Nicaragua in the cooperatives burned to the ground by his intrepid warriors, for example.

Departing from these impressive sources, we might inquire into the military victories that inspire Kondracke's admiration. The "most important military action we have carried out in the northern part of the country" according to contra spokesman Bosco Matamoros, duly reported as such by the *Times*, turned out to be slightly different as their correspondent later discovered on the scene: just another attack on "one of the most isolated villages in Nicaragua's northern mountains" in which the attackers never came close to "either the town's dirt airstrip or the small collection of shacks that serves as local headquarters for the Nicaraguan Army," but did succeed in burning down most of the houses in a nearby grain cooperative, stealing cattle from "distraught" peasants who report that "we came down here from the mountains to escape the contras" and cannot return "because they'll kill us," and killing three children and a pregnant woman with 18 other civilian casualties by shooting machine guns into houses as they ran by in this major military victory. Kondracke concedes that this military victory, with children killed "after *contras* threw grenades into houses"—the only victory he cites—will apparently not help his favorites in "attracting popular support"; so we are left with "overrunning cooperatives" as a sufficient basis for renewing support for the proxy army.

Other "military victories" prove to be similar on investigation. "In their April report on military actions," the *London Times* notes, "the Nicaraguan rebels listed as one of their main achievements the destruction of a "Sandinistan Army garrison at La Victoria." But when journalists visited this village in south-central Nicaragua, "they were able to find little evidence to substantiate the Contras' account." Rather, they found that in La Victoria, "formed two years ago by peasants fleeing from Contra raids in the North," there was no military garrison but rather a settlement of 45 families attacked by heavily armed contras who "came in shouting, 'Here come the sons of Reagan'." The sons of Reagan succeeded in overrunning the cooperative defended by untrained militia armed only with rifles, including a 13-year old boy who was killed, destroying many houses, killing, and burning crops. The CIA "has been frustrated in its attempts to stop American supported anti-Sandinista rebels attacking poorly defended state farms and cooperatives and killing innocent civilians, according to Western diplomatic sources with access to U.S. intelligence," the report continues (accepting this very dubious CIA claim as true), and has so far been unable "to change the image of the Contras from that of a ruthless horde to one of an effective military force with legitimate, populist aspirations" the latter obviously being a proper task for the CIA.

But the contra "image" is adequate for the enlightened editor of a journal that seethes with endless rage over PLO terrorism, because "under U.S. influence the *contras* are promising democracy, just as under U.S. influence El Salvador is creating it," one of these arguments being as compelling as the other.

Across the spectrum, it is recognized that success in the exercise of violence is the condition that the proxy army must satisfy to merit continued support, though it would be helpful if we could modify their "image." There are few qualms and no awareness of what is implied by these open commitments, as one should expect in a terrorist culture.

Similar assumptions prevail elsewhere. U.S. international terrorism has by no means been confined to Central America. As noted earlier, the worst single act of international terrorism in 1986 was the U.S. bombing of Libya, killing some 100 people according to Western reports. The pretext was fraudulent, as was known but concealed by the media at the time though the point is now tacitly conceded without, however, any capacity to draw the obvious conclusions. At the time, the most extreme critics of Reagan were enthusiastic, arguing that it is quite proper to kill "innocent civilians, or murderous states would never fear retribution". And though it is now conceded that the pretext was a fraud, respected commentators such as the 1987 Pulitzer Prize winner Charles Krauthammer continue to laud this "self-enforcement action" by the United States, which must play its role as global "enforcer," he blandly asserts. He goes on to denounce the United Nations for daring to condemn the attack as a violation of international law. The UN even stooped to the level of "condemning Western retaliatory actions such as the raid on Libya" without mentioning "the provocation" conceded to have been a fabrication, a matter of no account. These are simply further signs of the commitment of the UN "to undermine the legitimacy of Western ideas, institutions, and interests" and to carry out other "mischief" that should, he urges, impel us to eliminate this institution, now useless since it no longer follows American orders.

Within disciplined Western intellectual circles, few could comprehend that on the principle Anthony Lewis enunciates, innumerable people around the world are entitled to bomb Washington causing tens of thousands of casualties in retribution for the acts of the terrorist commanders who operate there with impunity. It is the hallmark of a terrorist culture that observations such as these may never be expressed, and must be incomprehensible when voiced far from the mainstream, where elementary rationality and minimal honesty are not excluded as intolerable affronts to decency.

We learn more about the nature of a terrorist culture by a closer look at the current interpretations of the consequences of the Reagan Doctrine in Central America taking care not to forget that these policies merely extend, to a higher peak of savagery, the Carter administration programs, which have ample precedent in U.S. history. Since the successful slaughters in El Salvador and Guatemala have been removed from elite concern and largely public awareness, let us turn to the attack against Nicaragua, still an issue because of the potential costs to us.

Documents circulated internally in the White House concede frankly that the contra armies organized by the U.S. government are a "proxy force" for which the U.S. must somehow construct a "political base" within Nicaragua, this task obviously being beyond the capacity of the "democratic resistance." Meeting at a sumptuous country club in Costa Rica with "catered buffet and open bar," the "collection of successful businessmen, bankers and attorneys" who make up the contra civilian leadership established by the United States as a classical Communist-style "front organization" explain the difficult problem they face: "to diffuse an impression of the contras as principally a military force with a vague, and largely conservative, political program" and to project a progressive image that might have some appeal within Nicaragua. The problems probably explain why their "exile Assembly" was largely ignored by the press; unreported, for example, was their conception of "democracy," to which we return. A further reason is that the "moderate" elements imposed for domestic propaganda purposes by the U.S. government (Arturo Cruz and Alfonso Robelo) "drew relatively cool receptions" and "a tepid response," while mention of the only civilian leader with real power, Adolfo Calero, elicited "thunderous applause."

Calero was not permitted to enter Costa Rica. An avowed proponent of terrorism as just noted, he is the ultra-right civilian leader of the major military force of the contras, the FDN, based on the Somozist National Guard and commanded by National Guard Colonel Enrique Bermúdez. A secret 1982 Pentagon intelligence report described its basic elements as a "terrorist" organization headed by former National Guard officers. Before taking on the role of civilian figurehead, the most respected contra leader, Arturo Cruz, recognized that the proxy army had committed "damnable atrocities" against civilians and that their victory might lead "to a possible mass execution of the flower of our youth." After joining as their spokesman with a handsome CIA subsidy, he explained that they cannot be dissuaded from atrocities without "demoralizing the fighters." Nothing has changed since, including the irrelevance of U.S.-backed atrocities to elite opinion. The horrifying record of contra atrocities compiled by human rights groups, priests in Nicaragua, and others, continues until the time of writing. Two investigators cite a high-ranking State Department official who describes the U.S. stance with regard to the atrocities of their proxy army as one of "intentional ignorance." The same has largely been true of the media and Congress. To select examples virtually at random, U.S. journalists reported the killing of four civilians and abduction of nine others from an agricultural cooperative at San José del Pueblo; I located no report in the press. A report released by Michigan Congressman David Bonior and Bishop Thomas Gumbleton of Detroit detailing contra murders, rapes, kidnapping and other atrocities in late 1986 appears to have passed unnoticed. A book by a Spanish priest with extensive testimony from victims of contra atrocities also appears to have passed without notice. And so on, along familiar lines. If these trivialities are brought up, they can be dismissed by the doctrine of "change of course."

Use of local collaborators and mercenaries to attack, suppress and control the domestic population is traditional practice. There are many examples. "Indian regiments were doing most of the work of conquering India for the English," who then relied on native mercenaries to keep the population under control. In the Congo Free State of King Leopold, who succeeded in reducing the population from 20 million to 10 million in two decades with Nazi-style atrocities, a native army of 20,000 men, given "a completely free hand to loot and rape," was instrumental in implementing the conversion of the country into a Belgian slave labor camp. In South Africa, the white regimes were able "to find African chiefs as allies and to make use of African levies pressed into military service," and black police and troops have conducted many of the worst atrocities until today. The Nazis in occupied Europe also relied on local forces to carry out their murderous chores. The same was true of the French and later the U.S. in Indo-China, and of imperial powers generally. In southern Lebanon, Israel employs local recruits to carry out torture, assassination, massacres and general intimidation. From the earliest days of the American colonies, indigenous elements were organized for terrorist operations, in the conquest of the continent and of the Philippines, and the attack on Indo-China, including the Hmong tribesmen, recruited by the CIA for a murderous "secret war" conducted by many of the same people now engaged in the private phase of the U.S. war against Nicaragua, then abandoned after their usefulness had come to an end.

The same practices have long been routine in the Caribbean and Central America. Official U.S. policy at the highest levels has been to rely on indigenous military forces to suppress the domestic population, a matter to which we return. Quite regularly peasants are organized for the task, as in the case of the terrorist Orden in El Salvador, or Somoza's National Guard in Nicaragua, recruited by Somoza "from the poor peasants of the region" for his earliest operations in 1926 and later consisting largely of "usually illiterate, poverty-stricken campesions." The same has been true in Haiti, where the Duvalier dynasty formed the dreaded Tontons Macoutes from similar elements—a force that still carries out its grim work, still granted "a licence to bully, extort and kill" for "a once-only payment of $15." In one July 1987 massacre, hundreds were cut to pieces with machetes by sharecroppers whipped into a frenzy by landowners to kill "Communist priests," employing a device that is often effective in rallying impoverished and frightened peasants, and incidentally destroying a Church-initiated effort to organize the poor in an area of vast inequality; shortly after, a respected anti-Communist political leader and two aides were "hacked to death by a frenzied peasant mob after the victims were accused of being Communists."

The enormous economic and propaganda resources of the dominant (often foreign) society combined with a depressed economy, ethnic rivalries, religious controls, exploitation of fear and ignorance, a mounting cycle of violence and other factors facilitate such efforts.

Apologists for U.S. terror and repression appeal to the fact that its agents are mobilized locally to justify the actions as "defensive" or even "populist." Nazis, the Belgian Monarch, South African racists, the U.S.-backed dictators of the Caribbean and Central America, and other torturers and mass murderers might have advanced similar arguments, with comparable justice. The sudden enthusiasm among U.S. elites for "tough peasants" namely, those recruited for U.S. terrorist operations is a noteworthy cultural phenomenon.

We read constantly in the U.S. media that the contra foot soldiers are peasants, as are soldiers generally in the

Third World, including the soldiers press-ganged for service in the Salvadoran army and those who filled the ranks of Somoza's National Guard, often recruited in the areas where contras supplied by U.S. air drops operate today. The ranching country of central Nicaragua was a "traditional recruiting ground for the brutal National Guard that sustained the dictatorship" of Somoza, and with its moderately well-to-do private farmers, is the main center of contra support today. Jorge Castaneda writes that the neglect of the Sandinistas for the "poor and backward peasantry of the northern reaches" in the first years after the fall of Somoza' "when linked with ties the Somoza National Guard had in remote, poverty-stricken areas traditional recruiting grounds for most Latin American armies made this sector of the population ideal for contra enrollment" before it was "neutralized" by land reform and resettlement from areas of conflict, thus reducing the "meager popular support" for the contras in scattered and generally remote regions. It comes as no surprise that "among the contras membership in the National Guard appears to hold little or no stigma," or that many joined the contras "because they were either members of the National Guard or had relatives who were," while others describe their service in the U.S.-trained elite battalions that have wreaked havoc in the Salvadoran countryside. The Miskito areas were an early recruiting ground for the contras, but no longer, it appears, as a result of Sandinista reforms and the moves towards autonomy, unusual if not unique in the hemisphere, hence a target for contra sabotage by kidnapping and terror. In fact, "during the past year, the number of volunteers dwindled to almost none, contra commanders acknowledge," despite the extraordinary level of support provided by the foreign master and the increasing harshness of daily life under wartime conditions in a country that was only barely beginning to recover from the ruinous conditions that were Somoza's legacy.

Americas Watch reports that contra terror continues to be the primary source of human rights abuses in Nicaragua, though they also condemn government practices. They know of no "systematic violations of the laws of war in the course of military operations by the government" and conclude that there are two "political prisoners in the sense in which that term is used in the United States," one since "released without charges" after having been arrested for draft evasion. Amnesty International currently has no "prisoners of conscience" in Nicaragua.

As in the Miskito areas, peasants sometimes joined the contras on the basis of real grievances, though these do not begin to compare with the abuse suffered under the reign of U.S. client states or its proxy army attacking Nicaragua. As to whether these grievances would have been properly addressed, we can only speculate, since the U.S. intervened at once to exploit and exacerbate them, in fear that Sandinista reforms might prove successful. That they are being addressed is sometimes ruefully conceded in the U.S. press, with the customary twist. A *Wall St. Journal* article, headlined "Managua Tightens Grip on Former Contra Strongholds," reports how the Sandinistas have proceeded to "build support by handing state farms over to landless peasants and offering foreign exchange incentives to cattlemen to boost meat production," and inaugurating new dairy projects, while in the Miskito areas, "the government is repairing and painting schools and medical clinics and bringing movie projectors for the first time to Indian villages" thus undercutting the U.S. goal of saving the people from oppression.

Eden Pastora, the darling of contra supporters when he was leading the southern front attacking Nicaragua from Costa Rica with CIA and South African support, lost his status as a "great Central American patriot" and disappeared from view after he was removed by the CIA for failure to follow orders. But he has not remained silent. He comments that in Nicaragua, the "contras" are referred to as "the guardsmen," which is not altogether wrong, because the former Somozist guardsmen force peasant youths to join their ranks and take them away to camps in Honduras. Instead of building up their morale to make them idealist guerrillas, they depersonalize and demoralize them. The peasants are turned into guardsmen, into a repressive and killing machine. The guardsmen murder prisoners of war and continue to say "yes, sir." The "contras" will never be able to enter Managua.

He describes contra chief Adolfo Calero as "a loyal soldier of the CIA, a pawn whose only merit is having been a Coca Cola salesman." He informed the French press agency that the "fascist contras" would "not respect their mothers" if they regained power. "The contras," he says, "are the ones that serve as instruments of Washington's policies against Nicaragua. They hold their meetings in the U.S. and receive thousands of dollars for putting themselves at the service of imperialism."

Pastora is also interviewed in the national U.S. media, with such comments omitted, however.

According to U.S. mercenaries serving with the contras, including Adolfo Calero's security chief Joseph Adams, Pastora is a prime target of "widespread assassination plots" involving "the most senior contra leaders," who also "maintain a list of Managua civilians including members of the clergy as well as Sandinista politicians who would be marked for assassination when FDN forces entered the Nicaraguan capital," to establish "democracy."

Pastora's views on the contras are echoed by others in the region, rarely heard here, and without affecting their status as the "democratic resistance." A coffee-grower in Honduras describes the contras as "moneyed commanders and the commanded poor, turned into the dogs of war," a "gang" without a "true ideology and with profound internal inequalities," who recruit by force and promise pay "with the victory" while the money "goes into the biggest pockets." An editorial in the right-wing Honduran journal *El Tiempo*, whose owner Chaim Rosenthal has called upon the U.S. to invade Nicaragua to overthrow the Sandinistas, states that "We know what is the cause of the terrorism that is flowering more rapidly than we had expected [within Honduras]: the presence of the contras with the complicity of the civilian and military authorities," describing popular discontent with the contras as a "powder keg" waiting to explode." A retired senior officer of the Israeli army, an arms merchant in Central America for 4 years, describes the contras as "an invention of the media and some people from the psychological warfare department in the Pentagon" who will fight as long as "the Americans give us a lot of money to play soldier for them and bullshit about democracy." Their commanders "sit in the jungle with a finger deep up their ass and think how to squeeze more dollars from the idiot gringos in Washington, just as the generals of South Vietnam did back then," while American journalists are led through Honduran jungles and told they are in Nicaragua among other less complimentary remarks based on his observation of the media at work in Honduras.

The most important currently available source of direct information about "the new contras," refurbished by official U.S. aid, is an account by Rod Nordland, an experienced correspondent with a distinguished record of important work, who spent a month in April-May 1987 with a contra unit in northern Nicaragua and then traversed the same area with Sandinista troops. He found the comparison striking.

As they departed from their Honduran bases, contra "morale seemed high, their new backpacks burst with up-to-date materiel, the skies droned with the motors of C-47 cargo planes dropping ammo to them, courtesy of the CIA" along with supply helicopters ferrying military supplies "in Red Cross disguise" (as shown in an accompanying photo, yet another violation of the laws of war in the familiar sleazy style of the Reagan administration; this violation of international law, a device also employed in Carter's rescue operation for commanders of Somoza's National Guard, was denounced by the Red Cross in Geneva in a response to the

Newsweek photo that received little notice here3). They were equipped with U.S. aerial reconnaissance maps showing the Sandinista base that was their assigned target "in such detail that the location of every latrine was noted" and were decoding messages on their portable computers.

But the contras soon degenerated into the same kind of "ruthless horde" described by the *London Times* reporter cited earlier, stealing food and cattle from terrified peasants, some of whom were "strong-armed" into serving as guides "and, worse, to walk on their point (the first man in the column) to make sure we weren't falling into a trap." The contras excelled at robbing the local peasants who were "paralyzed by our arrival, except one terrified woman who ground cornmeal for us so assiduously that she ignored her baby crying for attention," and whom they terrorized by their behavior as marauding bandits with their "skulls and crossbones tattooed on their arms," boasting names "like 'Exterminator' and 'Dragon'." They were "great at retreating; attacks, they never quite managed." They also never managed to impart any political message, nor did they appear to consider this as part of their task, even though "the independent-minded campesinos of the mountains are natural enemies of the Sandinistas," having been "hurt badly by the failing economy" and having received no benefits from the revolution. Nordland describes how the contras proceeded "to cement the loyalty" of a peasant who was bitterly anti-Sandinista for these reasons:

We ate his chickens, beans, tortillas, bananas, plantains, cassava, grapefruits and agreed with him that it was a pity other contras had already eaten the eligible pigs. We slept in his yard, despite standing orders to camp away from homes lest civilians are killed in an attack. We sent him out to scout the hills for Sandinistas at night, and before dawn we walked him out on the point. Small wonder that, taken aside, neither he nor his wife would speak against the Sandinista troops who come through. The compass speak softly, they said, and gave political talks, but normally ask only for coffee. In the battle for hearts and minds, the contras are still the losers even in the remote areas where they have potential support. They are still more "the losers" among the families whose children are kidnapped and forced into the contra army, including the family of one 14-year-old boy Nordland met with the contras, whom he later interviewed: "His family had been given a plot of land by the Sandinistas after their victory. 'How could they want to destroy the revolution,' wondered, 'when it has helped us and so many other people'."

Nordland also interviewed a "relatively big landholder" whom he expected to be anti-Sandinista and who told him: "Mister, if the war just drags on like this, soon it will degenerate into banditry." Nordland's final conclusion: "Mister, it already has."

Returning to the same region with Sandinista troops who quickly swept the contras from the area in a counteroffensive that was "the biggest of the war and the shortest," Nordland found a very different picture. Unlike the contras, who carefully avoid military targets, "concentrating on more lightly armed civilian militias and undefended targets" (when they are not simply marauding), the Sandinistas, whose conduct "made a striking contrast with the contras," "found contras and fought after only two days," and continued to do so. "Their discipline held firm after many months" in the remote mountains, though they were mostly "draftees on two-year tours of duty." "Where it had taken a mere three weeks for the contras we accompanied in the same mountains to turn into an unruly scourge, Sandinista troops on the march never even stopped at a peasant's house, except with permission from an officer and then only to wait outside for drinking water. When they did requisition food, the campesinos told us, they always paid." Peasants also agreed that only the contras "impress campesinos as guides or make them walk in front of the troops."

An accompanying story quotes a March, 1986 memorandum by Robert Owen, who described himself in congressional testimony as "the eyes and ears" of Oliver North. He had "few kind words for the Nicaraguan contras." For many of their leaders, Owen concluded, the war "has become a business"; "There are few of the so-called leaders of this movement who really care about the boys in the field." The commander of the Costa Rican-based southern front, Fernando Chamorro, "drinks a fair amount and may surround himself with people who are in the war not only to fight, but to make money." Another contra leader "had potential involvement with drug running and the sales of goods provided by" the U.S. government. More money to the contras "will be like pouring money into a sinkhole."

Nevertheless, the cost to the U.S. is limited, and the "ruthless horde" recruited for their services have been able, in part at least, to perform their assigned task of preventing Sandinista reforms and ensuring that "theirs must become a revolution of misery, a frightful object lesson to the people of the region".

Arturo Cruz was the indispensable symbol of contra democracy until he resigned from the leadership in 1987 accompanied by denunciations from Secretary of State George Shultz because his resignation "resulted from a failure to get his own way rather than a concern over democratic reforms in the movement." Jeane Kirkpatrick also discovered that the hero had feet of clay after his unconscionable dereliction. He was "a man of mercurial temperament" who "had lived outside Nicaragua for 20 years before he returned to work for the Sandinistas in July 1979" and "it seemed to many Nicaraguans that he was never comfortable working in the framework of Nicaraguan politics." He is "a technocrat" and "not a political man," a person who "seemed to evoke more intense admiration among North Americans than Nicaraguans," Kirkpatrick explained. At the same time, the congressional Iran-contra committee released a document showing that Oliver North's payments to Cruz began out of concern that Congress might disclose that he was on the CIA payroll, in particular, during the time when he was a candidate for President in the 1984 elections in Nicaragua. Reports that Cruz was on the CIA payroll had been dismissed as a canard by contra supporters, and neither these comments on Cruz's newly-discovered weaknesses nor others reminded the reader that during the 1984 elections, Cruz was presented by the U.S. government, the media and the journals of opinion as the only hope for democracy in Nicaragua, with largely fabricated accounts alleging that the Sandinistas blocked his campaign by violence and other means because of his great popularity in Nicaragua, suddenly dissipated now that he is failing to perform his duties under U.S. orders.

Cruz describes the contra movement as "very ill." Its main problem is that "it was artificially formed too soon by the US" which "used as its core a group which the Nicaraguan people had rejected the Somocista National Guard." Its civilian leadership is "a mere 'clique' of businessmen and old-line politicians who were incapable of articulating a coherent political message." After a new contra directorate was formed at U.S. initiative in May 1987, "the senior US official who has worked with the contras for many years says, 'Unity will be the merest façade, kept together at least until the US elections by the ringmaster, CIA"'; the leaders are "opportunists," lacking "political or moral principles, or any real sensitivity to the Nicaraguan poor," a "liberal contra official" adds, referring to the new democratic hopeful, Alfredo Cesar. "The contras suffer from political anemia," Philip Bennett reports, and "continue to neglect military objectives while raiding poorly guarded symbols of the Sandinista revolution such as farm cooperatives, often killing innocent civilians." Trips to the war zone reveal that "roaming contra units rarely impart an explicit political message." "Some contra leaders point to the difficulty in devising a political formula to match the concrete promises of land and social services espoused by the Marxist insurgency in El Salvador." A "leading US intellectual" who supports the contras and presumably qualifies as a "leading intellectual" for this reason complains that they cannot "figure out a social program that would appeal to people, and then put it into some kind of context," and have no interest in a political program or a grass-roots structure. Another problem, this leading thinker explains, is that it is hard to arouse Nicaraguans against the government because of the social services they are provided with. Thus, the Sandinistas have been able to keep the opposition at the level of mere grumbling. How does one oppose such a regime? I don't think the contras have any idea.

In fact, they and their backers, including this "leading intellectual," have a very good idea: you oppose such a regime by random terror and the resources that can be mobilized by a violent superpower, in accordance with William Casey's insight that "It takes relatively few people and little support to disrupt the internal peace and economic stability of a small country."

With his departure from the directorate formed by the U.S. government to mislead Congress and the media, Cruz will presumably forfeit his $7,000 monthly (tax-free) paycheck and perhaps the "several million dollars from a private aid network over the last three years, money that has never been publicly accounted for," though Alfonso Robelo, the wealthy businessman who stayed on to provide a facade of "democracy," will presumably continue to receive the $10,000 per month provided for his services.

At the "exile Assembly," Cruz at the time still playing his assigned role and thus a heroic defender of democracy told the delegates that "all the conditions [for victory] are present, except only that we have failed until now to define clearly and consistently our own political positions," a minor defect. Meanwhile senior U.S. officials bewail the fact that "the contras can demonstrate no major political gains" and "have almost no support systems" within Nicaragua. They do not understand why the proxy army attacking Nicaragua from foreign bases is "not as effective as the leftist rebels in El Salvador," who have always fought within their own country, receive virtually no known outside aid, and face a military force far better equipped than the army defending Nicaragua from terrorist attack, with nearly 80 helicopters, 11 A37 bombers and 12 C47 gunships, and direct participation of the U.S. Air Force and other U.S. military forces in surveillance, coordination of bombing, and ground operations.

Contra commanders complain of "the lack of airplanes and pilots" for their "rudimentary air force" and the lack of "small boats for river patrol." The problem they face is that they need dozens of flights per month to keep their troops functioning within Nicaragua, this "aerial resupply network" being the "key to the contras' ability to keep large numbers of fighters in the field." "The air operation is the key to the war," according to a Western diplomat in Managua who monitors the rebels (presumably a U.S. Embassy official, probably CIA): "Without it, the contras couldn't make it." According to Nicaraguan and Western estimates, U.S.-run supply flights reached the level of 30-40 flights monthly, delivering hundreds of tons of equipment, from April 1987, in an effort to ensure that the much-heralded Spring Offensive would be sufficiently violent to impress Congress. The CIA "has equipped the rebels with a computer center that intercepts and decodes hundreds of Sandinista messages a day," information that is dispatched "via portable computers with special encoders to rebel units in the field." In addition, extensive U.S. surveillance provides the proxy army with up-to-the-minute intelligence on Nicaraguan army deployment. While the government must cope somehow with CIA commando operations, the constant threat of invasion, and other conditions that are also unimaginable in the case of an authentic guerrilla force. British journalists who travelled with the contras report that they are often "better equipped than the Sandinistas," describing their high-quality "state of the art" weapons and communication systems, and also explaining the basis for recruitment: "Sandinista price freezes on agricultural products mean that many peasants make less money now than they did under former dictator Anastasio Somoza" a result of the effort to maintain subsistence levels under wartime conditions for the poor who are left to starve in U.S. domains, in accordance with the approved "Central American mode."

Meanwhile contra supporters assure us that it was "the abuses and horrors of the commandants" that "led to what has to be seen as a civil war not, as the Sandinistas claim, the U.S. aggression against Nicaragua."

Despite the resources flowing in lavish abundance and the direct U.S. participation, it doesn't work. Even journalists impressed with their achievements agree that "without continued airlifts and renewed American support, it is virtually impossible that the contras can survive as an effective guerrilla force," thus tacitly conceding that they are not "a guerrilla force" in any meaningful sense of the term. U.S. officials fear that these incomprehensible failures are "going to have long-term costs for us," the same correspondent reports.

The failures of the proxy army are particularly dramatic in comparison with neighboring El Salvador. Close by areas where thousands of government troops carry out ground sweeps, guerrillas "non-chalantly held a town meeting" in a village just four miles from a government military base that they had "devastated," carrying out "a frank, if highly political, discussion of the basic needs and social issues affecting the majority of Salvadorans," with their audience plainly interested and supportive. Meanwhile, government "Army patrols continue to enter areas of conflict as a raiding force, rather than a governing presence with a political vision that appeals to the peasantry," according to military analysts; "both American officials and members of his own party say Mr. Duarte has failed to administer effective social programs, despite ample American aid," and "his ruling Christian

Democratic party, they say, has become a corrupt political machine in a land where most Salvadoran peasants cannot find work, clean water or health care." U.S. economic aid supports "the businesses of the rich," whose "wealth is safe because taxes are collected irregularly and dollars can be quietly tucked away in Miami bank accounts" and whose sons "are safe because there is no draft and the army press gangs do not pick up young men in affluent neighborhoods, one expression of the class character of the war." Little U.S. aid "appears to reach the impoverished majority of Salvadorans who live in the urban slums and the countryside," where U.S. aid officials rarely travel. "The poor are press-ganged into military service" and "political power remains in the hands of the urban elite," while "most Salvadorans are afraid of policemen and soldiers, and few of the poor would dream of seeking legal redress against a landlord because virtually no judge would favor a poor man."

The armed forces, who "once applied scorched-earth tactics" and "supervised death squads on the ground and bombed from the sky," can now "afford to be more lenient" in areas where they have established control, the *Wall St. Journal* reports; "but as long as the left is a political threat, the army doesn't dare let go of the leash entirely" (my emphasis). A Catholic priest describes the rebuilt village of El Barillo, devastated by government terror, as now "a concentration camp." Villagers say that they are "afraid to talk" to an American journalist. They are "under the boot," an international human-rights worker observes. "The army fears that El Barillo's relatively efficient organization is a sign of continuing leftist influence," since nothing of the sort could be expected under government rule.

These comparisons reveal, once again, the true "symmetry" between El Salvador and Nicaragua. It is not, as the ideological system contends, that in each country there are guerrillas fighting the central government in a reflection of the global "East-West conflict." Rather, in each country the U.S. has organized and directs a terrorist force that must use violence to achieve the ends of the foreign master and the local elites that rely on external power, unable to enter into a political struggle since they have nothing to offer the population beyond a renewal of misery and subordination. We can begin to speak of "symmetry," of "the East-West conflict," and of "U.S. security concerns," when the Soviet Union organizes a mercenary force to attack El Salvador from Nicaraguan bases and to terrorize the population, supplying them with sophisticated modern equipment in daily air drops, while the KGB runs sabotage programs in El Salvador with its own assets" and forces a state of mobilization there by a constant and credible threat to invade outright, constructs a permanent Soviet military base in Nicaragua, runs military exercises there involving tens of thousands of Soviet troops, maintains threatening naval forces off the coast, floods the Salvadoran airwaves with hostile propaganda, conducts regular over flights to gather intelligence on Salvadoran army operations to be dispatched to "the sons of Gorbachev" marauding in the countryside, coordinates military attacks by its proxy forces in El Salvador, and so on. Then the conventional picture will be more than an object of ridicule. As of now, it hardly has the merits of complaints in *Pravda* about U.S. aggression in Poland, a pitiful victim of the East-West conflict.

Furthermore, the real world pattern is traditional, adequately explained in the documentary record of secret planning and even public commentary, and a predictable consequence of the roots of intervention within domestic U.S. society. Such facts cannot be perceived within educated circles if they hope to retain respectability. There, we can at most only contemplate "the mystery" of "why is it that the United States so often supports dictators," leaving it to "political scientists, philosophers and wise men to answer the question," which is too deep for ordinary mortals to comprehend. And we may ponder the question of why Nicaragua remains "beyond the reach of our good intentions." We might observe that business circles abroad seem to have little difficulty in penetrating the mystery that so troubles Americans. Discussing U.S. support for Ferdinand Marcos, which elicited the thoughts just quoted, the London *Economist* observes simply that "For many years Mr. Marcos was good for American business and America's bases.

Contra supporters, some of whom describe themselves as liberals or democratic socialists, find it natural that the U.S. should create a "proxy force" and attempt to construct a political base for it, because this reflects their conception of how the lower orders are to be managed. Correspondingly, they are enthusiastic about "the attractive new civilian leaders of the *contras,*" who essentially share this conception. One of the few independent U.S. journalists accurately observes that the official contra leadership represent Nicaragua's old business and land-owning classes, the kind of Third World that American officials and businessmen like to deal with. That is why they were picked in Washington to head the contras. What Cruz, Robelo and Calero all reflect is the plantation mentality that infected Nicaraguan political life during the many decades of U.S. manipulation and intervention. They share the assumption that Nicaragua really belongs to the United States, and that it is valid for would be leaders to turn to Washington to find shortcuts to political legitimacy.

The same is true of those who praise them here as virtuous democrats while applauding or averting their gaze from the social and political system imposed and defended by the United States in El Salvador, a system similar in character to what it hopes to restore in Nicaragua.

An American academic specialist on Latin America observes that the contra civilian leadership "tends to be or was prior to 1979 economically affluent, representative of a tiny elite or a small middle class," men who were "alienated" by the revolution "because it challenged their privileges," creating "a topsy-turvy world in which their own welfare was being considered the equal of the formerly dispossessed." "Almost all the contra leaders are on the CIA payroll. Each of the seven members of the FDN directorate receives an annual salary of $84,000, tax free, compliments of Uncle Sam." Alfonso Robelo was a wealthy cotton grower and cooking-oil processor, formerly "president of the Superior Council of Private Initiative, the umbrella organization for most of organized private initiative." Arturo Cruz, who spent one year in Nicaragua from 1960 to 1985, "worked as an international civil servant and for the Inter-American Development bank." Adolfo Calero managed Coca-Cola of Nicaragua and had long-standing CIA connections. Aristides Sanchez was a wealthy landowner and close associate of Somoza. Most of those who finally opposed Somoza did so for the same reasons that led similar elements to oppose Trujillo, Marcos and other U.S.-backed dictators and state terrorists: he was robbing them, not merely the poor. It is hardly surprising that "they have never issued a detailed program of their social, economic, and political goals." Edgar Chamorro, who left in disgust after two years service as the contra spokesman selected by the CIA, states that they offer Nicaragua "nothing but a return to the past"; the contras "are being used as instruments of U.S. foreign policy by the CIA and the Reagan administration...and by the old Somozista gang to get back the money and power they lost in 1979." Before joining the U.S.-directed civilian front for the contras, Arturo Cruz had described leading elements among them as "civic cadavers," noting that "most of these persons in positions of military authority within the FDN are ex-members of the National Guard, who unconditionally supported Somoza until the end against the will of the Nicaraguan people" in fact, 46 out of 48 of the *contra commandantes* as of mid-1984. In October, 1985, Cruz expressed his continuing unhappiness that the contras "are almost totally controlled by right-wingers, many of them followers of" Somoza, views that he reiterated after resigning from the CIA civilian front.

The device of historical amnesia. and tunnel vision cultivated in intellectual circles protects the press and other commentators from perceiving that the curious technical problem of inspiring "our friends" and constructing a political base for them has always bedevilled U.S. planners conducting their exercises of international terrorism, described with such euphemisms as "covert action," "low intensity warfare," "counter insurgency," "pacification," or "containing Nicaragua." Throughout the Indo-China wars, government experts struggled with the same problem: the U.S. is militarily strong but politically weak, as regularly discussed in captured Vietnamese documents as well as U.S. government analyses. Secretary of Defense McNamara pondered "the discouraging truth" that "we have not found the formula, the catalyst, for training and inspiring [our Vietnamese] into effective action"; all we can do is kill, he added, President Eisenhower attributed the high morale of the "Communist forces" in comparison with "the democratic forces" to the "sense of dedication" mysteriously produced by "the Communist philosophy." General Maxwell Taylor bemoaned the "national attribute" that "limits the development of a truly national spirit" among the South Vietnamese while speculating about "the ability of the Viet Cong continuously to rebuild their units and to make good their losses," "one of the mysteries of this guerrilla war" for which "we still find no plausible explanation"; the apparent contradiction with regard to the "national attributes" of the South Vietnamese is readily resolved when we recognize that the Viet Cong are by definition not South Vietnamese, since we are massacring their families and destroying their homes (in South Vietnam). In his Ten Point Program for Success in 1965, U.S. Ambassador Lodge proposed as Point One: "Saturate the minds of the people with some socially conscious and attractive ideology, which is susceptible of being carried out" the same perceptive advice now offered by Arturo Cruz and the "leading US intellectual" cited earlier. Somehow, it couldn't be done, so it was necessary to saturate the countryside with bombs along with general terror.

The U.S. propaganda services were no less baffled. John Mecklin, who was responsible for their operations in South Vietnam in the early 1960s, described the Vietnamese peasant as a man whose "vocabulary is limited to a few hundred words," whose "power of reason develops only slightly beyond the level of an American six-year old," whose "mind is untrained and therefore atrophies." How, then, could they comprehend the benevolence of our intent while we were forcing them into concentration camps and slaughtering their families, or our sophisticated measures of "nation building"? But oddly, the political and military tactics of the Viet Cong, making use of techniques that were "skillfully entwined in the life and character of the Vietnamese peasant," "confounded not only the U.S. Mission but also the aristocratic leaders of the [U.S.-imposed] Diem regime." Their forces "were developed to a surprisingly sophisticated degree with jungle arms factories, radio nets, clandestine hospitals, propaganda printing presses, V.C. cameramen filming the action" in ambushes, and other such exploits. To the U.S.-organized military forces, the Viet Cong—South Vietnamese peasants with "atrophied minds" seemed to be "eight feet tall." What could be the explanation for this curious paradox?

Much the same was true in Laos, where the U.S. subverted the elected coalition government in 1958 because it was dominated by the left and later conducted one of the most intensive bombings in history to demolish the civil society of northern Laos as the sole means of blocking social reform and popular organization in this primitive peasant society; and in Cambodia shortly after, at an even higher level of slaughter. U.S. reporters were no less baffled over the familiar pattern than the American command. In his final summary report from Phnom Penh as the direct U.S. bombing ended, Sydney Schanberg raised "the key unanswered question: How have the insurgents without any planes of their own, and without the extensive artillery support the Government troops have, with only small arms and mobile weapons been able not just to match the Government forces, which are more than twice their size, but to push the Government forces back and sustain the offensive for six months without any significant lull?" Exactly the question now raised by his *Times* colleagues with regard to El Salvador and Nicaragua. "Since the insurgents are not superhuman," Schanberg muses, "there must be other explanations for their success." Perhaps they are so "determined and capable" because they "are less fatalistic than the Khmers on this side" and "believe they can change their environment" (U.S. Embassy official). In this regard, "the enemy" from the peasant society of inner Cambodia are quite different from those who Schanberg calls "the Cambodian villager," who "usually has no politics" and "is not interested in taking sides, only to be left alone to farm and fish and feed his family and once in a while to celebrate on a Buddhist holiday." Just as in Vietnam and Laos, and now in Central America.

Over and over again, we discover that "our side" is unable to develop popular support or to survive political competition, unless, of course, popular organizations have been demolished and the ideological system, the military, production, commerce and finance in short, the entire decision-making apparatus, the means of life, and the means of violence are firmly in the hands of approved elements. This inability has always been incomprehensible in an intellectual culture committed to the rule of force, and to "reform" dictated from above in the interests of the foreign master. The current bafflement over the failures of the proxy army despite its extraordinary advantages, and the endurance of the Salvadoran guerrillas who lack anything remotely comparable, is a familiar refrain.

The constant perplexity over these paradoxes is not difficult to resolve, but the solution is unacceptable, therefore impossible to perceive, even when presented by respected mainstream figures. The bitterly anti-Communist French military historian and Vietnam specialist Bernard Fall explained the point lucidly during the early stages of U.S. aggression in Vietnam. He raised the question why the Americans, like the French and British before them, "must use top-notch elite forces, the cream of the crop of American,

British, French, or Australian commando and special warfare schools" who are "armed with the very best that advanced technology can provide" to defeat local insurgents in Vietnam, Algeria and Malaya, "almost none of whom can lay claim to similar expert training and only in the rarest of cases to equality in fire power." "The answer is very simple," he wrote. "It takes all the technical proficiency our system can provide to make up for the woeful lack of popular support and political savvy of most of the regimes that the West has thus far sought to prop up," or the civilian fronts for the proxy armies it has mobilized. He might have added that. it also takes all the eloquence that advocates of state terrorism can muster to disguise the facts, just as the stern commitment of a terrorist culture to ignorance and insulation from unpleasant reality is required if we are to miss the obvious point of the lesson. The very same problem, Fall warned, would soon be faced by the U.S. in South Vietnam, as it was; and in all of Indo-China, in Central America today, and in other tortured lands tomorrow.

In Indochina, Australian journalist Denis Warner, also passionately anti-Communist, could perceive the source of the problem: "in hundreds of villages all over South-East Asia the only people working at the grass roots for an uplift in people's living standards are the Communists," while the U.S. is dedicated to restoring the old order of suffering and corruption. This perception being unacceptable, U.S. ideologists were compelled to provide a different answer: the war in South Vietnam was simply an expression of the East-West struggle, with the South Vietnamese its passive victims; and the sly Communist leaders in Moscow and Peking are more adept at manipulation than their innocent American counterparts, while "our Vietnamese" (and Laotians, and Cambodians) are "fatalistic" or "corrupt." Similarly today, it cannot be perceived that the situation in Central America has the same essential features as the U.S. attack against South Vietnam. Rather, it must be that the Salvadoran and Nicaraguan people are passive bystanders, victims of the East-West conflict, with the innocent Americans unable to match the trickery of the devious Communists of the Soviet bloc.

And so we are informed by "objective journalists," merely describing the facts. James LeMoyne explains that "creating a base of popular support appears essential to guerrillas" a remarkable discovery of the 1980s and "it is one of the fundamentals that Cuban trainers have emphasized to both Salvadoran rebel leaders and Sandinista commanders," who plainly could not have achieved this profound insight by themselves. "The contras' American advisers," he continues, "appear to have been far less expert in the art of guerrilla war" and have not given adequate thought "to making democracy, with its emphasis on individual choice, into a doctrine of revolutionary war." Thus "the Nicaraguan contras need to study the Salvadoran rebels' success in organizing popular support," just as Americans in Vietnam tried to ape the methods of their South Vietnamese enemy.

LeMoyne, however, goes a step beyond his predecessors in the Indo-China Agitprop system. The contras, he explains, face problems beyond those confronting the guerrillas in El Salvador, namely, the repressive apparatus of the Sandinistas which has "hindered the contras" and impeded their efforts to construct a political base. "The rebels face similar restrictions in El Salvador," he notes, "but they are less consistently applied there." The physical elimination of the independent media by violence, the murderous attack that destroyed the national university, the outright murder of the political opposition by the security forces, the assassination of the Archbishop who attempted to defend the "popular organizations" that were effectively demolished by U.S.-organized terror, the slaughter of trade union activists, journalists, human rights workers, priests and nuns, students and teachers, and tens of thousands of peasants, the scorched-earth tactics that devastated the countryside and created hundreds of thousands of refugees, the torture and mutilation and savage terror that traumatized the society all of this is slight in comparison to Sandinista repression, in the eyes of the *New York Times* Central America correspondent. In the same issue of the *Times*, LeMoyne denounces Salman Rushdie for "writing a great deal of admiring drivel at the knees of various Sandinista commanders" which makes it "easy to consign his brief book to the bonfire where accepted truths belong," as he is "swallowed by an exotic revolution whose darker sides he barely manages to glimpse" in contrast to this tough-minded journalist, who is not fooled by the "Communists" and surveys the Soviet-American conflict in Central America with clear eyed objectivity and no failure to "glimpse the darker side" of the U.S. operations in defense of democracy.

These are persistent themes of the reporting from Central America by the leading *Times* correspondent in the region which, it should be noted, is of high quality by general media standards. We return to further examples.

As noted earlier, it is a truth, whatever the facts may be, that Nicaragua is a Stalinist prison camp while El Salvador is struggling towards democracy with U.S. assistance. A review of the U.S. ideological system shows that this required picture has been presented with dedication and skill.

According to the official view, Nicaragua is a Hitlerian state in its internal practices and its threat of foreign adventures. "There is no comparison between South Africa and Nicaragua," President Reagan explained in a press conference. "In South Africa you're talking about a country, yes, we disagree, and find repugnant some of the practices of their government but they're not seeking to impose their government on other surrounding countries" in the manner of the Nicaraguan aggressors; one finds no South African troops in Namibia in violation of international law, for example, and no South African moves to destabilize Botswana, Lesotho, Angola, Mozambique, and other states of the region.

The U.S. government view is expressed in a joint State Department-Defense Department document entitled "The Challenge to Democracy in Central America," distributed in celebration of International Human Rights Day on December 10, 1986:

> *In the American continent, there is no regime more barbaric and bloody, no regime that violates human rights in a manner more constant and permanent, than the Sandinista regime.*

Commenting, Americas Watch observes that civilian noncombatant deaths attributable to government forces in Nicaragua over seven years, in the course of an attack of mounting intensity by the United States and its proxy army, might possibly reach 300, most of them Miskito Indians in 1981-82; in comparison some 40-50,000 Salvadoran civilians were "murdered by government forces and death squads allied to them" during the same years, along with "a similar number" during Somoza's last year, "mostly in indiscriminate attacks on the civilian population by the National Guard," and still higher numbers in Guatemala all of these atrocities supported or directly organized by the United States, contrary to much illusion.

Furthermore, those responsible, in Washington as in Central America, remain in power today, apart from the Somozist National Guard and wealthy business elites that the U.S. government is laboring to reinstall in accordance with its conception of "democracy." When Morton Kondracke visits El Salvador to rejoice in its march towards democracy, he is greeted by President Duarte, who presided over most of the slaughter, and his defense minister General Vides Casanova, who supervised it in accordance with his principle that "the armed forces are prepared to kill 200,000-300,000, if that's what it takes to stop a Communist takeover." Kondracke concludes that the Reagan administration deserves credit for the wonderful achievements of the 1980s, having "handled El Salvador better than the Democrats managed Nicaragua." His fellow-editors assure us that "the depredations of the *commandants*" in Nicaragua are "greater and more systematic depredations by far than Somoza's," including the slaughter of some 40-50,000 people by the Somoza regime after years of torture, killing, robbery and enrichment of the "democrats" while the population starved.

The editors of the *Washington Post* conclude that Duarte "has worked hard, governing in a democratic manner, starting to tame the criminal right and to subordinate the armed forces, prosecuting a war and a social revolution, and cushioning as best he can the cruel economic effects of war, backwardness and social change." In the real world, the "criminal right" are elements of the security forces whom Duarte lauds for their "valiant services" in their murderous assault against the population while laboring to ensure that Congress provides them with the necessary means, the rule of the armed forces remains absolute as demonstrated by their complete immunity from prosecution for past or present atrocities, and Duarte's constructive policies are a figment of the editors' imagination, as they can learn from the occasional news reports they publish. But Duarte is doing the job for which he was commissioned, and therefore, they continue, "the United States has a firm obligation to support an imperfect but striving democracy in El Salvador," where, they assure us, the guerrillas could not possibly remain a "major presence" were it not for the "Sandinista government in nearby Nicaragua," evidence as always being an irrelevant annoyance when the state has spoken.

Duarte's popularity in the United States is not matched in El Salvador, where a 1986 poll by his Christian Democratic Party indicates that less than one-fourth of the country's voters would support him in new elections; what the figures would be if the left were not excluded and the population not traumatized by terror, no one can judge, though we may recall Duarte's admission that "the masses were with the guerrillas" when he joined the government and the onslaught of terror began in full fury. And while the remarkable democratic achievements under his government are praised with enthusiasm in the Free Press, the population of El Salvador perceives something rather different. Public opinion polls conducted by the Institute of Public Opinion of the Central America University in El Salvador in January-February 1987 reveal that 10% of the population "believe that there is a process of democracy and freedom in the country at present" while 18% think the situation has deteriorated and 28% believe "that there have been improvements, but that repression continues"; the remainder, almost half the population, "think that nothing has changed." A majority believe that Duarte's new economic policies will harm the poor, while few think the rich will be harmed (63%, 9%, respectively), and a substantial plurality say that the agrarian reform "might have helped" but the Duarte governments "promises were lies" (41%, as compared to 22% who see advantages in the reform).

Duarte is also less than a hero in South America. Throughout his recent trip to the emerging democracies of South America, he was shunned by moderates and plagued by angry crowds. As he attempted to address the Argentinian Congress, over half the representatives filed out of the chamber. In Uruguay, he was denied permission to address the General Assembly and denounced by the Christian Democratic Party for his "obvious alignment with the Reagan administration." Similar displays of opposition were evident in stopovers from Brazil to Peru.

"Arriving in Uruguay, Argentina and Brazil, Duarte received unwarm welcomes," the Costa Rican journal *Mesoamerica* reports. A labor union official declared that "the working class of Uruguay condemns his arrival to the country because he does not represent democracy" but rather "heads a regime characterized by notorious violations of human rights" and "he facilitates Reagan's penetration into Nicaragua." "Duarte's daughter broke into tears in Brazil amidst boos and hisses by angry crowds waving signs saying 'Duarte is a murderer, a genocide'" and "the strong objection to Duarte's presence in Brazil forced him to change or cancel some public ceremonies planned." "The greatest embarrassment endured by Duarte came when the Brazilian Congress was summoned to pay tribute to the visitor and a ridiculously low number of representatives turned out: 30 of the 479 representatives and seven of the 69 senators!"

In Uruguay, Argentina and Brazil, where there is a good deal of experience with such matters, they know a killer when they see one.

Duarte's popularity in the U.S. is reminiscent of Anwar Sadat, also a great hero in the United States, considerably less so in Egypt as American reporters discovered to their surprise when they travelled to Cairo to cover the memorial after his assassination. Duarte remains indispensable to the military because of his ability to ensure the flow of funds from Congress, and business circles have offered him ambiguous support for similar reasons. The general population has little choice. As long as he remains an outstanding democrat within the U.S. ideological system, fulfilling his assigned role, his prospects are reasonably secure.

Contra lobbyist Bruce Cameron charges the "liberal-left" with a double standard because it regards human rights violations by the Sandinistas as "less serious" than in El Salvador, while democratic socialist Ronald Radosh explains that "The need for pressure against the [Sandinista] regime" and "U.S. protection to the democratic resistance" is "more necessary than ever"; "The Sandinistas should be pressured to do no less than the Duarte government did in El Salvador," he adds. Again we see how easy it is to tolerate, indeed not even to perceive the most gruesome atrocities as long as they are committed by "our side." If such statements at first seem shocking, we should bear in mind that Radosh's insight is perceptive. Suppose that the Sandinistas were to adopt the methods of the Duarte government, as Radosh advocates, resorting to physical destruction of the independent media and murder of the political opposition along with savage terror and mass slaughter of the population generally to destroy popular movements and to restore the old order under the control of the military and privileged civilian sectors dedicated to enriching themselves and serving the foreign master, while the pack animals die of disease and malnutrition and semi-slave labor and pesticide poisoning in the approved manner. Under these conditions, the U.S. would be pleased to support their "imperfect but striving democracy," to the polite applause or indifference of American intellectuals who assure us of their profound dedication to the cause of the suffering poor of Central America.

❒❒❒

2

Damage and Destruction Control by Terrorism

Introduction

We have seen, many crucial issues are simply off the agenda: the historical and documentary record that reveals the general and largely invariant guidelines for U.S. policies; the institutional setting within which policy develops; the recent application of these policies in Guatemala and El Salvador; the normal conditions of life within the Caribbean and Central American domains of long-term U.S. influence and control and what these teach us about the goals and character of U.S. government policy over many years; and similar matters elsewhere that might yield a degree of understanding of the origins and nature of the problems that must now be addressed. Such matters are not fit topics for reporting, commentary and debate. Rather, the agenda must conform to elite requirements, generally set by state propaganda, though debate is permissible insofar as dominant elites disagree on tactical and procedural matters. Within these limits, basic doctrines are beyond question and controversy, for example, the firm commitment of U.S. policymakers to democracy, economic development and human rights. Contemporary events must be reported and discussed in these terms, and historical memory must be shaped so that these doctrines are not called into question, or even considered controversial.

The project of damage control is much facilitated by the technique of historical amnesia and tunnel vision. This allows us to avoid what might otherwise be embarrassing (and surely pertinent) questions. Among those that come to mind at once are these:

What explains the sudden conversion of U.S. elite opinion to profound concern for human rights and democracy in Nicaragua precisely in July, 1979, when the Somoza clan, our long-term allies, were driven from Managua, and the Carter administration failed in its effort to retain his hated National Guard, so that it would be in a position to restore the old order with new faces?

What were the U.S. and Israel doing in Iran before they began the scandalous arms dealings with Iran in 1985, according to the chronology provided by the Tower commission and the congressional hearings—that is, when there were no hostages to rescue?

Why was there great outrage over the suspension of the pro-contra journal *La Prensa* the day after Congress issued what U.S. government officials described as a virtual declaration of war against Nicaragua, but total silence when Israel, at the same time, permanently closed two Jerusalem newspapers on the grounds that "although we offer them freedom of expression, it is forbidden to permit them to exploit this freedom in order to harm the State of Israel" and as the High Court held, "It is inconceivable that the State of Israel should allow terrorist organizations which seek to destroy it to set up businesses in its territory, legitimate as they may be"?

A crucial condition of respectable discourse is that such questions as these be suppressed.

Let us consider some features of the technique of damage control. In Congress, a leading critic of Reagan policies, Rep. Michael Barnes, expresses his support for the "noble objective" of the Reagan administration: "to somehow 'democratize' Nicaragua." But the contras, he adds, "are not the instrument that will achieve that objective." He sees the democratic process in operation among "our friends" in the region Honduras, Guatemala and El Salvador, where no reasonable person could utter the word "democracy" without a shudder. And we must persevere in our commitment to bring democracy to Nicaragua, undeterred by contemplation of what is revealed by a record of U.S. intervention extending over 130 years.

Turning to the media, in the "ultraliberal" press, a critic of the Reagan administration writes in a news analysis that Lt.-Col. Oliver North, who was at the "vortex of scandal," "became increasingly committed to democracy in Central America, especially the cause of the contras." Even before Col. North's testimony, which revealed his utter contempt for democracy with brutal clarity, what was the evidence that he cared about democracy in Nicaragua or the United States or even knew what the word means, or that the contra leadership or the U.S. government are interested in democracy, or ever have been? None is necessary, since we are dealing here with doctrinal truths.

It is an important feature of American culture that these doctrines serve as the presuppositions of discourse, entirely beyond the reach of discussion. It is a doctrinal truth, whatever the facts, that the Reagan Doctrine was "designed as a foreign policy tool to bring democracy to places where Soviet-sponsored regimes came to power in the 1970s," though there are questions as to whether we should aid "the resistance in Nicaragua", that is, the proxy army attacking Nicaragua from its foreign bases, maintained in the field by supplies flown in daily thanks to the bounty of their superpower sponsor. We must support the "elected governments in the region," the editors of the *New York Times* demand, strengthens the "democratic regimes" in El Salvador, Honduras and Guatemala and their "elected presidents," and protecting them from the depredations of "the Sandinistas," not an "elected government" with an "elected president," and surely not "a democracy" such as our client states. The editors of the *Washington Post* agree. The Central American conflict pits "the Marxist regime" in Nicaragua against "the elected government of El Salvador" and "the Nicaraguan resistance," and we must help "friendly governments in the region cope with the overflow of Sandinista power" not the overflow of American power in violation of international law, as determined by the World Court with overwhelming UN endorsement while assigning to "Nicaragua's fellow Latins the burden of moving it along a democratic path" as proposed in the Arias plan, which, outside of the Free Press, treats the governments in Central America on a par, with no mention of Nicaragua. "Admiral Poindexter believed that the President's general policy was to help the contras democratize Nicaragua," James Reston informs us after listening to Poindexter's remarkable testimony; "Maybe the tragedy began first with the corruption of language," he adds, though surft without understanding why these words have a certain merit.

When the intellectual elite turn to their task of restoring the faith, we descend to low comedy. In the *New York Times Magazine, New Republic* literary editor Leon Wieseltier assures us with perhaps a touch of desperation that "It would be hard to exaggerate the purity of heart that the Reagan Administration feels" as representatives of "a great and good power." "The pure hearts dream of democracy in Nicaragua" and proceed with "exaggerated humanitarianism," but they err in the atmosphere of "intellectual righteousness of Mr. Reagan's Washington," soon to be displayed, even more vividly than before, in the congressional hearings. To recover from "the moral and intellectual intoxications of the

Reagan years," we must add a touch of "realism" to the "lofty idealism" that has inspired the Reaganites as they exulted in the slaughter of some 150,000 people in Central America, enthusiastically supported Israeli massacres, and in general, became apologists "for some of the worst horrors of our time" in the words of international human rights monitors, and agents of these horrors. But in their dealings with Iran, Wieseltier continues, the Reaganites "have made a mockery of one of the administration's finest articles of faith, that terrorists and their taskmasters not be appeased." This is a common refrain, never accompanied by the observation that if international terrorists are to be shunned, then Washington must close down.

With regard to Nicaragua, Wieseltier urges that we replace the "lofty idealism" of the Reaganites by a "realist anti-Communism." Sober realism dictates that we act "to prevent the final integration of the Sandinista state into the structure of Soviet domination and to prevent the Sandinistas from interfering in the lives of their neighbors," goals that cannot "be accomplished without the tightening vise of the contras." Turning to the real world, we quickly discover that one consequence of Reaganite policies from the outset, predictable and predicted, was to compel the Sandinistas to rely on the USSR, abandoning their efforts at neutralism, so as to justify the attack launched against them for quite different reasons. This is, furthermore, a standard pattern of U.S. intervention, Guatemala in 1954 being one familiar case. As for the idea that the U.S. must prevent Nicaragua from interfering in the lives of its neighbors something we would never do it is worthy of note that the doctrinal truth remains unaffected by the absence of credible evidence of such interference, including the pathetic efforts of the most recent State Department propaganda. The remainder continues in the same vein, in conformity with the norms of educated discourse.

The norms are not entirely exception less, as earlier references indicate, and are quite different from those to be found in the professional Latin Americanist literature. But the uniformity is nevertheless striking and instructive, revealing features of the dominant intellectual culture that receive much less attention than they merit.

We might note that the effects of Reaganite programs in ensuring Nicaraguan dependence on the USSR, imperceptible to elite opinion, are obvious enough to the Nicaraguan opposition they profess to support.

This country has little alternative to tying itself more and more closely to the military and economic community of eastern Europe. The fruit of the US strategy will be if Nicaragua truly becomes, at some point, a part of the East-West confrontation. I am not opposed to support from the socialist countries. Certainly, if the Sandinistas were not getting arms from the Warsaw Pact, our country would be in the hands of the FDN, that is clear. And the FDN is not a democratic option. Eduardo Frei died hoping that Pinochet would give power back to the civilians. We know that something equivalent or worse would occur here in Nicaragua. We are against the FDN and we are against the counter-revolutionary option.

The alleged commitment of the United States to bring democracy to Nicaragua, a crucial principle of damage control, is assumed with virtual unanimity by commentators, untroubled by the question of its curious timing and the demonstrable efforts of the U.S. to destroy meaningful democracy in Latin America and elsewhere, a fact that also cannot be perceived, indeed an idea that cannot be entertained. Editorials assure us that the "unchanging goal" of the administration is "democracy and free elections in Managua," though the "Reagan administration must take care that its efforts to bring democracy to Nicaragua are not at the expense of democracy already in place in neighboring Honduras." In the news columns, we read that the U.S. "has been seeking a comprehensive regional treaty that will compel the democratization of the countries, particularly Nicaragua," and that Congress sees diplomacy as "a fresh approach to the US policy of using the contras to press Nicaragua's leftist government into becoming more democratic." In the case of official enemies, or even foreign states that are not simply U.S. clients, the proclamation of some alleged intention does not entail that it is the actual goal of policy, but when Washington pronounces its objectives, the claim becomes unchallengeable fact and no rational analysis is permissible, even thinkable.

Dozens of similar examples can be cited, and one will be hard put to find any deviation in the media from this mindless incantation of state propaganda even after the stark revelation of the disdain for democracy in Reaganite circles during the Iran-contra hearings as if the factual record of the 1980s, or the historical record, did not suffice to allow a rational assessment of this passion for democracy.

In such cases as these, as in the call that the U.S. remain true to its vocation of "protecting freedom" and so on, we see illustrated the great advantages of adherence to the Party Line: no facts are necessary, history is as irrelevant as elementary rationality. The principles of the doctrinal system are Higher Truths, requiring no argument, susceptible to no challenge.

This rigorous adherence to doctrinal truths, repeated day after day, no doubt succeeds in its purpose of establishing state doctrine as sacrosanct. The perpetrators as well no doubt come to internalize what they say and to lose the ability to call it into question. The very absence of argument helps instill required beliefs, assigning them the status of background assumptions that it would be bizarre to question. Given the tacit elite consensus on fundamentals, and the subordination of the political and information systems to concentrated state and private power, closely linked, there is little danger that alternative conceptions will reach a large audience, and if by chance they do, they must bear a heavy burden of proof not required by the chanting of authorized slogans. The system works very well to constrain independent thought and keep it within approved limits, at least among articulate and political active segments of the population.

The contras are "the rebels" or "the resistance," or even "the democratic resistance" (Ronald Radosh) or the "Nicaraguan freedom fighters". Elsewhere in Central America the "leftist insurgents" are "subversive groups," in the terminology of news reporting. It is only in internal documents by their lobbyists that the contras are correctly described as a "proxy force" for which we must somehow construct a popular base.

As noted earlier, critics are concerned only that Reagan's "active promotion of democracy" may be too "aggressive." At the dissident extreme of the media, Tom Wicker criticizes the Reaganites on the grounds that the U.S. has no "obligation to install democracy by force in Nicaragua," and Sol Linowitz, another critic, urges that the U.S. and its Central American allies should not "desist from their goals of political reform" in Nicaragua so that it can become a "democracy" like Honduras, El Salvador, and Guatemala, safely ruled by the military and the U.S.-linked oligarchy. He explains further that we should support the Arias plan, which "certainly does not mean abandoning the goal of advancing human rights and democratic politics in Nicaragua" in accordance with Reaganite humanitarian passions: "Indeed, the centerpiece of the Arias plan is democratic change in Nicaragua," the standard misrepresentation of the wording of the plan, to which we return, in the U.S. doctrinal system, and noteworthy again for the tacit assumption that "democratic change" is a lesser problem in the U.S.-backed terrorist states. Editorials and commentators assure us that "Washington's overriding goals are the security of Nicaragua's Central American neighbors and the stability of democracies throughout Central America," and that Congress has supported "stepped-up military pressure" in the hope that it "may influence the Sandinistas to leave their neighbors alone and re-establish internal democratic freedoms."

Examples are legion. The authors are aware or could easily become so that the Sandinistas have been requesting international supervision of the borders since 1981 so that the Central American countries would "leave their neighbors alone," a proposal always rejected by the United States, which is committed to military intervention in the region as it has been for over a century. They might also learn though not without some effort that as of mid-1986, Nicaragua was the only Central American country to have accepted the Contadora treaty (rejected by U.S. clients), which would bar arms imports and remove foreign military advisors from the region, a fact virtually suppressed in the U.S. media; and that in December, 1986, Nicaragua once again requested that the UN send an independent fact-finding mission to the border after a conflict there, "in order to determine the causes of tension and recommend relevant measures to prevent a further worsening of the situation", a proposal rejected by Honduras with U.S. backing, as always, and also unreported.

The authors of these typical commentaries could also easily learn, if they do not already know, the facts cited earlier concerning Nicaraguan trade with the Soviet bloc when Reagan announced the May 1985 embargo, also declaring a National Emergency in the face of the threat to our existence posed by Nicaragua, renewed yearly since; but to consider these and similar facts would clearly be improper, inconsistent with the required image of an agent of the Kremlin conspiracy. It would also shed too much light on the real purpose of the embargo: to overcome this neutralist stance so as to justify the U.S. aggression undertaken for quite different reasons.

They know, or can easily discover, that U.S. allies such as Israel enforce measures at least as harsh under far less onerous circumstances and that the United States too adopted such measures at home during World Wars I and II, though it was not under attack by a superpower; in fact, its national territory had not been threatened since the War of 1812. One can only imagine what the internal policies would bc if a terrorist army organized by the USSR were rampaging through Arizona and Montana with a base in Idaho, heavily supplied with air drops, with Canada serving as a major Soviet military base with massive permanent Soviet military maneuvers preparing for an invasion, Soviet fleets of unimaginable power cruising offshore and regular Soviet reconnaissance flights coordinating the terrorist attacks of their proxy armies, and U.S. air waves dominated by hostile radio and television from abroad. Would the U.S., under those circumstances, permit free travel by Russians who have published outrageous lies about the U.S. in the course of their lobbying and apologetics for the terrorist forces, and who are visiting with the open intention of digging up further information or inventing it, if necessary that can employed to gain support for the attack on the border states? Or would it permit the publication of a major journal of wealthy Communists who had managed to hoard American capital, funded by the Soviet Union, lining up in the terrorist crusade? Given the actual record under vastly less provocative conditions, the questions are hardly worth raising, though it should be noted that a realistic analogy is impossible to construct.

The authors could also easily discover that repressive policies were not only the predictable effects of the two-pronged U.S. war against Nicaragua, combining terrorist attack with barriers to trade and aid, but also the intended effects from its earliest days. In the World Court proceedings, former CIA analyst David MacMichael testified that the 1981 CIA program ratified by the administration had as its purpose: to use the proxy army to "provoke cross-border attacks by Nicaraguan forces and thus serve to demonstrate Nicaragua's aggressive nature," to pressure the Nicaraguan Government to "clamp down on civil liberties within Nicaragua itself, arresting its opposition, demonstrating its allegedly inherent totalitarian nature and thus increase domestic dissent within the country," and to undermine its shattered economy. We hardly need the testimony, since these predictable effects were surely the intended ones. But to understand such matters, it is necessary to escape the confines of the ideological system and to question the sanctity and nobility of U.S. intentions. That is excluded, as an intolerable departure from civilized norms.

A closer look at the substantive content of formal civil liberties is also excluded, though it is hardly an insignificant issue, even in states such as Costa Rica, which have an impressive democratic record (or in the U.S., for that matter). The Council on Hemispheric Affairs and the Newspaper Guild (AFL-CIO) discuss the topic in their regular surveys of the Latin American media. They point out that in Costa Rica, where civil liberties "have been observed to a degree unmatched by any of the Spanish-speaking republics of Latin America," the population "in practice-often can obtain only one side of the story, since wealthy ultra-conservatives control the major daily newspapers and broadcasting stations"; here the effective control over information is guaranteed by the "free market of ideas" as it functions in a society with concentration of resources in private hands, and therefore no limits on freedom of the press would be perceived from the Orwellian standpoint of U.S. ideology on the matter.

In El Salvador, which the Council lists as the worst violator of press freedoms after Chile and Paraguay, reporters continue to "work under the constant threat of harassment and death" with at least 20 journalists killed since the 1979 coup and a greater number "disappeared" or forced into exile. The "prevailing sense of insecurity has profoundly affected moderate and right-wing journalists" while other publications "have been forced to close as a result of right-wing death-squad violence" and those that remain are largely "controlled by wealthy ultra-conservatives"; and, of course, "freedom of expression remained. suspended in 1985-1986 under a state of emergency" that had been in effect since March, 1980, but was virtually unmentionable in the U.S. Similarly, "restrictions on press freedom in

Honduras remain unofficial but pervasive, producing a system of self-censorship," because of government blacklists and general fear.

Others have made similar points. In the journal of the Committee to Protect Journalists, Alan Nairn writes that "The main method of censorship employed by the Guatemalan army [who effectively rule the country behind a democratic façade] is murder, directed primarily at the local press." He notes that "since 1978, about 47 Guatemalan journalists have been assassinated, many of them in quite spectacular fashion radio broadcasters dragged out of the station while on the air, prominent newspaper journalists machine-gunned while they are driving downtown." The mass slaughter of civilians by the ruling generals had never been discussed in the Guatemalan press radio, T.V. or newspapers. And that had been accomplished without a system of formal censorship. There is no ministry of censorship in Guatemala. It's simply an ad hoc system where journalists who dare to discuss such things are killed.

Writing on El Salvador in the same journal, Ruben Martinez concludes that the situation is improving in that terror has declined from the peak years of U.S. sponsored atrocities, but "press freedom is still very limited for those who do not echo the official line." The two largest dailies are "extreme right-wing," and their editors laud the freedom of the press, observing that they can criticize the government as harshly as they like "since current conditions do not inhibit the political right from speaking out," Martinez adds, meaning that they will not be assassinated or "disappeared" by the security forces or the terrorist squads associated with them. These journals do not even accept paid ads from left-of-center opposition groups, nor does a smaller one, close to Duarte's PDC. Another smaller journal, *El Mundo*, is "by far the most open of the dailies," accepting ads from opposition unions and human rights groups that call for freedom for political prisoners, an end to the war, and measures to deal with "the economic hardship of the working class." The "most daring source of information" is the small weekly news bulletin of the Catholic University of Central America (UCA), "limited in circulation" but willing to accept articles from opposition unions and political opposition groups. The most "significant sign of *apertura*" in the press is an editorial in *El Mundo* adapted from a UCA piece, in which the most extreme statement quoted is that the army "has succeeded only in not losing the war," a statement that "would have been impossible to make publicly in the terror-filled atmosphere of the early 1980s." Americas Watch also observes that state terror has sufficed to ensure that "since 1981 the Salvadoran press has either supported the government or criticized it from a right-wing perspective."

These matters are never discussed as we laud our achievements in bringing "democracy" to El Salvador, just as heavy censorship and closing of journals, detention and expulsion of editors, even refusal to grant permission to publish, is off the agenda with regard to Israel. One will search the U.S. media in vain for impassioned demands that *La Cronica* and *El Independiente* be permitted to reopen in El Salvador, protected by an international military presence from the Duarte security forces, which continue to reign unchallenged. Indeed, who has even heard the names of these journals destroyed by state terror, their editors and staff murdered and mutilated by the security forces, driven from the country, or intimidated into silence, the physical plant demolished? In contrast, violations of press freedom in Nicaragua that evidently fall far short of murder and general terror evoke unbounded outrage.

These are crucial requirements for the operation of damage control. The Reagan administration has assumed from the start that it could count on domestic hypocrites to feign indignation over the intended consequences of its terrorist acts, applying lofty civil libertarian standards that they do not for a moment accept (as is easily demonstrated by comparative analysis) while blaming the travail of Nicaragua on "Communist mismanagement," "Sandinista paranoia" or their "inherently totalitarian nature." Everything has proceeded exactly as anyone familiar with American history and culture would have anticipated.

The concern of the editors of the *Christian Science Monitor* that we act to "re-establish internal democratic freedoms" in Nicaragua is widely echoed. Thus, the *New York Times* endorses the Arias plan because it calls for "restoring freedoms and holding elections in Nicaragua." there having been no elections according to *Times* doctrine. Such hopes for *restoration* of democratic freedoms in Nicaragua must be a reference to the Somoza period, if words have meaning, hence an appeal for a return to those happy days, when, in fact, there was little concern voiced over conditions in Nicaragua; "from 1969 to 1977 the networks spent a total of one hour on Nicaragua all on the 1972 earthquake," while El Salvador was also ignored. These interesting formulations are standard not only in editorials but also in what are called "news columns," where we read, for example, that the Arias plan calls for "the creation of a democratic system *in Nicaragua*" and that Guatemala "favors *re-establishment* of a democratic system" in Nicaragua. The *Washington Post* also demands that we must turn "Nicaragua *back toward* democracy" and assures us that the U.S. "is working through the contras to *restore* democracy to Nicaragua" as under Somoza, presumably; and Reagan is also laboring to "break the Sandinistas' Cuban and Soviet ties" which, of course, the Reaganites relish and have desperately sought to strengthen in the traditional pattern discussed earlier.

There is, in fact, a way to give some sense to the pretense that that the U.S. is concerned to bring democracy to Central America and that elite opinion truly feels concern over the lack of democracy in Nicaragua (under attack by a superpower). It is only necessary to understand that like most terms of political theology, the term "democracy" has two meanings: its dictionary meaning, and a technical sense devised for indoctrination exercises. In the technical sense of the term, as discussed earlier, "democracy" exists only when elements favorable to the interests of U.S. investors are guaranteed the capacity to rule the political system. At home, that means that the political and ideological systems must be under business control, a result achieved long ago. In the Third World, "democracy" requires that the media and political system be in the hands of local oligarchies or similar elements committed to the form of "development" favored by U.S. investors, that the public be marginalized (by violence, if necessary), and that the military, with its long-established links to the U.S. system of violence, be granted free rein.

We can therefore understand how, on the one hand, Ronald Radosh and others can describe the contras as the "democratic resistance," while on the other, Edgar Chamorro, the CIA-appointed contra spokesman "who knows the contras far better than anyone in Washington," can characterize them as "the most 'undemocratic force' in Central America, the combined product of the CIA, Somoza, and the Argentine military." Both usages of the term "democracy" are appropriate, the first in the Orwellian sense of approved discourse, the second in the dictionary sense of the term. The Orwellian sense is required for damage control, standing alongside the term "people's democracy" flaunted by other commissars.

In the technical Orwellian sense of the term, the "fledgling democracies" of Central America much lauded by elite opinion are indeed "democracies." Similarly, the "collection of successful businessmen, bankers and attorneys" who met at a Costa Rican country club to propound a "progressive" political program under the watchful eyes of their masters are surely "democrats." The reason is that they can be counted on to oppose reform measures that would direct the resources of Nicaragua to the poor, and they insist upon domestic advantages that would guarantee something like the traditional system of rule but with *them*, rather than the Somoza clan, in the driver's seat, subordinated, of course, to the Ruler of the Hemisphere, the "enforcer" in Charles

Krauthammer's apt and admiring phrase, always on call to break the bones of anyone who gets out of line. Nicaragua, in contrast, is not a "democracy" for the sufficient reason that business- and landowner-based groups were not represented much beyond their numerical proportion in the pre-election system of governance, as Thomas Walker observes, and in the 1984 elections, privileged elites linked to U.S. state and business interests were not guaranteed the required advantages: domination of the media and the political system in addition to the power that flows from control over economic life all of this a severe affront to "democracy." That is presumably why the "moderates" left the pre-election junta and why they refused under heavy U.S. pressure to take part in the 1984 elections while the "leader" chosen by the United States, Arturo Cruz, was funded by the CIA elections that did not take place according to the U.S. doctrinal system because the right outcome was not guaranteed by the distribution of power. Similarly, the "moderates" remain admirable democrats despite their lack of a political program and their insistence at the "exile Assembly" that in contrast to the victorious Sandinistas in 1979, who gave business elements a place within the ruling coalition, they will exclude the Sandinistas totally from "any representation in the governing junta" after their victory. That stand is entirely consistent with "democracy" in the Orwellian sense of U.S. usage, just as other measures to exclude "Communists" (another term of Newspeak, referring to anyone who does not accept "democracy") are considered legitimate, at home as well, including measures of extreme violence in our dependencies. It is therefore unnecessary to demonstrate the democratic credentials of the official "democrats," or to consider any additional facts about Nicaragua.

On similar grounds, we can understand the perceptions of U.S. government officials struggling to bring "democracy" to the Third World, for example, the legendary General Edward Lansdale, who was dedicated to these tasks for many years in Southeast Asia. Explaining his progress in laying the basis for democracy in Laos after the U.S. had succeeded in subverting the coalition government established by a democratic election, he reported proudly, in secret, that "There is also a local veteran's organization and a grass-roots political organization in Laos, both of which are subject to CIA direction and control and are capable of carrying out propaganda, sabotage and harassment operations." As in Laos, so in Nicaragua: democracy under CIA control.

The same principles explain why the liberal press finds nothing odd in running an article on the opening of Congress in the Philippines, lauding "the return of fall democracy" and quoting Rep. Stephen Solarz, who says that this "marks the transition of the Philippines from dictatorship to democracy" with a headline reading: "Aquino's decree bans Communist Party," and a lead paragraph reporting that President Aquino, in a presidential decree, stipulated penalties of imprisonment for membership in the Communist Party, thus reversing the policy of the Marcos dictatorship, which legalized the party in the mid-1970s. One may imagine the response to similar moves in Nicaragua, outlawing the domestic political opposition.

On the same principles, we can explain State Department concerns that the government of Guatemala in the early 1950s was too democratic (in the dictionary sense of the term), treating the Communist Party "as an authentic domestic political party and not as part of the world-wide Soviet Communist conspiracy." As a secret State Department intelligence report commented in 1955, a year after the successful destruction of Guatemalan democracy, Arevalo, faithful to his program, insisted upon the maintenance of an open political system; and neither the military, debilitated by internal rivalries, nor self-seeking politicians were able to circumscribe his policy. It was in this atmosphere of *laissez-faire* that the communists were able to expand their operations and appeal effectively to various sectors of the population, so Guatemalan democracy obviously had to go. On the same essentially invariant principles, we can understand why democracy is untainted, and hence no critical commentary is heard, when the military retains tight control over communities in El Salvador where fear of leftist *political* contamination remains. If we proceed to less obvious cases, where more subtle questions arise, we can also understand how it can be that, in the cause of establishing democracy, U.S. occupation forces worked with considerable success to restrict democracy to limits acceptable to established privilege in Japan and Europe in the early post-World War II period, at the direction of the civilian leadership in Washington.

3

Contemporary Terrorism and Mass Media

Introduction

If we examine the larger patterns of selection by the mass media, one of its most notable characteristics is stress on "enemy" misbehavior and problems and a corresponding deemphasis of misbehavior and problems of "friends." Terror abroad can be classified roughly but usefully as *constructive, benign* and *nefarious.* Constructive terror is defined as that which positively serves important domestic interests; benign terror is that which is of little direct interest to the U.S. elite but may sometimes serve the interests of a friendly client; and nefarious terror is that committed by enemy states (or by bearers of hostile ideologies).

Constructive terror would include the holocaust in Indonesia in 1965-1966 and the large scale. political murders in Chile in 1973-1974, where the terror in both instances decimated a political opposition deemed threatening to U.S. and western interests, and was quickly followed by an opening of the door to relatively free western economic penetration. In such cases, where business and government *like* the political outcome, and in fact make notable contributions to the origination and implementation of the terror, the mass media play down the violence irrespective of its level. Reports on the scope and character of the terror are few and antiseptic, details of the human suffering involved are sparse, indignation and rage at the human agony are rare, and no sustained campaign of daily information or appeals for intervention is mounted. Government attitudes range from mild expressions of regret at the alleged excesses, interspersed with a hard-headed recognition of the (implicitly) just grievances that led to the violence, (communist provocations and threats), to even more explicit apologetics. Thus, Robert McNamara, the U.S. Secretary of Defense at the time of the 1965-1966 Indonesian coup and massacre of an estimated 500,000-1,000,000 people, described these events as a "dividend" showing that our military aid and training there "was well justified." James Reston of the *New York Times* wrote of "A Gleam of Light" rising in Indonesia as a result of "developments" in process there. It is worth noting and reflecting on the fact that the numbers slaughtered in cold blood in Indonesia in 1965-1966 exceed by a substantial factor any official U.S. or scholarly estimate of numbers *deliberately killed* in Cambodia by the Khmer Rouge. As regards the Chilean massacres of 1973-1974, probably in excess of 20,000, William Colby, then CIA head and formerly manager of a national system of death squads in South Vietnam, explained to a Congressional committee in late 1973 that the ongoing mass murder by the Chilean junta was a "good" thing, as it was "rooting out Marxist influence" and reducing the possibility of a civil war which might otherwise have taken place.

Benign terror is well exemplified by the Indonesian invasion and occupation of East Timor from 1975 up to the present time. As Indonesia is a friendly client, its aggression in East Timor aroused negligible interest in the west (with the exception of neighboring Australia), because the health and welfare of the Indonesian NSS was important to western interests (notably those of the United States and Japan), whereas East Timor was otherwise of little concern. The Indonesian invasion was a blatant act of aggression that resulted in the deaths of somewhere between 100,000 and 200,000 victims. U.S. arms were extensively employed in this invasion and occupation, in violation of U.S. law, but U.S. officials, including Presidents Ford and Carter, Vice-President Mondale, and Secretary of State Kissingen, colluded with the Indonesian generals in playing down the aggression, its illegalities and its savagery. In fact, during the Carter years 1977-1978 arms flows to Indonesia were sharply increased, facilitating the huge massacres of that period. It has been shown in detail elsewhere that, given western support of the Indonesian NSS, and thus the "benign" character of the terror brought to East Timor by the Indonesian military, this quite brutal and illegal state terrorism was off-the-agenda for the western mass media. And just as the media played down this terror, similarly, any explanations and questions about the selective suppression were also duly suppressed!

In sharp, even startling, contrast with western media silence on the events in East Timor was the attention given to Cambodia. There undoubtedly was a holocaust in Cambodia during the same period in which Indonesia was invading and attempting to subjugate East Timor, with many thousands executed and a great many more dying of disease and starvation. A question that western patriots hate to confront, however, is: why the immense attention to the Cambodian violence and the virtually total suppression of discussion of the Indonesian violence in East Timor? It should be noted that the indignation over Cambodia had no practical significance for the victims, as events in that country were beyond western influence after April 1975, and no useful suggestions for alleviating Cambodian misery were even put forward; whereas, in contrast, East Timorese deaths were being carried out in the U.S. sphere of influence, with U.S. weapons, and therefore under circumstances where western indignation and pressure might have had an impact. (It may also be asked, similarly, how we reconcile the outpouring of compassion and indignation over Cambodia and the placidity and apologetics about *dividends* and the *gleam of new light* in reference to the even larger massacre in Indonesia in 1965-1966?) Patriots react negatively to a focus on this *selectivity* of concern because it obviously compromises the idea that western benevolence is pure or perhaps even real and suggests essentially political definitions of worthy victims, and a large measure of hypocrisy. This is not to imply that many individuals concerned about Cambodian violence were not sincere and honorable. What happens, however, is that the more powerful forces in the system succeed in mobilizing human decency in a highly selective and politically skewed manner. Sometimes decent things are done for those selected as *worthy* victims. But victims of benign terror (East Timorese) or constructive terror (500,000 or more Indonesians, 20,000 or more Chileans, many millions of dispossessed and abused peasants in Brazil, Chile, Paraguay, Indonesia and the Philippines) are frozen out of this system of channeled benevolence.

Returning to the contrast between devoted mass media attention to Cambodia and neglect of the East Timor massacres, it will not do to pretend that this can be explained by the level of violence, or by our "sense of responsibility" to the Cambodians, or by our "ignorance" about East Timor. The numbers killed by deliberate acts, as opposed to deaths by the war-related ravages of disease and starvation, which were of predominant importance in Cambodia, do not appear to be of different orders of magnitude. Furthermore, the western sense of concern toward Cambodians was not evident during the huge B-52 bombing campaign of 1973, when 240,000 short tons of bombs were dropped on rice fields, water buffaloes and villages over a 160 day period, killing large numbers of Cambodians and setting the stage for the later and *further* terrible events, especially the massive starvation. Why did the west feel "responsible" for the death of Cambodians only after the Khmer Rouge took power, not during the Lon Nol regime when the deaths were the United States' direct responsibility?

Western "ignorance" about East Timor can hardly be advanced as a serious explanation of non-concern-this differential knowledgeability is precisely what has to be explained. Cambodia is a very remote and small country, and U.S. citizens could have been allowed to remain in ignorance of the sequel of events there (as they have about events in, say, Burma, or Thailand since 1975). What is more, media attention to East Timor was not negligible in 1974-1975, during the period of Portuguese withdrawal, when the fate of Timor was of some interest to the west. East Timor became "remote" *after* the Indonesian invasion, and western media coverage was inversely related to the extent of the Indonesian massacre!

It is clear, then, that if the *Readers Digest*, *Time*, the *New York Times*, the U.S. government, or important businessmen in the United States had concluded that the Indonesian invasion of East Timor was detrimental to U.S. interests, or that political capital could be extracted from focusing on its victims, the U.S. public would have become quickly "knowledgeable." But the, important power interests in the United States, including multinational investors and the military-security complex, were closely tied to the Indonesian invaders, and there was certainly no political advantage to be gained from focusing on the abuses of a NSS. U.S. policy, in fact, was supportive of the invasion and the massacre, both in the U.N. and via arms transfers (provided in violation of U.S. and international law). The mass media saw, things in the same light, and decided to "lay off." This was helped, along by the fact that primary government sources also clammed up, provided no news, and were obviously interested in a coverup which ensued.

This spectrum of power interests had no reason to "lay off" Cambodia. This was *nefarious* terror, the form which serves primary system propaganda needs, and which, according to my hypothesis, the mass media will rush to exploit at the slightest opportunity. Circumstances in Cambodia were especially favorable for a propaganda campaign. There was not only a substantial bloodbath of vengeance killings, ruthless and murderous treatment of the former urban elite, but there was also a vast residual toll of disease and starvation that was already foreseen and predicted by U.S. and other experts even before the Khmer Rouge took power. There were large numbers of refugees in Thailand and elsewhere whose stories (many no doubt quite accurate) could be selected, embellished, processed and retailed to produce a desired line and effect. In a sustained mass media campaign that might be a propaganda model of its kind, the extreme violence of the earlier conflict, and the U.S. bombings and sponsored invasion very important contributors to postwar events were quickly set aside; Pol Pot murder totals were inflated, as standards of evidence were suspended for this special case; and, in the end, the western propaganda machine succeeded in attributing every Cambodian victim of disease, starvation and retaliatory killing to Pol Pot and/or the inherent qualities of "Communism."

My purpose here is not to debate the facts about Cambodia or East Timor, but to use them to illustrate the hypothesis that mass media attention is a function not of terror per se but of the relation of terror to larger "national interests." The point is also strikingly evident in the case of "martial law" in Poland, which dominated the headlines and aroused the mass media and political leadership to a state of frenzy in the United States in 1981 and early 1982. In contrast, martial law imposed in Turkey in 1980-1981, accompanied by mass arrests, torture and executions (which threatened to engulf a good part of the trade union leadership by early 1982), aroused little attention and no indignation.

"Frightful abuse" in the enemy sphere equals a "return to stability" in the client state.

In short, what the general public knows and is interested in is managed. A small elite sets the agenda for discussion, and while there are limits on its ability to make people think in a certain way, through the mass media it is "stunningly successful in telling [the public]... what to think about." The U.S. people knew about and were interested in Cambodian atrocities, because the mass media latched on to Cambodian violence and made it familiar ground (although the level of distortion was extraordinarily high). They are able to prove the evils of Communism by focusing attention on negative events in Poland, and by simultaneously "blacking out" the facts on the literal murder of hundreds of trade union leaders and permanent martial law of varying levels of intensity in more than a score of western client states. This is a system of self-fulfilling "news interest management" in which constructive and benign terror are never allowed to become the subject of intense scrutiny and concern.

As the NSS has come into being and is protected and supported by the economic and political elite that defines the national interest, its ugly proclivities produce "dividends" and are "constructive." As was the case with the huge bloodbath in Indonesia, therefore, the mass media of the United States will not characterize its organizers as madmen, mass murderers and terrorists. By one route or other the Suhartos, Pinochets, Stroessners and their NSS colleagues and operatives will be protected. I will consider first the forces that drive the media into this apologetic function. Then I will examine the devices used that allow the media to combine massive bias with the outer garments of objectivity.

Mass Media as Protectors of the Real Terror Network

Bias is built-in by a number of basic structural facts. One is the close relationship and literal overlap between the leaders of the mass media and the businessmen and officials who like the NSS. The dozen or so top level mass media enterprises that have: real Clout are all large, profit-seeking businesses, with boards of directors that interlock with the rest of the business community. Most of them have diversified out of single media operations, some of them out of exclusive media activity, so that they are: generally business conglomerates. Some of them are in the defense business (most notably, RCA, the parent of NBC), and a number have substantial foreign interests that make them dependent on the goodwill of host governments. The second tier of mass media enterprises includes even more diversified, defense oriented and multinational enterprises most significantly Westinghouse, General Electric, Avco and Kaiser Industries. This commonality of corporate purpose, structure of interlocks, and geographic and product diversification make it likely that the mass media leaders will have the same values and the same vision of the national interest as the general community of large corporations. Eric Barnouw goes farther in his survey of TV, the most powerful of all media forms.

The symbiotic growth of American television and global enterprise has made them so inter-related that they cannot be thought of as separate. They are essentially the same phenomenon. Preceded far and wide by military advisers, lobbyists, equipment salesmen, advertising specialists, merchandising experts, and telefilm salesmen as advance agents, the enterprise penetrates much of the non-socialist world. Television is simply its most visible portion.

A second structural fact is the importance of the sponsor. The mass media depend heavily on advertising, which produces well over 50% of their gross revenue. Advertisers are mainly business firms, although the NSS governments also advertise fairly heavily with large ads and supplements in newspapers like the *New York Times* and *Wall Street Journal* and business oriented publications like *Business Week*. The general interest and even the specific interests of these advertisers are likely to have an impact on mass media selection processes. Thus, during ITTs time of troubles in the early 1970s, sponsorship of its Big Blue Marble program on TV led to a significant drop off in mention of ITT on TV news programs. Far more important, however, is the general effect of sponsorship as the prime source of TV revenue—the need to produce programs that will not seriously offend sponsors, and the mutual interest of network and sponsor in providing an environment congenial to selling advertised goods. CBS president Frank Stanton explained in 1960 that "Since we are advertiser-supported we must take into account the general objectives and desires of advertisers as a whole." Barnouw gives persuasive evidence that the sponsor exercises a huge influence on TV programming.

Their influence over it is spearheaded by "commercials"—the "focal point of creative effort"; protected by "entertainment" designed to fit sponsor needs; bordered by a fringe of successfully neutralized "public service" elements; and by a buffer zone of approved "culture."

Barnouw uses as an illustration of sponsor impact the long-time suppression by the TV networks of any negative or minimally objective analysis of the implications of nuclear power. Until the end of the 1960s, "nothing seen or heard on television could lead viewers to think that atomic energy involved risks of any serious kind. Documentaries and public service messages had come overwhelmingly, perhaps exclusively, from those who had a stake in promoting the industry;" and, "As in the early stages of the Vietnam war, the medium had served largely as a transmission belt for official and corporate promotion, closely coordinated."

On foreign news and conditions in the NSSs, the situation tends to be even worse than in the handling of domestic issues like: nuclear power, as negative impacts on distant peasants have no, political consequences in the home country. As *Time, Readers Digest* and dozens of U.S. multinational banks and non-financial corporations have extensive interests in Brazil, built up under the auspices of the hospitable generals ruling that NSS, these important members of the mass media and powerful advertisers have an important vested interest in the NSS status quo. The mass media may occasionally bite the hands that feed them, but not very hard or long, and they more than make up for these small falls from grace. They do not focus on dispossessed Brazilian peasants.

The ideological range of the top media leadership extends from enlightened cold war and corporate liberalism to militant conservative or reactionary. For the latter, in large circulation publications like *Readers Digest*, *TV-Guide* and within the Hearst and Luce empires, news and opinion bias is blatant and oriented to conservative ideological mobilization. In these publications, the death squads of Latin America, the systematic torture, the looting, and the condition and treatment of the lower 80% of the population, are for all practical purposes completely suppressed. Retail terror and Communist abuses are given enormous and highly emotional play. The *Readers Digest*, for example, over the decade 1971–1980, had more articles on Castro's Cuba than it did on all 26 U.S. client states that were using torture on an administrative basis in the early and mid-1970s.

This large and blatant brainwashing by the right has no counterpart on the left in the United States the "left" in the mass media is cold-war liberalism, strongly pro-free enterprise and devoted to the national interest as it would be defined by the progressive managements of large multinational corporations such as IBM or Bank of America. Not exactly a real left in the sense of a critical opposition. Therefore, in the mainstream respectable mass media, abuses in the NSSs are mentioned, and on rare occasion are even highlighted, but always episodically, never in a sustained manner that would build up public indignation and bring political consequences. Relatively miniscule abuses in the Soviet Union can produce day-in-day-out coverage in the, mass media; huge and sustained abuses in the NSSs cannot. That the NSS abuses were a result of U.S. intervention, as in Guatemala, where the CIA-sponsored coup, military aid and training, and the huge U.S.-managed counterinsurgency operations of 1966–1968 were absolutely decisive factors in maintaining 27 years of rightwing terror, is rarely noted and never given its proper weight.

A third structural constraint is the nature of mass media sources. Analysts of the mass media point out that they need steady and reliable sources to meet their day-by-day demands for news, and that the only sources that can produce large volumes with some minimal credibility are very powerful and rich cntitics likc govcrnmcnts and, secondarily, business firms. Thus, 46.5% of the information sources for stories appearing in the *New York Times* and *Washington Post* between 1949 and 1969 were U.S. government officials and agencies, and the trend toward reliance on government sources during that period was upward. The business community is the next most important information source. *Foreign* news is even more thoroughly dominated by a small and powerful group with vested interests in the NSS U.S. government officials, the three western news services (A.P., U.P.I. and Reuters), businesses operating abroad and foreign governments. The big news services rely heavily on the local governments for news about events in the NSSs, as do the small contingent of western reporters located there. The news services depend on these governments not only for news, but they also sell news *to* these governments, who are frequently owners of large media units. The news services are also sold to private NSS media. Any sustained focus by the media on torture, or on the parlous state of the NSS peasantry, would jeopardize relationships with primary and efficient news sources (and, for the wire services, buyers of news services). The U.S. government and businesses' operating in the NSSs are the other leading news sources the former is the Godfather;

the latter are the Godfather's progeny obtaining the benefits of the immiserating economic growth in the NSS's.

The lower echelons of the mass media are given a fair amount of freedom of action by the top managements. The top managements themselves, or at least some of them, accept an ideology of staff freedom to do things based on news value, postulated as an objective standard. Is it not possible that this ideology allows reporters, writers, editors, analysts, researchers and broadcasters to disseminate a broad range of views, some hostile to establishment interests? There is some truth in this, and I have noted that NSS abuses can be aired it is a question of how frequently and in what terms relative to the newsworthiness and human values involved. The terror that has engulfed Guatemala under the Garcia regime (to go back no farther in time) has involved *thousands* of deaths, unimaginable violence against ordinary civilians in a region of predominant U.S. influence and frequent intervention. Trade union leaders have been murdered by the hundreds, peasants have been killed, robbed and pushed off their lands by the thousands with Nazi-like ruthlessness; the center parties have been decimated by scores of murders. By any standard of human values and responsibility Guatemala deserves more indignation than Poland. I have offered the simple and obvious explanation of the lack of attention and indignation in the U.S. mass media: these terrible events and large social processes of abuse in states like Guatemala are serviceable to important domestic economic interests. The abused do not advertise, vote, threaten or complain in ways that can be heard; Bank of America, Dow, GM, Westinghouse, the U.S. Chamber of Commerce and the U.S. government can be heard, often and with compelling force. In the face of this complex of interests, well intentioned individuals in the mass media, while they can occasionally help lift the lid a little, can have only marginal impact; they cannot alter the overall drift of mass media priorities, which rests on basic structural facts and constraints.

Media staff are also predominantly middle class people who tend to share the values of the corporate leadership, and they are affected by the fact that approval,' advancement and even job survival depend on acceptance of certain priorities. The biases at: the top are filtered down by long term penalties and rewards. The mass media top leadership puts into key positions individuals who reflect their values: "I surround myself with people who generally see the way I do ...," says Otis Chandler, publisher of the *Los Angeles Times*. Bias is also a consequence of the nature of mass media news sources and the subtle impact of depending on and entering into relationships with them. In the NSSs primary news sources are government officials and local and multinational businessmen, not peasants or disaffected intellectuals. News people who actively sought out abused people would run into difficulties: (1)They would weaken their links to primary sources in these states. (2)This might result not only in loss of availability of ready information but possibly also complaints to the head office, ouster and even physical damage. (3) They would have to work harder, in contrast with the case of reliance on official sources. (4) Their stories might well be rejected at the top as (a) too controversial; (b) lacking in adequate source confirmation; or (c) not of general interest. Reports seriously critical of the NSSs would elicit flak from the powerful friends of the NSS, including enforcers like Accuracy in Media, Freedom House, the U.S. government, the governments of the NSSs, businesses and banks operating there, and advertising firms and their customers who have relationships with the NSSs. In consequence, the sources for stories describing abuses must be extra authoritative. But most dissident sources are inherently unauthoritative and will be contradicted by official sources. The Latin Church is, of course, an exception a credible source of abuses which is why it is feared and persecuted by the NSSs, and why it is under increasing attack by current U.S. leaders now aggressively protecting NSS terrorism. It takes a combination of extreme abuse, exceptional reporters and receptive home office people in the media agency for such news to surface. Since this kind of news does not surface that often, it tends to be unfamiliar and is therefore not of "general interest." Thus we have a full circle, in which NSS abuses are suppressed by a built-in process.

My conclusions then, are first, that most members of the mass media avoid a focus on NSS terror for ideological reasons; terror that is "constructive" from the standpoint of important U.S. interests is seen as a regrettable necessity serving the "national interests." And although some of the leaders and a still larger number of the lower echelons of the mass media find the reality of terror reprehensible and push for some coverage, since terror is a regrettable necessity, the primary route taken is looking the other way. Second, this ideological bias is strongly reinforced by the fact that primary sources of information on which the mass media depend are either pro-NSS or have ties of interest and reciprocity that compromise any ability to focus on serious abuses. Third, as the generation and production of information on abuses would involve extra costs in search, and assured negative repercussions from the vocal supporters of the NSS, even episodic treatment of NSS abuses is further constrained, and tends to be handled with a balance and a degree of understatement that is not required of enemy terror. Fourth, this system of watered-down and episodic treatment of terror, in the larger context of mass media protectiveness of the NSS, may actually serve the interests of the real terror network. The muted treatment of friendly terror gives the mass media more credibility as purveyors of "all the news that's fit to print" than would total suppression. The dispensing of small doses of the uglier aspects of the NSSs makes the central apologetic and diversionary role of the mass media less obvious. This allows the more liberal western elites to deceive themselves into thinking that the United States has been a neutral bystander, not an active sponsor of these unfortunate NSS "abuses," which are discussed and debated so, openly here at home. We may even be too harsh in criticizing human rights violations which seem to arise so naturally in these backward cultures.

Principles of Apologetics for the National Security State

I turn now to an examination of the methods used by the mass media to cover up and divert public attention from the abuses of the NSS. I will use this format, first, as a means of further documenting the fact that there is massive bias and a de facto cover up. My second aim is to alert readers to the variety of tricks employed and to sensitize them to the forms that bias takes. For these purposes I have organized the treatment around ten "principles," to dramatize the many varieties of bias. This list is hardly exhaustive, and the categories also overlap. I have "stripping of context" as one principle and the "United States as disinterested party" as another, but a common form of stripping of context is pretending that the United States is not an active, interested and responsible party to ongoing terror. I do not include "lying" as a. separate category as it appears directly or indirectly in most of the others, in "objectively" transmitting lies of the government, or suppressing available information that would call into question a government lie or half-truth. Most of the principles enumerated below are really sub-categories of the first "averting the eyes," or plain suppression. There can be direct suppression of important facts or evidence, which is what I encompass in that principle, or there can be eye aversion by a variety of deceptions, misrepresentations and diversionary ploys. If 20 human beings on a given day are murdered and mutilated in El Salvador, averting the eyes includes not merely failing to give these major crimes front page and detailed attention, it also includes choosing something in their place as fitter news to print such as shortages and arrests in Poland, Andrei Sakharov's hunger strike or house arrest, or State Department handouts on the Cuban threat.

It is extremely difficult for readers and observers of the U.S. mass media to get outside of the medias' premises, to look at their priorities and tricks from any critical perspective. The mass media are so powerful that their choices seem natural and the enormous everyday bias becomes a background norm like the rising and the setting of the sun. Thus when they deign to lift the veil a bit and write up in some detail events in Guatemala, such as the murder of the 76 Christian Democratic leaders in 1980, the question "where was the reportage, detail and indignation for each one of these murders?" is rarely raised.

A useful device for getting a feel for the dimension of the normal massive bias is to substitute the facts of NSS violence into a Soviet context, and try to imagine western mass media responses. I refer the reader back to the Preface where a translation is made between Lech Walesa and Brazilian labor leader da Silva, who somehow doesn't qualify for U.S. media attention, and the labor leaders in Guatemala, murdered 30 at a crack without eliciting a word from the mass media or Lane Kirkland. Or the reader might experiment with the language of Edward Schumacher's warm accolade in the *New York Times* for General Robert Viola, one of the principal organizers of Argentine torture and murder since 1976, analysed below under Principle 6 ("With the NSS let us look at the bright side"). Test out how Schumacher's wording sounds when applied to other statesmen hangmen-say, that "gruff Georgian with a warm but sly smile and walrus mustache, Joseph Stalin," or the stern gauleiter Reinhard Heydrich, a "quintessential German," beneath whose tough exterior beat a heart that had a warm spot for the music of Mozart.

1. The principle of averting of the eyes from NSS terror

The primary method of protecting Pinochet, Viola and Marcos is averting the eyes, or, in less metaphorical language, suppression. Most of the other principles examined below are more or less refined modes of achieving the same broad end, but the rudimentary and basic route is simply non-reporting or under-reporting. I described in the last chapter the extensiveness of terror in the NSSs, the use there of the most horrendous forms of dehumanization, and the fact that this terror serves the terrible: end of keeping millions of people in a deprived and miserable state. Important mass media publications engage in complete or close to complete suppression of facts about the real terror network the *Readers Digest*, for example, had a grand total of three articles describing abuses and direct violence in the NSSs through the entire decade 1971–1980. The more news-oriented and quality mass media present a much more complex picture, but suppression is still the most important single ingredient of the package they offer as news and commentary on countries like Brazil, Indonesia and Guatemala. There is total suppression of thousands of details of specific events and larger sequences of abuse that would be newsworthy if they occurred in an enemy state. I referred in the Preface to the First Congress of Relatives of the Disappeared, held in Costa Rica in January, 1981, an exceedingly dramatic occasion with all the ingredients of newsworthiness, except for that one key variable the murderers are our allies, and their murders are therefore "constructive" or "benign," as I defined these terms earlier. The murdered Christian Democratic politicians in Guatemala fall into the same category. When the numbers murdered reached 76, and with the internal conflict and slaughter in that country attaining high levels of ferocity, the victims became newsworthy, as an aggregate; but the public's eyes were averted from the individual murders. Even larger massacres are suppressed by the U.S. mass media, one of the most notable being that carried out on May 14, 1980 on the banks of the Rio Sumpul river by the El Salvadoran National Guard, where,

On that day, fourteen National Guard trucks arrive around 7:00 A.M. in the villages of San Jacinto and La Arada. All the inhabitants, men, women and children, are gathered by the river that partially follows the border. The massacre lasted ten hours. In total, more than 600 people murdered, houses looted and destroyed, corn fields burned with gasoline; a policy of "total scorched earth". Corpses were either left lying to be eaten by predators or thrown in the Rio Sumpul. Honduran peasants caught in a fresh-water fishing net the bullet-riddled bodies of five children. Area inhabitants affirm that Honduran soldiers were posted up on the hills and watched the massacre without intervening. How could they have intervened without starting an armed conflict with unforseeable consequences? But, about ten days beforehand, Salvadorian and Honduran officers met at El Poy, a border town. On the eve of the massacre, over 150 Honduran troops had arrived in the area, forbidding the population to move.

This huge crime was unmentioned in the U.S. mass media at the time, and has been mentioned only briefly and rarely since, although it was newsworthy in Latin America and Western Europe. This was constructive terror, and occurred shortly after new Carter administration moves to step up military assistance to the El Salvadoran military regime, as well as to Honduras. At the Rio Sumpul massacre, as with Operation Condor murders, we can see U.S. efforts at training, aid and inter-NSS coordination coming to fruition, bearing "dividends." Armstrong and Wheaton point out that during the day-long slaughter " U.S. made trucks, jeeps, communications equipment and helicopters were used by the Honduran forces who maintained ongoing communication with Salvadoran armed forces via U.S.-made walkie-talkies."

In Guatemala, Church and other sources have collected and eagerly offer innumerable well-documented and detailed accounts of army and paramilitary murders, rapes and thefts that occur on a daily basis against the Indian and peasant populations. These are almost entirely ignored by the western media, but show up occasionally as dry statistics matte-of-fact notings that 30 or 40 bodies were found on Guatemalan roadsides today. When these daily murders are spelled out and humanized, they can make an impression. Thus in an article entitled "Violence Batters The Church

In Guatemala", June Carolyn Erlick writes, Father Carlos Galvez was on his way to baptize a child in a Guatemalan rural community on May 14. Suddenly shots rang out. He, like seven priests in Guatemala before him, was murdered in cold blood.

"There were only horrified neighbors who could do nothing to keep his life from spilling out onto the stones of the street," wrote a nun who works in Guatemala. "When his body was removed the parishioners circled the pool of blood with rocks and filled the circle with flowers. But soon no blood was visible. It had been reverently gathered up with the dust of the road and carried home by grieving townspeople in much the same way that the early Christians gathered the blood of their martyrs as relics of their witness to their faith on the sand of the coliseum."

The funeral in Tecpan, where Father Carlos worked, was massive. Three bishops and over 30 priests concelebrated the Mass, even though they knew they were risking their lives to do so.

"But the greatest tribute to Father Galvez, the sixth priest to be killed since May 1980, was the enormous crowd of townspeople at the Mass," writes the nun. "Shoulder to shoulder stood wealthy and poor, young and old, men and women, Indians and mestizos."

Multiply this story by 2,000 or more a year for Guatemala alone, adding in the frequent pre-killing violence of rape and torture, the subsequent mutilations, the widespread thievery, and we see at picture of the human but de-humanized Guatemala but we also see why it is important that the U.S. public be spared such details.

Indonesia is another country almost completely "blacked out" by the mass media of the United States. This is in perfect accord with a hypothesis proposed here: namely, that a friendly NSS which allows easy penetration by western economic interests can engage in virtually unlimited abuse of its own citizens without attracting substantial attention or expressions of concern, let alone denunciations, by the U.S. mass media. Really sensational events can occur;

people of the same high quality and nobility as Sakharov can be harassed, arrested, tried, imprisoned and killed in Indonesia, *and the U.S. public will never know about it.* I will give two illustrations. One is the arrest and trial in 1979 of Heri Akhmadi, general chairman of the Students' Council of the Bandung Institute of Technology. This episode directly followed widespread student protests at Suharto's unopposed election for President in 1978. In retaliation, and to help return the students to the proper state of fear and quiescence, the army invaded dozens of college campuses in January, 1978 and arrested scores of student leaders. This was followed by an even more violent invasion of the campuses in February 1979, when many students were injured, hundreds more were arrested, and the army units confiscated and took off "evidence." (At his trial, Akhmadi asked: "Does the law actually provide for such a method of confiscation?", but he never received a reply.) The protesting students, largely middle-class, were objecting to a comic opera election by generals without legitimate authority, who had chosen (in Akhmadi's words) "the easiest and laziest way" of growing, namely, attracting as much foreign investment as possible without regard to domestic impact, and who had been looting on their own without restraint, in a system of managed privilege, while doing very little to alleviate truly massive poverty and distress.

The trial of the most prominent student leader in Indonesia had three features that one would have thought would make it newsworthy. First, it was a trial of someone protesting political tyranny, which is supposedly a western value of importance. Second, Akhmadi was being tried for allegedly "insulting" the head of state, Suharto, again presumably a basis of arrest and trial contrary to western ideals. And, third, Akhmadi put up a bold and eloquent defense, of sufficient interest and quality that the Cornell Modern Indonesian Project published a translation in 1981 under the title "Breaking The Chains of Oppression of the Indonesian People, Defense Statement at His Trial on Charges of Insulting the Head of State". If Akhmadi had been a communist, allegedly conspiring against the state, perhaps his trial would have been newsworthy; but as he was a strongly anticommunist nationalist, who presented a serious indictment of the Suharto regime for looting and selling out the national patrimony to foreign interests, his dramatic statement and his victimization failed to make the grade in the western media. Once again, the reader is urged to translate to a hypothetical "Moscow equivalent" student leader, and trace out the probabilities of equivalent media suppression.

Another illustration concerns the distinguished Indonesian novelist Pramoedya Anata Toer, a nominee for the Nobel prize in literature, referred to in the *Far Eastern Economic Review* as Indonesia's "best living novelist," who, "from the beginning of his literary career has been functioning behind bars." His first major works were written in a Dutch jail in 1949. Between 1965 and 1979 he was imprisoned by the Indonesian generals without charges or trial (along with tens of thousands of others). During this 14 year imprisonment, Pramoedya wrote, among other things, four historical novels. Two of them, *World of Man* and *A Child of All Nations*, were secretly published in 1980 and widely distributed, even though quickly banned by the authorities. Pramoedya was subject to multiple interrogations and harassment following a lecture in September, 1980 at the University of Indonesia, and four students who arranged the talk as well as his publisher were arrested. The publisher was held incommunicado and had not been released by year end 1981. Ten thousand copies of Pramoedya's two novels were burned by order of the Attorney-General of Indonesia in October 1981.

Keith Foulcher, commenting in the *Times Literaty Supplement* of August 7, 1981, wrote on the ban on Pramoedya's two novels:

> *His situation, just eighteen months after his release, may again be precarious. For the rest of the world, the ban serves as an indication that Indonesia`s one major novelist to date still awaits the basic freedom to practise his art, let alone official recognition of it.*

Once again, the dramatic event of the arrests, the nobility and prestige of the victim, an official book-burning, would seem to define a newsworthy violation of human rights. Benedict Anderson of the Cornell Modern Indonesian Project even received a call from the *New York Times* to get his confirmation (which he gave) of the fact of the book-burning. The *Manchester Guardian*, in England, carried a letter of protest against the treatment of Pramoedya with distinguished signatories from 16 different countries. But nothing materialized through 1981 in the *New York Times* or elsewhere in the mass media of the United States. Pramoedya chose the wrong country in which to suffer repression, and his condition is what we may call "structurally unnewsworthy."

I will give one final illustration, of averting the eyes by underreporting, a case that is of interest because it combines partial suppression with hypocrisy. In October, 1979 a political refugee from Paraguay living in Brooklyn recognized there Americo Pena-Irala, a police inspector general from Asuncion and a member of a team that tortured and murdered assorted opponents of General Stroessner. Pena had been accused by the father of one victim, a 17-year old boy named Joelito Filartiga, of kidnapping, torturing and murdering him. The *New York Times*, in a small back page article of April 5, 1979, noted that A confidential report prepared by the Inter-American Commission on Human Rights of the Organization of American States, contended that Mr. Pena and three other policemen kidnapped the Filartiga youth on March 19, 1976, with the intent of forcing him to incriminate his father falsely in sedition charges. The report, obtained by the *New York Times*, asserted that the boy had died of a heart attack after being beaten and receiving high-voltage electric shocks.

The boy's father, a physician and painter of renown, started an international campaign to bring charges against Pena, and the case was investigated by Amnesty

International as well as by the OAS. Pena was under such pressure that he decided to leave Paraguay temporarily, and the kindly U.S. consulate in Asuncion gave him a visa to enter the United States. Following the sighting noted above, Pena was eventually taken into custody by the U.S. Immigration and Naturalization Service, which held him on bond pending deportation hearings. The father of the murder victim brought a suit for damages against Pena in a U.S. court to prevent his deportation to the safety of Paraguay and, hopefully, to try to obtain justice by law in this country. This effort failed as the suit was lost on appeal to the Supreme Court and Pena was allowed to leave the country.

Several points are worthy of special note here. First, this case involved facts of huge dramatic potential, human interest, and state terror in its most terrible form. A young boy tortured to death in a police state, with photos available of slashes, whip wounds, an erect penis from unremoved wires still in the dead body. The father pursuing justice and catching up with the torturer-murderer, who, according to the Council on Hemispheric Affairs, was not only one of the most detested and feared police killers in Paraguay but also a drug dealer and pimp, very possibly bringing into New York City unsuspecting Paraguayan teen-age girls for sale as prostitutes.

Point two, however, is that this remarkable story was not found very newsworthy in the United States. The *New York Times* gave it an aggregate of four small back-page items of coverage and failed to interview Dr. Joel Filartiga, the father, and get his views on these events, despite his distinction, the nobility and justice of his effort, and his presence in New York City. This conforms to an earlier pattern noted by Richard Arens in his *Genocide in Paraguay*: namely, that the U.S. press in general, the *New York Times* among them, "shamefully buried" stories about the destruction of the Aché Indians that were found newsworthy in Great Britain, West Germany, Switzerland and elsewhere.

It also conforms to the hypothesis advanced here, that the leading mass media enterprises have a strong propensity, to suppress or play down terror in U.S. client states. From the media's viewpoint, Dr. Filartiga chose the "wrong country" in which to have his son tortured to death.

A third point concerns the protective cover given this client state terrorist by the United States government. Pena was initially provided with an entry permit on the basis of a fraudulent claim. When he was discovered in Brooklyn, it took months, and the impetus of aroused congressional interest, before the Immigration and Naturalization Service took Pena into custody. The government then tried as hard as it could to get Pena deported back to the safety of Paraguay, and fought the attempts by the father of the torture-murder victim to keep Pena in the United States to stand trial.

This,brings us, finally, to the matter of hypocrisy. On August 20, 1980, the *New York Times* had an editorial entitled "Foreign Torture, American Justice", dealing in large part with the Pena Filartiga case. It describes briefly the background and legal process, but focuses on a decision by Judge Irving Kaufman in the Court of Appeals, that allowed Pena to be sued as a violator of international law if ustice is unobtainable in the home country of victim and victimizer. The hypocrisy rests in the fact that at the time Pena was in the United States, when a trial against him would have been meaningful, and when extensive news coverage and editorial indignation would have been of practical significance, the *New York Times* was exceedingly quiet. Its editorial on the case features U.S. judicial nobility in the cause of justice, whereas U.S. *practice* sustained by the *New York Times* features the glossing over and protecting of friendly terror, no matter how outlandish.

2. The principle of reliance on government as the source of the relevant and the true

This is a principle with obvious exceptions, but the exceptions do not vitiate its importance as a powerful basis of brainwashing under freedom. The *main* exception is the government of enemy states, whose pronouncements are normally neither sought out nor taken at face value. In reporting on Vietnam and Cambodia, U.S. reporters and western wire services almost never communicate with and convey the explanations and rationales of the leaders of those governments on internal economic problems or sources of violence. There, refugees and western official sources have sufficed. Whereas, on economic problems and violence in the NSSs of Indonesia, Thailand and Chile, the views of the NSS officials are important, both directly and *via* wire service reports. This was applicable, for example, in the case of the South African incursions into Angola in mid-1981, where, as I described earlier, the press gave dominant coverage not to the Angolan victims, the damage sustained by Angola, or Angola's accounts or explanations of events, but rather to South Africa's views. There was heavy front page play to the South African capture of "Soviet advisers" and attention was given to the "spoils" captured by the apartheid regime in its invasion. As in the case of East Timor, there was a minimum of indignation.

The U.S. government, as sponsor of the NSS, provides it with a protective propaganda cover. And it succeeds because of its power as a preeminent news source, its special relations with the mass media, and their patriotic refusal to challenge patriotic lies. When they do raise questions about really egregious lies, they do it in so muted a fashion while continuing to allow the government unlimited space for reiteration that the public is still hardly aware of the fact that the government is lying. There is an important difference in this regard even as between the western European and U.S. media, with the former tending to look more closely at U.S. government claims, the latter more likely to do very little independent search and more inclined to transmit the official line. A comparative study by Moraes and Lawton of European and U.S. press coverage of the 1973 Chilean coup, for example, shows clearly that the major U.S. papers followed at "line" that stressed Allende mismanagement as the root of the coup, deemphasized internal and external opposition and destabilization efforts as factors contributing to Allende's difficulties, and, following the coup, underplayed the torture and murder and stressed the "return to normality," precisely in conformity with "one of the major themes appearing throughout the junta's own propaganda." Moraes and Lawton show that the European. press used a wider range of sources and disputed this State Department-Pinochet party line disseminated by the U.S. press.

When the U.S. government wants to establish some policy justifying "truth" e.g., that the problem in South Vietnam in 1961–1962 or 1964–1965 was North Vietnamese aggression, or that the rebels in El Salvador are "extreme leftists" under the "discipline" of World Communism the U.S. mass media cooperate and the patriotic truths are established. This is accomplished. by the sheer volume of government claims and handouts and their uncritical transmission by the media that count. A study by Gusmao and Benjamin of the *New York Time's* 1980 coverage of El Salvador, for example, found that 60% of the attributed sources represented the official government viewpoint, and that although the majority of the victims of violence in El Salvador have been peasants, the *New York Times* quoted only two peasants in 75 articles on that country. With this dependence on official sources, the mass media can be "used" to convey a propaganda line. When the State Department wanted to show that the Nicaraguans were helping the El Salvadoran guerillas, a beach landing of "well-armed guerillas" and a huge battle was reported by Christopher Dickey in the *Washington Post* of January 14, 1980, based on telephone calls from his hotel room in San Salvador to U.S. officials. On January, 19 Dickey reversed himself, still claiming an engagement of troops, "But where they came from and who they were has not been established and U.S. officials here now are saying that White 'overemphasized' the supposed invasion and no longer thinks the evidence about it as 'compelling' as the day he spoke." This is "news" in a Pickwickian sense, depending on the fluctuating emphases desired by various U.S. officials. Maslow and Arana, in their examination of the media's gullibility on El Salvador, conclude that "Dickey, it seems, had been used by intelligence agencies to spread the evidence of Nicaraguan intervention and thus bolster the case for renewing military aid to the junta." Former CIA employee Ralph McGehee noted that, Although the reported battle between the invading guerillas [allegedly 100 or more men] and the Salvadoran security forces lasted all day, the Government troops failed to kill any guerillas, capture any prisoners, or recover any weapons. A second sea raid was reported on January, 22 again without casualties or prisoners. This was considered sufficient evidence, and on January, 24, the United States signed a $65 million aid package with the Salvadoran Government. On January, 29, two Salvadoran government officials resigned, charging that the two "invasions" were staged in order to justify the sending in of American troops.

According to a "Dissent Paper on El Salvador and Central America," put out by individuals in the State Department at odds with official policy, there has been a deliberate effort by the authorities to "misrepresent the situation in El Salvador," and, with the help of "liason and public relations" efforts, "media coverage of El Salvador has been responsive to official government policies." This is clearly evident in the media's handling oil the El Salvador White Paper. The government issues White; Papers that offer alleged proofs of its claims in a charged atmosphere that produces enormous headlines. There may have been "leaks" to favored reporters and columnists in prior weeks. The mass media uniformly feature these claims as hot news irrespective of their plausibility or validity. In the lesser media (from the standpoint of circulation) the government's charges are often contested and are sometimes shown to be the inverse of the truth. Thus the Johnson adminstration's White Paper of 1964, was utterly devastated by I. F. Stone and by the editors of the *New Republic* (among others), but the charge of North Vietnamese aggression was nevertheless institutionalized. The El Salvador White Paper of 1981 has been similarly taken apart and shown to be crude even by traditional White Paper standards by James Petras, John Dinges and Philip Agee. Somewhat later the *Wall Street Journal* itself featured a long news article that pointed up the careless packaging of this propaganda piece. The Reagan administration apparently understands that fact and consistency are irrelevant, and can be overridden by the mass media's deferential role playing as conduit for whatever claims the authorities wish to disseminate. Thus once again, as with earlier White Papers and the Red Scares of 1919–1920 and 1949–1955, the mass media of the United States failed to examine the foundations of a party line that was not true.

The government White Paper claims of a large-scale outside Communist arms flow into El Salvador are based on alleged captured documents. The secret of U.S. mass media apologetics is to pass on official claims and interpretations of documents immediately as truth, without even examining the documents, without independent checking of the claims, and without any context. The *Baltimore Sun* carried a front page article headlined "Haig Describes Salvador Insurgency As Soviet Attempt To Overthrow Junta"

Overthrow Junta," and Roger Mudd conduited the State Department view on NBC: "The [State] Department said weapons are being supplied by the Soviet Union, Vietnam and East Germany among others, and that the whole operation is being coordinated by Cuba." Juan de Onis of the *New York Times*, also "objectively" conveyed the message that the Soviet bloc nations had pledged arms to the Salvadoran rebels according to captured documents which "are considered authentic by U.S. intelligence agencies." This last point is not knowable by de Onis—it would be more "objective" to say that the documents are *alleged* to be considered authentic by these agencies, as a de Onis knows that such agencies may occasionally leak fabrications to people like himself.

Both John Dinges and James Petras have shown that even taking the documents at face value, all they demonstrate is an effort to mobilize support abroad by the rebels; an effort not confined to the Communist powers, and one that met with only modest success. The Soviet Union is mentioned in the documents only in a report of El Salvadoran Communist Party chief Handal's tour of the Communist states, in which he expresses disappointment at a refusal of a high official of the Soviet Union to meet with him and in "the non-resolution of the request for help." Nothing in these documents anywhere suggests that the Soviets have made more than token moves to aid, or that either the Soviet or Cubans initiated or coordinated anything. In short, the Haig claims of a Soviet attempt to "overthrow the junta" is demagogic lying of the most egregious sort.

The White Paper's evidence for a large and rapidly growing Communist. arms flow to the rebels is extremely muddled and obscure, but it took an outsider, Christopher Wren of *The Times* of London, to look at the facts on the scene. He went to the head of the Salvadoran National Guard, which had allegedly captured the documents, and he looked over the captured weapons themselves which he found to be in small quantity, many home-made, and including a British Lewis machine gun of First World War vintage. The White Paper charges that some 800 tons of arms were promised to the rebels and 200 delivered, but the *documents* give evidence of perhaps 10 tons having crossed over the borders. Those who have looked closely at the arms flow to the rebels find the distinctly small flows to be coming from Costa Rica, Panama, Florida, and, in general, mainly from a flourishing international black market in which the rebels appear to be buying. The White Paper focus on Cuba and Nicaragua as major sources of arms is unsupported by the allegedly supporting documents and is contrary to independent evidence on the arms flows.

The White Paper is a throw-back to 1965, when the U.S. Indo-China assault was preluded by similar claims of an enormous flow from North Vietnam, also not sustained by the accompanying "documents." I.F. Stone went to the trouble of actually inspecting the documents, which the mass media did not do and still do not do and was able to compute that approximately 2 ½% of the captured weapons of the previous 18 months were of Communist origin, 80% were captured from the United States or one of its proxies. With only rare exception, it is outsiders who investigate and contest major government claims that prepare the ground for foreign intervention; the mainstream reporters, publications and stations are part of a national institutional apparatus whose function in such cases is the institutionalization of patriotic truths. The main qualifications to this normally cooperative relationship occur when the government is threatening encroachments on mass media prerogatives, or in those very special cases where the government is operating in a manner deemed threatening by important domestic power groups. Ordinarily foreign policy rests on an elite consensus, and a symbiotic relationship between government and the mass media follows. The threat of sharply escalated intervention in El Salvador in 1981 and early 1982 led to heightened public attention, some elite reservations and suggested caution, and an opening up of publicity on details of the junta's anti-civilian violence. At the same time, U.S. government claims were allowed full head, and its misrepresentations of the nature of the junta, the rebels and the threat of "foreign intervention" were the dominant factors shaping general public understanding of the issues and allowing continued U.S. support of state terrorism in its ugliest form.

3. Stripping away of context

Facts have meaning only in context. Mindless reporting of Haig claims that X-tons of arms are flowing into El Salvador from the' Communist powers is not "objective," even apart from veracity it allows a propaganda source to define which facts are important and which are to be ignored. As a propagandist, Haig's aim is to push into the background the U.S. role in El Salvador, past and present, to create a context in which whatever we may be doing or have done we have a right to do; whereas Cuban and Soviet intrusions are a priori illegitimate. As in Guatemala, however, the El Salvadoran "security forces" that have been killing peasants by the thousands and ravaging the countryside for quite a few years are products of an exclusively U.S. investment in military training and arms, which became especially heavy and intense in the "counter-insurgency 60's." Security assistance was only $16.9 million between 1950 and 1979, but over 2,000 El Salvadoran officers were U.S.-trained and the paramilitary security force, Orden, was encouraged in the 1960s as part of post-Castro counter-revolutionary strategy. There was a cutback ' in military assistance to El Salvador during the early Carter years, but it was never terminated, and the slack was taken up by U.S. "surrogates" like Israel and Brazil. U.S. military aid to the El Salvador junta in 1980 totalled only $5.9 million, but economic aid amounted to a substantial $72.5 million and additional multilateral aid brought the grand total to $183.9 million. It is elementary that a dollar provided to a general pool releases a dollar to acquire "lethal" weapons.

The U.S. mass media pretend that third party supply by our clients and surrogates is not a worthy subject for discussion. An arms shipment from Nicaragua to the rebels is newsworthy and somehow sinister arms transferred from Honduras or Brazil to the El Salvador junta is not news. Rebels and governments opposed by the United States, such as the Arbenz government of Guatemala in 1954, are subject to serious military threats by generous U.S. supply and training of rightwing forces and by U.S. encouragement of neighboring clients to invade or threaten groups or states on our hit list. The latter will have to seek arms to survive. Boycotted by the U.S. and its clients, the rebels will reach out to any friendly powers for arms and other assistance. But arms coming from Czechoslovakia in 1954, and trickling in the early 1980s from Nicaragua, Cuba and more distant Communist powers show the international Communist conspiracy at work trying to undermine Free Societies., This parody is close to the workings of the propaganda machine. Since the mass media will allow a Dulles, a Rusk and a Haig to get away with identifying any trickle of arms from the Communist world as sinister and proof of some dangerous Red plot, even if defensive and provoked by gross U.S. and U.S. client intervention and threats, the system will always work to create a propaganda rationale for anything the United States chooses to do.

In short, if arms to El Salvador were discussed in a full context, it would be seen that the United States has been the only serious supplier of arms to that country over the past several decades, that the murderous central regime of El Salvador is a product of long and extensive U.S. training, supply and political manipulation, and that the only long-term conspiracy to dominate from the outside is quite clearly located in Washington, D.C.

The stripping away of context has long been a feature of U.S. mass media reporting on Indo-China. As indicated earlier, deaths under the Khmer Rouge regime were ultimately attributed to Communism and Pol Pot period. Antecedent factors involving the west, such as the murderous warfare prior to April 1975, the devastation of the land, and the already endemic starvation conditions were set aside to allow a focus on the desired locus of terror. A superb recent example was provided by Henry Kamm in his article in the *New York Times* of November 8, 1981, "In Mosaic of Southeast Asia, Capitalist Lands Are Thriving." Kamm finds, "sadly," that conditions of life in Vietnam, Cambodia and Laos are bad, in contrast with the rising living; standards and a "state of peace in the countries of the region that reject Communism." I think we must concede that 10 million tons of bombs, supplemented by a boycott of the victims of the! bombs, is less serviceable to per capita income growth than no bombs and positive external aid. But Kamm does not even mention that the countries which failed to "reject Communism" were invaded by a distant great power and subjected to a bombing onslaught unparalleled in human history. He even states with great matter-of-factness, as if part of a long and undisturbed historical process, that in the countryside of Indo-China, "even working animals are rare, and men, women and children do the work done elsewhere by machines or beasts of burden." That the vast proportion of these beasts of burden were killed quite recently, during more than a decade of warfare-a large fraction by U.S. bombs is unmentioned, as is the fact of a post-1975 U.S. boycott and deliberate effort to impede the replacement of beasts of burden by other states. This, I believe, carries "stripping of context" to the limit of its theoretical potential.

Kamm also provides some observations on changes in the level and distribution of income in Southeast Asia that are worthy of note. He tells us that a first-time visitor to Manila or Jakarta will be impressed by the prevalence of luxury motor cars in the midst of penury; but longer term observers (i.e., Henry Kamm) can see that "the floor has risen for the many." What is the proof? Motorbikes owned by the "average man" clogging the streets, people better dressed, and cassette recorders and cameras more prevalent. In the villages, bicycles and frequent sewing machines "tell of a gradual, if uneven, amelioration in the standard of life." This evidence leaves something to be, desired on matters of representativeness, rigor and consistency with more detailed studies. Motorbikes observed on the main streets of cities with millions of inhabitants, even if measured closely rather than by casual impression, hardly tell us much about the human condition of the 99% of unobserved cases, possibly living in the huge shanty towns that have grown on the periphery of NSS big cities. There is no indication in Kamm's reporting that he ever gets off the main streets. One wonders, also, how many of the thousands of villages in rural Indonesia and the Philippines Henry Kamm has visited, and how many households he checked out concerning the number of sewing machines. If he visited as many as one tenth of 1% of the villages, and checked as many as 20 households, I would be surprised.

The World Bank 1980 report on Indonesia, which goes as far as one can go in looking at the bright side without doing gross violence to the facts, gives a quite different picture from Kamm. In contrast with Kamm's "gradual amelioration" up and down the line, the World Bank says that "the overall impression one gets [from studying data on the wages paid by business firms and governmental bodies] is that real wages of unskilled workers in these firms have at best stagnated." The "at best" is generous as virtually all sectors, including the government, "show a decline in real wages between 1973 and 1977 ranging from 3% in government administration to over 50% in a large hotel." The Bank also concludes that improvements which have occurred "still amount to only a tiny diminution in the problem of poverty in Indonesia with 50.1 million people altogether existing on less than US$ 0.25 per day." The situation in the Philippines has been worse, with virtually nobody claiming any improvement in the condition of the huge numbers of destitute, and with that total itself increasing. Szal shows that urban real wages fell for both skilled and unskilled workers during the 1970s, and he cites Philippine evidence of serious levels of malnutrition.

On the question of the distribution of income between rich and poor, Henry Kamm puts the matter this way: "there is ample proof [not anywhere cited by Kamm] that the floor has risen for the many, while the ceiling has gone higher for the few." He thereby carefully side-steps the question of differences in the degree of benefits between classes, although every serious observer of the facts (including the World Bank) is very clear that in both Indonesia and the Philippines the "few" have significantly increased their proportion of the total. And Kamm gives no figures on the actual distribution of income, although data are readily available.

The NSSs in Kamm's beat have also been characterized by elite looting and conspicuous consumption of really notable proportions, but Henry Kamm has long steered clear of any close look at the details. Ingrid Palmer suggests a phenomenal 30% of national income corruption drain in Indonesia, where the: generals have a long established record of venality, and the lavish life style and large scale corruption of Marcos and his cronies is also well known. In the Kamm article, there is an antiseptic statement about luxury motor cars and "economic injustice evidenced by this conspicuous consumption in the midst of penury" but this exhausts his discussion, and it is surrounded by the claims of an alleged rise in the bottom, the average man's motor bike in Jakarta, and a statement on income distribution that suppresses evidence of a redistribution upward. No statements on magnitudes, or suggestions of venality, or details regarding housing conditions, servants, forms of elite consumption and outlays for entertainment, size of Swiss bank accounts, or other matters that would give any substance or life to NSS inequality and other abuses.

It is not that Henry Kamm never gets indignant over unequal life styles e.g., on March 3, 1980 Kamm had an article on "Pol Pot Living in Jungle Luxury in Midst of Deprived Cambodia," in which he is quite sarcastic about the plush conditions of the Khmer Rouge leadership, with "smiling waiters" in a camp that is "the latest in jungle luxury," the visitors received in a room with "a handsome vaulted roof of dried leaves over a table at which coffee was served to refresh the visitors." Each of four guest bungalows had four beds made of wood and bamboo, with homemade mattresses, blankets and pillows. And bamboo vases contained flowers "that must have been brought from Thailand." Thus Kamm is capable of providing details of luxurious living, but he selects according to the principles that I have already spelled out. Even in the article I am focusing on here on Capitalist Lands Thriving, while Kamm provides no detail on the elites of the NSSs, he does get a bit angry at the high living of the bureaucrats of the Communist states, juxtaposing a remark on the badly fed condition of the people with the assertion that "motorized transport [is] reserved for high Government and Communist Party officials."

It is fitting that Henry Kamm should close out his 12 year stint in Southeast Asia with an article covering up the structured deprivation and injustice of the NSSs, and discoursing at length on the performance differentials between the Indo-Chinese states and the U.S. clients without once mentioning any possible relevance of the 10 million tons of bombs dropped on the former.

4. The principle of balance

The classic modes of expressing balance to protect NSS violence are to pretend either that there is an equivalence of state and "left" violence, or that the government stands in the middle between a left and right that is independent of the government and which the government is trying to control. As I described earlier in the case of Sterling, this can be done with a further apologetic twist in which leftist terror comes first, then the military reluctantly enters to rectify matters. Why the military keeps on killing, as in Uruguay, long after the extermination of the leftists, is not discussed. In treating Brazil, where state terrorism produced a responsive left terror that had not existed previously at all, Sterling suppresses the causal sequence and then attributes the further abuses of the military regime.

The principle of balance invariably involves lying, as the balance usually does not equate, or the matters put in the balance are not comparable. Thus, Warren Hoge suggests that Guatemala is "in the grip of an escalating balance of terror" between incompetent terrorists and an "inept" army. This balance is false, first, because official killings have exceeded the killings by the "left" (which actually includes the middle) by an enormous factor; surely better than 25 to 1. Between 1966 and 1976 some 20,000 people were killed by government forces, initially in a huge counter-insurgency campaign which eliminated a guerilla force estimated at a peak level of 450, plus thousands of "others." More recently, just since Garcia came to power in 1978, his program of political murder has resulted in over 7,000 deaths. "The bodies of the victims have been found piled up in ravines, dumped at road-sides or buried in mass graves. Thousands bore the scars of torture, and death had come to most by strangling with a garrotte, by being suffocated in rubber hoods or by being shot in the head." These are victims of rightwing-state terror. Even the Guatemalan government does not pretend that these are victims of leftists its claim is that they are the results of the actions of autonomous rightwing death squads.

The second deception of the "balance" line in its application to Guatemala is its failure to recognize that the guerillas have come into existence once again under the most extreme provocations most notably, pacification by deliberate and extensive murder. Many of the thousands of murders have been indiscriminate, carried out sometimes on whim or on the basis of rumor or alleged associations. This is especially true of people of low status, who have constituted "the vast majority" of victims of official violence. The precarious balance for the poor in Guatemala between life and death at the hands of the security services is illustrated by the testimonies in this report. The former soldier describes house-to-house searches in which the discovery of certain "paper" leaflets or circulars was sufficient reason to wipe out an entire family. The prisoner [who described his ordeals to AI], who was brutally tortured and escaped only the day before he was due to be executed at Huehuetenango army base, believes that a neighbor denounced him as "subversive" because of a dispute over the village basketball court—a good enough reason, as far as officers of the Guatemalan army were concerned, for him to be tortured and put to death.

But official violence in Guatemala is not entirely random. According to AI,

> *By far the majority of victims were chosen after they had become associated or were thought to be associated with social, religious, community or labor organizations, or after they had been in contact with organizers of national political parties. In other words, Amnesty International`s evidence is that the targets for extreme governmental violence tend to be selected from grass roots organizations outside official control.*

This system of anticipatory pacification by systematic murder has been carried out under conditions of appalling exploitation and oppression of the Indian and peasant population. The remarkable inequality of income distribution in Guatemala and the horrendous conditions of the majority as measured by unemployment, malnutrition, child mortality, life expectancy, illiteracy and curable disease rates. This is a NSS at its most violent, rapacious and cruel, with large scale expropriations of peasant and Indian lands by force (as in Brazil and Paraguay), extensive and uncontrolled use of pesticides like DDT and Endrin on open fields in which Indian men, women and children are working, and regular murder of any elements of the lower orders that raise their voices or attempt any self-defence. No independent political activity has been possible in Guatemala since the U.S. sponsored rightwing coup of 1954. As noted, even the modestly liberal Christian Democratic Party had virtually its entire body of officials murdered by the Garcia government, and it has closed down its office in Guatemala City. In this environment "guerillas" have emerged, have killed a few score members of the "security forces" and their supporters and sponsors, and thus we have a state of offsetting terrorism of the left and right!

Warren Hoge quotes an unnamed scientist who suggests that the Indians of Guatemala will be hard for the "guerillas" to mobilize as "they are real good at stepping aside and getting out of the way." No suggestion of the possibility that the *guerillas* may be Indians, although Church and other independent sources in Guatemala say that the escalating abuses both forcible expropriations plus continuous search and destroy missions involving arbitrary killing and regular thievery are literally forcing them into self-defense, and that many Indians have already joined the guerillas. Although Hoge gives a few rather antiseptic figures on the concentration of wealth and the imperfections of the electoral process and human rights situation, there is nothing on the quality of treatment of the Indians, the forms of exploitation, or the extensiveness, character and role of political murders in Guatemala. He does cite an expatriate who had worked for a social action group: "The head of one such group who has just left the country because his life was threatened said the overreaction to ordinary organizations occurred after the Sandinista victory in Nicaragua and civil war in El Salvador. 'Suddenly, everything that had been normal became suspicious to the army,' he said." Notice how the cause of the violence in Guatemala is shifted to the outside; the death squads are just "over-reacting" to what is, by implication, a legitimate external threat. The over-reacting implies that the prior behavior of Garcia and company was perhaps reasonable. So does the quoted phrase about what had been "normal" in the! past. This is classic apologetics. And, having quoted the "opposition" (or misquoted it, or paraphrased it to apologetic purpose), Hoge can close out this article with two paragraphs on the views of the Reagan administration.

Flora Lewis, an old hand at apologetics for U.S. intervention in Guatemala, provides a genuine classic in the use of "balance" in her article on "The Danger of Absolutes", in the *New York Times* of October 16, 1981. This article is, in fact, an absolute gold mine of clichés. A delightful one of ancient vintage takes this form: "The left, with considerable historical support, attacks America [sic: she means the United States] for supporting dictators. The right complains we don't support them enough." Her fair-mindedness is demonstrated by the concession that there is "considerable" historical support for the left contention of U.S. aid to dictators; but, as the right claims a deficiency of U.S. support, does this not suggest to a reasonable person that actual policy, condemned by both extremes, is not far off the mark?

In her balancing act on Guatemala, Flora Lewis writes, Jacobo Arbenz, the Guatemalan President overthrown in 1954, turned up later in Prague and openly discussed his ties to the Soviet bloc. But the fact that the C.I.A. arranged the coup to oust him has converted his memory to one of mild liberalism for many who are now shocked by Guatemala's ruthless right-wing regime. The habit of absolutes makes people imagine that if one side is bad, its adversaries must be all good.

Observe, first, that while pretending to be interested in contesting the tendency of people (unnamed) to take absolutist opposite positions (if the United States was bad, Arbenz must be good), she herself uses relativism as a means of blatant apologetics. If Arbenz was also bad, maybe the United States is not so bad after all. This little trick allows her to bypass the questions of just how bad the U.S. sponsored terror regimes have been, and, even if Arbenz was proved bad (which she does not do), why the United States chose to organize and support the thoroughly vicious system of gradually escalating terror that developed after 1954. Notice how the United States is only implicated in the *coup;* the "ruthless right-wing regime" is placed a bit apart, as something that emerged perhaps inadvertently and not as a planned result of the coup and definite U.S. follow-up policies. This is dishonesty by omission. The United States did not just organize the coup and leave. It shaped the course of terror in crucial ways, and, instead of constraining counter-revolutionary terror, U.S. leaders displayed obvious distress only at the unwillingness of 'the newly chosen managers to kill with sufficient energy. Thus, U.S. Ambassador to Guatemala, John Peurifoy, presented to interim post-coup president Colonel Carlos Enrique Diaz a long list of "Communists" to be killed within 24 hours. Diaz' refusal and his expressed intention to proclaim a general amnesty were the "last straw" for Peurifoy, and Diaz was quickly ousted. Even Castillo Armas, carefully selected by the U.S. authorities, and generally following orders in detail, offended Dulles by his unwillingness to seize the 700 or so Arbenz followers who had taken refuge in foreign embassies after the coup. Kinzer and Schlesinger point out that Dulles advanced a new doctrine: communists should be automatically denied the right of asylum because they were connected with an international conspiracy. . .In the end Castillo Armas disregarded Dulles' advisories. He himself was a product of widespread belief in Latin America that embassy asylum and safe exits were a fair resolution to political conflicts.

But Dulles and Peurifoy felt that Armas had "betrayed them." In short, book burnings, the murder of numerous trade union leaders, the termination of political freedom, elicited not a word of complaint from U.S. authorities in 1954. Only restraint in seeking vengeance bothered them.

The first durable state terrorist, Castillo Armas, was directly chosen by the United States. But the United States also arranged a further coup in 1963 when, in the words of Kinzer and Schlesinger, "Kennedy gave his approval to dissident Guatemalan army officers to overthrow Ydigoras" in order to prevent an election campaign by the popular former president Arévalo. The U.S. chosen successor to Ydigoras was "an officer decidedly more reactionary than Ydigoras," under whose auspices "the Guatemalan dictatorship took on new zeal," and "murdered hundreds of anti-government activists." In 1966 U.S. intervention intensified, Green Berets were introduced, military aid was stepped up, familiar anti-guerilla warfare tactics were used on a large scale, "but a new weapon was also introduced: political assassinations on a mass scale." "Thousands of people suddenly met death at the hands of unseen gunmen" as the new campaign began to reach "anybody tinged with liberalism." In brief, the progress of Guatemalan terror from 1954 onward was a result of steady U.S. intervention, carried out by U.S. trainees, with U.S. arms; and at each major political turn 1954, 1963 and 1966 the United States played a decisive role in consolidating the power of forces that carried terror to greater heights. The U.S. choices and the "absolute" level of exploitation and murder are of enormous importance and relevance; the bringing in of Arbenz is a classic use of "relativism" combined with a red herring.

Returning to Flora Lewis' equation, how does she prove that Arbenz was bad? The answer is that she does not rather, she uses a McCarthyite trick that does not withstand the most superficial inspection. Her language is an interesting exercise in deceptive ambiguity: Arbenz "turned up later in Prague and openly discussed his ties to the Soviet bloc." From this she implies that he was a Soviet puppet while in power at an earlier time in Guatemala, though she avoids saying this directly. Notice her failure to spell out just what Arbenz *said* in Prague. Did he say more than that he was happy to be in a country with which Guatemala under his regime had had friendly and sympathetic relations? Observe the phrase "openly discussed his ties," with the sinister connotation that "ties" (unstipulated) which of course the United has in great number with the Soviets (trade, loans, exchanges both political and cultural) must have been sub rosa and illicit. The historical context of Arbenz in Prague is also ignored Arbenz was a refugee, ousted from his legal position in Guatemala by completely illegal U.S. subversion, which suggests several further questions: What weight do we give his statements as a refugee-dependent? (I repeat, though, that Lewis' evasions suggest that Arbenz said nothing incriminating anyway.) Had he become embittered as a result of his experiences? If so, were his views as a refugee and victim of U.S. intervention the same as those he held in Guatemala some years earlier?

Flora Lewis also carefully avoids discussing the evidence regarding Arbenz in Guatemala. She makes no mention of the fact that he was elected democratically and received 65% of the vote in the last free election seen in that country. Nor does she discuss the fact that Arbenz was doing a great deal of very decent things for the long-repressed majority, who were allowed to unionize, to vote, and given land in a land reform that conformed rather closely to that urged at the time by the World Bank. The rabid hostility of United Fruit to these policies was far more important than any alleged Communist ties in determining U.S. hostility, and all of these reforms were quickly and savagely undone in the counter-revolution that followed under U.S. command. I mentioned earlier that the propaganda line pursued by the PR counsel for United Fruit and its government allies, with careful calculation, was to play down the land reform and union threats, which were the substantive issues of real concern to United Fruit, and to stress the "international Communist conspiracy." Even the CIA-sponsored study by Ronald Schneider made no claim of Soviet control or significant influence over Arbenz, and the recent study by Kinzer and Schlesinger shows more directly that the alleged control was a propaganda fraud unsupported by any evidence. The latter authors do establish the fact of a very important set of ties underlying the early sequence of events in Guatemala they point out that "almost every one of the significant figures [in the United States] behind the Guatemalan coup was intimately acquainted with high United Fruit executives," leading them to conclude: "The takeover of United Fruit land was probably the decisive factor pushing the Americans into action." But Flora Lewis operates on the selection principles described earlier she is interested only in enemy terror, and as the Guatemala story indicates, if she cannot find it in the real world she will construct it out of the whole cloth.

Another irresistible classic is provided in Edward Schumacher's reporting on El Salvador, where "balance" is regularly achieved through two routes: by offsetting nasty facts with propaganda claims of the authorities (not "apples versus oranges" "apples versus wisps of hot air"), and by a highly selective culling of alleged facts to achieve the preconceived result. Only once, to my knowledge, did Schumacher ever actually refer to direct evidence from a peasant. On that occasion, the woman stated that regular soldiers brutalized and murdered her 67 year old husband, and beat her, for no reason. Before even concluding his first-ever first-hand report paragraph, Schumacher remarks with even-handed balance that this peasant woman's testimony demonstrates "what high Government and military officials say is their frustration in trying to control their own troops without destroying morale." Note that Schumacher repeats this government claim as truth, never raising the possibility that it could be a propaganda ploy. Nor does he raise the deeper question if this is the way government troops behave in fact, killing the innocent without discrimination, does this not constitute a criminal operation whatever its pretended goals?

Having inserted uncritically a government propaganda claim, Schumacher then quickly adds further balance to the empirical fact of an indiscriminate murder. He presents an account of an interview with Archbishop Arturo Rivera Y Damas, who he designates as "a critic of the government." Without quotations he claims that the Archbishop said that "while killing by Marxist guerillas appeared to be increasing, killing by government forces was decreasing. He attributed the decline to the government's efforts to curb the security forces." Examining Schumacher's use of the Archbishop more closely, some questions arise. Why no direct quotations? The phrase "Marxist guerillas" is used by the State Department and Duarte, but does the Archbishop use it? What else did he say? The line which Schumacher attributes to the Bishop, without quotation marks, is an exact replica of the one that the U.S. government and the El Salvador junta were trying to peddle at that time. If Schumacher were lying or stripping context, the Archbishop could not easily reply because he is in a highly vulnerable situation. Critics of the government in El Salvador are often murdered, including Archbishop Damas' predecessor. This threat of murder might be mentioned in a honest news account. So would the fact that Archbishop Damas was "under instructions" by the Vatican to work for the unity of the Church, and that he has taken a centrist line in a desperate effort to use a nominal even-handedness to preserve his credibility and bargaining power with the right and the United States. According to a Catholic church official in the United States who met with the Archbishop shortly after Schumacher's article, "Rivera's public indecision (he's much clearer in private) is designed to enable him to function within the dialog process." Is it not a bit unscrupulous on the part of a news reporter to use this compromised political position to extract "facts" that can be put forward as by a "critic of the government." Instead of asking somebody on the left, or somebody in the Church's Legal Office who follows political murders closely and asking them off the record Schumacher sticks to the very decent but politically confined Damas to give a. critic's position.

We may note also that in Schumacher's paraphrasing of the Archbishop, no numbers are given, only an alleged direction of movement. It would be consistent with the Archbishop's alleged statement if government murders had declined from 500 to 480 whereas rebel killings had increased from 6 to 10.The implication in Schumacher is that the Archbishop is attributing the bulk of the killings to the rebels, not the government. As both the Archbishop and the Church Legal Office keep saying the opposite, Schumacher is lying by omission as well as by implication.

Another reason why Schumacher carefully avoids citing the Church's Legal Office is that it not only attributes the vast bulk of civilian killings to the military junta, it keeps suggesting quite openly that the *United States* is at the root of the murders, that this is a "prolonged, cruel and bloody *North American* military intervention," and that it is "military regimes educated, financed, advised and armed by the United States who are the ones who have generated the violence." Clearly this will not do. Such a view, although as obvious as the sun at noon on a clear summer day, has no place in a Schumacherized version of murder in El Salvador. Neither do Al's outcries, which have also stressed the blind indiscriminateness of the official killings in El Salvador of a death machine run amok. In a letter to Alexander Haig in June 1981, Al points to the large scale killings of people who have no connection with guerillas of conclusive evidence of "a consistent pattern of killing by the security forces of peasants, young people and other victims who had no part in guerilla activity." This is "constructive" terror, however, supported by the United States, and Edward Schumacher suppresses accordingly.

5. The principle that the NSS is led by moderates standing between two poles of extremists

This classic ploy is used even for Guatemala. The former press secretary of the Ministry of the Interior, Elias Barahona Y Barahona, claimed that one of his prime concerns while in that office was to get the media to swallow the notion that there were left extremists and right extremists *independent of the government.* He told Al that this ploy was based on a direct lie; that the names to be used for death squad murders were prepared from the records of Military Intelligence and National Police, and the blank letter-head stationary of the leading death squads were stored in the office of the Minister of the Interior, who was in charge of internal security. Nevertheless, Associated Press reports from Guatemala continue to say that "The violence appeared part of the terrorist war that has been raging for years between leftist and rightist groups."

This technique has also been used heavily in reference to Argentina and Brazil, where the extremists were long alleged to be a left and *segments* of the military who do the killing, regrettably out of control of the "moderates" who otherwise exercise supreme power. This propaganda device allows a distribution of functions between government torturers and killers, the bad guys, on the one hand, and the struggling moderates, on the other. We may sympathize with the latter group, and align ourselves with the government, without implicating ourselves in the torture or compromising our well-known dedication to the rights of each and every individual. More important, we can convey this distributed function picture to the rest of the world, along with our support for the struggling moderates, which makes us moderates.

The difficulty has always been that the distinction between rightwing terror and government terror, and the alleged struggle between the forces that kill and the moderates, are both largely fraudulent. As I discussed earlier in connection with the death squads of Latin America, many of them are regular military cadres, and all of them regular and irregular are under the general direction of their respective governments. And while there has been infighting at the top of these military gravy trains, there is no evidence whatsoever suggesting that death squad and detention center torture and murder have not been under top level general control and direction.

The "moderate center" gambit reached its propaganda zenith in the Carter-Reagan effort to apply it to the murderous thugs ruling El Salvador. The State Department Dissent Paper stressed that a "moderate and reformist image of the current regime" was one of the deliberate misrepresentations that the government has foisted, with the aid of the media. The U.S. government propaganda line is that the violence and killing by the military and paramilitary forces are not actions of the "government," but of a "right" that is either separate' from government forces or regrettably "out of control" (there has been some confusion on which line to take, but the media have not pressed the point). According to William Bowdler of the Carter State Department, "we have vigorously supported the Junta and opposed a repressive or non-reformist solution for El Salvador the former [sic] association of elements of the security forces with the extreme right has left suspicions that undermine the moral authority of the new regime." This separation has never been accepted by any serious investigator or respected foreign journalist Orden and other paramilitary forces work in tandem with the regulars, are supplied by the government, and there is no reported case of incarceration or other serious action taken against any member of these rightwing groups for murder. AI is explicit that they are under the direction of the top military command. Even the apologists usually don't pretend with Bowdler that there has been a separation as shown in discussing Schumacher's "balance," his contention and that of El Salvadoran authorities is that indiscriminate murders by regular and irregular forces are being *brought under control,* not that these irregulars have been disbanded or pushed out of the orbit of government authority. The truth is, however, that in the last two or three years, rightwing that is to say, government sponsored and controlled murders of civilians have escalated greatly. The Salvadoran. Church's press bulletin, *Solidaridad,* estimated that the rate of political assassination of civilians rose from 144 in 1978, to 768 during the first nine months of 1979. After the ouster of Romero in September, 1979 and the takeover of the U.S. sponsored "moderate center" the murder rate rose to 1,800 in 1980, then to 1,200 a month in 1981 (an annual rate of 14,500). According to *Solidaridad,* "In the first nine months of 1981, 10,714 defenseless people were executed" by government forces, with 4,000 more killed by "unidentifiable paramilitary bands."

Despite the almost uniform opinion of close observers that paramilitary murders are government murders, the U.S. mass media have usually followed the Bowdler-official propaganda line, although inconsistently stumbling a la

Schumacher between an independent paramilitary and a government arm under tightening discipline. The content analysis of the *New York Times* by Guzmao and Benjamin reveals that just as the U.S. government and Duarte junta "displaced the responsibility for the violence onto nongovernmental sources," so did the *Times*' news reports, attributing the killings to government forces in only about onethird of its news articles whereas El Salvador church sources attributed over 80% of the violence to those forces.

A second facet of government and mass media misrepresentation of the centrism of the junta is in their analysis of junta composition and power. The coup of October, 1979 led to the formation of a relatively moderate junta, which included several reform-minded civilians and a diversified group of military personnel. That junta was decimated by resignations only three months later, in January 1980, based on the inability of the reformers to stem the increasing tide of official murders or to institute any reforms. The subsequent ouster of the only military moderate, Majano, would seem to have left the rightwing military in even firmer control. The belated arrival of Duarte, in the midst of an intensifying war and in the wake of the departure of all known moderates, would suggest that Duarte is a figleaf for a victorious rightwing military elite. This point is reinforced by the fact that Duarte, although the President, is not Commanderin-Chief of the armed forces; that post is held explicitly by army Colonel Gutierrez. Gutierrez was one of the two rightwing generals, the other Garcia, both affiliated with U.S. business firms operating in El Salvador, who were pressed by U.S. officials upon the original organizers of the reforming junta in October 1979, a highly significant U.S. intervention that effectively cancelled out the power of the military and civilian moderates. Thus, if a "center" ever had any potential to influence the course of events in El Salvador, this was precluded from the beginning by the direction of U.S. influence.

Complementing the treatment of the "centrist" government has been the media's regular characterization of the Democratic Front as "Marxists" or "extreme left." When several moderate civilians joined the junta in October, 1979, this was used as evidence of its broad-based and centrist character. When these civilians resigned and joined the FDR, by some miracle this did not reduce the centrism of the junta or broaden the base of the Front. The Front also included representatives of 49 unions and a large array of peasant, student, health, teaching and other professional organizations, as well as other political groupings. It even included 80% of the splintered Christian Democratic Party. The European and Mexican press featured the breadth of the Front and the integration of the far left and the moderate democratic oppositon. This did not happen in the United States, where much attention is given to the fact that the Communist Party is a part of the whole (without discussion of its weight, which is small), and words like "leftist" and "marxist" have generally been used as descriptive adjectives. The Front's composition, program and support base is distorted or suppressed, and the savageries being carried out against its leaders and mass constituency are being downplayed.

The analogy with U.S. intervention in South Vietnam is fairly close. There also moderate reformers or unduly independent nationalists were eventually squeezed out in favor of murderous thugs willing to pursue a savage antipeople's war against their own rural population. In Vietnam there was also a "land reform" foisted from Washington D.C., that was a complement to the primary program counter-insurgency warfare. In El Salvador the land reform program was enacted in March 1980 simultaneously with the army's primacy being enacted by law and the army carrying out the occupation of the large plantations to be reformed, and the whole national territory. John Bushnell of the State Department stressed to Congress the linkage between security assistance and "our support of reform" in

El Salvador, both of which give us "unique opportunities to change the political balance in our favor." The "protection and security provided by the Salvadorean army" is an integral part of reform in the U.S. arranged package, and it was this central role of the military arm and its assured primacy that won rightwing support in El Salvador, while the "reform" aspect immobilized liberals in congress. Armstrong and Wheaton note that "It is instructive to recall that this is precisely the form and sequence of the U.S. model of rural pacification used in Vietnam and the Philippines: Reform with Repression. In the case of the Phoenix program in Vietnam, at least 35,000 Vietnamese peasants were systematically murdered."

The special feature of the El Salvador political scene, in contrast with Vietnam, is the up-front man Duarte. But the official position of Gutierrez as Commander-in-Chief, the predominance of the military in the El Salvador political environment of intense warfare and a State of Siege, and the departure of all independents from the junta point up the fact that only a propaganda system could maintain the fiction of a centrist government ruling that country. What remains in El Salvador in 1982 is a highly militarized right, representing under 10% of the population, and a left-oriented coalition that represents a large majority. And as in Vietnam and Nicaragua, the only important external force the only thing keeping the rightwing death machine functioning is the United States.

6. With the NSS let us look at the bright side

As a focus on the many unpleasant aspects of the NSS would offend important people, and thus the "national interest," the mass media tend to accentuate the positive. There are exceptions to this principle, but the exercise of the power of positive thinking about the NSS is impressive. This has three main variants a focus on personalities and pleasantries, alleged "improvements," and a look at the details of economic progress. A good illustration of the first is Edward Schumacher's October, 1980 article in the

New York Times describing Roberto Eduardo Viola, the "newly named" President of Argentina. He is portrayed there by Schumacher as a warm human being, a "quintessential' Argentinian, with immigrant Italian parents, a "populist," a "compromiser," a peace-maker in the conflict with Chile, a man of the people, loving the "working class" passions of soccer and pasta. Schumacher neglects mentioning that this man of the people owns a 10,000 acre estate on the pampas, and that this man with "working class" passions led the army in the liquidation of hundreds of working class leaders, the serious weakening of working class power, and a large decline in working class real income and employment. Schumacher also fails to note that Viola, as Army Chief of Staff, was in charge of the counter-insurgency war of torture and disappearances. He does mention that there was a dirty war, but he carefully avoids linking Viola, as he should be linked, to its precise quality of dirtiness. Viola, as Penny Lernoux observes, "was a pillar of the institutionalized terror as army Commander-in-Chief," and he still "adamantly refuses to discuss the fate of the thousands of disappeared Argentines kidnapped and murdered by the security forces."

Schumacher does say that Viola, while a compromiser, "can be tough." This is as close as he gets to suggesting that he may have been an organizer of mass torture and murder. The word "tough" is one the Nazis liked to apply to themselves: in contrast with words like murderer, killer, or madman, the word tough implies the ability to do things that are unpleasant but necessary. As Himmler noted, executions have been "necessary and in many cases will continue to be necessary. Most of you will know what it means to see 100 corpses piled up, or 500, or 1,000. To have gone through this and to have remained decent, that has made us tough." Apropos of the Nazis, in one of his speeches Viola remarked that "There wouldn't have been a Nuremberg trial if the Reich armies had won the war. Nobody investigates a victorious army." The Buenos Aires *Herald* pointed out in response that "Viola is supposed to be a moderate, and if moderates think that the only thing the Nazis did wrong was to lose, the normal mind would find it hard to imagine what the view of the hard-liners must be." This is a reflection that escapes Schumacher and the U.S. mass media in general.

Viola is quoted by the kindly Schumacher as favoring "a stable, and modern democracy, authentically representative," etc., but he is against "demagogic populism." Although Viola was a leader of a carefully planned coup that eliminated democracy and unleashed a reign of terror, his muddy vacuities are given full head by Schumacher, without comment. There is even a nice touch of apologetics for the coup, which Schumacher says had "great popular support," but which has since then "dwindled." Viola would say the same, and perhaps this is Schumacher's source for these findings.

Schumacher also suppresses the fact, widely disseminated in Latin America, but ignored in the United States, that Viola was a major figure at a secret conference of Latin American intelligence services held in Bogota in November 1979. Out of the conference came a "Viola plan" for extending the National Security Doctrine and curbing any further democratic threats in the region, a plan which had its first material impact in the Argentina-sponsored coup in Bolivia in July, 1980 (discussed in chapter two). Colombia's Conservative Party ex-Foreign Minister Alfredo Vasquez Carrizosa told *Latin America Press* that The moment has arrived to give warning that Colombia figures in the "fascist international" in Latin America. For General Viola to think and do as he wants in his own country is another matter. We Colombians need some explanation about his coming to Bogota and outlining models to which the intelligence services of countries of the region must be coordinated under the direction of the military junta of Buenos Aires.

Clearly this kind of information also has no place in an article that could have come out of the public relations arm of the Argentine National Security State. Another good illustration of looking at the bright side is provided by Juan de Onis' article "Chile's Regime Sees New Economic Hope", published in the *New York Times* of February 28, 1980. It is a fairly representative sample of the more sophisticated type of mass media apologetics for the development model in application, and I will use it to show how bias is implemented. The article is characteristic de Onis in that the view of Pinochet and the NSS leadership is paramount the frame is their problem and the reader is asked to identify with Pinochet, recognize his legitimacy, and accept his alleged concern for the Chilean people. De Onis mentions that "the armed forces took power six years ago" very neutral, with no mention here or elsewhere in the article of extensive torture and murder, or that the taking of power involved the overthrow of a democratic and legally elected government and this neutral phrase is preceded by the claim that "prospects look brighter" for Pinochet and company, enveloping the fact of an illegal seizure of power with a warm and optimistic glow.

The article starts out in an even more positive vein, remarking that there had been a riot in an overcrowded jail in Santiago, embarrassing Pinochet, but that he "ordered the immediate construction of a new prison, the first since 1893." This act was encouraged by an alleged new "sensitivity" of the regime to criticism "and a new ability to pay for public investments." De Onis goes on in the same warm tone, telling us that "President Pinochet feels that he is in a position now to convince a majority of Chile's 11 million people that the free market capitalism being practiced here offers solutions to basic: problems like jobs, housing, health and social security." Sustained growth and a better distribution of wealth "are now being promised." And although "no elections are foreseen" under military rule, "public support" is contingent on fulfillment of economic promises.

Perhaps the most notable thing about this article is de Onis' willingness to cite at length somebody's "promises," "feelings," and "sensitivity" on his own say so. That de Onis does this for the leader of a police state noted for its cruel violence speaks volumes about his own (and Free Press) principles. De Onis points out that the U.S. Embassy in Santiago had just issued a "highly favorable" report on the NSS program that "accepts uncritically" Pinochet's estimates of prospective investment, income redistribution, etc. This, of course, places de Onis in the middle between the "extremes" of harsh critics and the uncritical Embassy, although Sherlock Holmes would be hard pressed to detect the critical elements in this news report. What the Embassy accolade really shows is not de Onis' moderation but the root of his apologetics namely, that he is a reporter for a newspaper in a country whose dominant economic-political-military leaders are extremely well satisfied with fascist Chile.

A second notable feature of de Onis' article is that it contains a political contradiction which he leaves unresolved. He cites Pinochet's claims of a commitment to jobs, social justice, etc., and the necessity of meeting these promises in the interest of obtaining "public support." But no elections are foreseen. Why not? If Pinochet is serious about the new promises, why fear elections? If elections are not to be allowed, why any need to worry about "public support"? De Onis goes on to say that elections and union autonomy are ruled out because "the success of the program depends on stability and investor confidence." But if these criteria still rule, why will they now be compatible with improving the distribution of wealth, health and social security, and jobs? De Onis doesn't attempt to reconcile these two irreconcilable strands which of course suggests that he is allowing himself to be used to create a propaganda aura for the Chilean NSS.

While he cites Pinochet's promises of "improvements" de Onis carefully avoids discussing *what has happened* in

Chile that might make improvements needed. The one spot where de Onis injects a critical fact about Chilean developments reads as follows:

> *Critics of the present economic "model" generally agree that the situation today is an improvement over the breakdown in 1973, but they emphasize persistent unemployment, which is about 15 percent of the labor force, and indications that wealth is increasingly concentrated in an elite, with wage earners and peasants making less than before.*

Observe that the single critical fact, about the rate of unemployment, is preceded by a "positive" claim that critics all say that the situation is improved from the "breakdown" of 1973. The choice of base of comparison is a marvel of NSS apclogetics not only does de Onis select a completely abnormal point in time, he neglects mentioning that the "breakdown" was engineered by the same forces that introduced the NSS. Quite a few critics claim that the Chilean NSS performance has been a human catastrophe and a failure even on NSS principles but de Onis does not cite one of them. Note also the terseness of de Onis' reference to persistent unemployment of 15% a figure at the low end of credible estimates, and with no comparative data for reader context and the lack of any detail on income redistribution or its human consequences. Unemployment, which averaged under 6% between 1960–1973, was somewhere between 15 and 30% in 1980 depending on how one handles disguised unemployment and the significant numbers hired under the Program of Minimum Employment (PEM), which pays nominal wages (and no social security or related benefits) for arduous jobs in the public and private sector, and which accounted for about 7% of the workforce in 1980. Unemployment among farm workers was about 35% in mid-1980 and underemployment was even more widespread.

As noted, although de Onis says that "economic prospects look brighter" for Pinochet and "Chile" he gives no details that would support the brightening, except for the fact that copper prices were rising and might allow Chile "to cover the higher cost of petroleum imports." This provides the basis for his statement about a "new ability to pay for public investment." Again he makes no mention of what *actually happened* to public investments after the coup. The public sector was sharply reduced by the NSS in a massive sell-off of public enterprises, often at bargain prices. A huge readjustment in the shrunken public sector saw all social service outlays fall (health by 22% and housing-sanitation-community services by 60% of the reduced total) while defense expenditures increased by 100%. The social security system is in the process of being dismantled and turned over to the private sector.

A few other points that de Onis neglects to mention give a different picture of NSS developments and prospects. First, it took the Pinochet NSS until 1980 to get Chilean domestic output per capita back to the 1970 level of the Frei regime. And, despite the terror, the drastic fall in real wages, and the large upward redistribution of income, in 1980 domestic saving and investment were both below their late 1960s levels. It should be recalled that supply side economics with machine guns is supposed to stimulate saving and investment. Second, the real value of imports was up by 38%. Most of this import increase was in the form of luxury consumer goods motor cars, household durables, sumptuary goods, beverages, and clothing with capital goods imports that would bear on "development" increasing negligibly. Between 1970 and 1978 capital goods imports fell from 20 to 13% of total imports; luxury goods imports increased by 276%. The shifts in the composition of Chilean output reveal growth largely in financial, service and trading activities, with the goods producing sectors of the economy showing absolute declines. Between 1972 and 1979 employment in industry in Chile fell from 24.6% of total employment to only 16.5% while employment in commerce and services together expanded from 38% to 52.3% of total employment. There has been a surge in foreign credit, and transnational credit has been the motor for whatever feeble growth has taken place, but a large portion has been used to finance the import of high-priced consumer goods, luxury housing, takeovers of local firms and speculation. An internal tight money policy, and relatively easy credit from abroad available to large interests and transnational corporations, have combined to decimate local small and medium sized businesses NSS economics in Chile has led to the most concentrated market system in Latin America.

Third, foreign debt has risen enormously, equalling 2.3 times export receipts in 1980; and in that year the Chilean ratios of debt-service charges to exports and debt to GNP were the highest in Latin America. The current account deficit was 8 percent of gross domestic product in 1978 and rising rapidly. Between 1977 and 1980 Chile's gross foreign debt doubled in size. This debt is indexed to the exchange rate, and the junta has therefore kept the peso overvalued, which has stimulated imports, increased the pressure on exporters, raised the unemployment rate, and reduced the rate of inflation. But the size of Chile's debt and debt service requirements are so great that at present new debt is needed to service old debt a situation referred to as "Ponzi financing," and widely regarded as a perilously speculative and hazardous condition. The economist David Felix contends that "The choice now is essentially how Chile wants the crisis to come."

The negative human impact of the Chilean counter-revolution has been enormous. The union and peasant movements have been crushed, thousands of their leaders tortured and killed, and peasant cooperatives and union membership decimated (the number of unionized farm workers fell from 65 percent of the total in 1972 to 10% in 1980). NSS economics has produced a huge reserve army of unemployed, which, along with the pacification of the labor movement, has caused the real wages of the employed to fall sharply (as noted earlier, estimates range from 20 to over 50%). The upward redistribution of income from labor to property has been of major proportions, although estimates are necessarily tentative given both the authoritarian conditions of research in Chile and the natural reluctance of the leadership to divulge the impact of direct class warfare. But it clearly manifests itself in the sharp rise in imports of advanced consumer goods, which has taken place even while the Chilean economy stagnates and approaches a debt crisis. Chicago School economist Arnold Harberger, in fact, points to the enhanced availability of elite boutiques and stylish goods as proof of the success of the Chilean NSS:

> *Santiago has never looked better. Consumer goods from all over the world are readily available at cheap prices. All the things you get from Japan Sony tape recorders, televisions, Honda cars are readily available.*

This language should, I think, take its place alongside of Vittorio Mussolini's description of the impact of a western bomb unfolding like the petals of a rose among Ethiopian natives.

As described earlier, the NSS systematically ignores the needs of the majority, but in a case like Chile the function of state terror was to reverse a welfare state tradition and reduce the well-being of the majority absolutely and substantially. There is evidence that all human needs trends in Chile have been adverse. No word about this from Juan de Onis. He tells us that prospects for improvement are bright, which flies in the face of the economic realities of the debt-ridden economy with its "low investment rate and flabby productive structure that lies beneath the glittering facade of ostentatious import-intensive consumerism and financial wheeling and dealing." He tells us that Pinochet intends to solve basic problems, but he makes no effort to reconcile this with the Pinochet policies on the record or with the model and economic strategies pursued. He suppresses almost every relevant fact about the impact of NSS economics on the majority, and the gains accruing to the joint venture partners.

7. With the NSS the relevant world is that seen by the elites

This principle, closely related to looking at the bright side, also follows from the fact that the dominant forces in the United States are allied with these elites. Since things are going pretty well for the military leaders who have seized power, and the businessmen with whom they are aligned, they find the NSS good. A steady stream of such articles by Everett Martin in the *Wall Street Journal* stick to this perspective almost exclusively; to such a degree that Martin frequently forgets that there are any "people" beyond the tiny business elite with whom he is preoccupied. Thus in Argentina, under inflationary conditions "They [i.e. the Argentine people] also started playing the stock market with a vengeance. It looked like a reasonable gamble." Frequently the NSSs are personified, with "Argentina," "Brazil" and "Chile" transformed into entities that are then identified with the business leadership or the ruling generals and their policies "Brazil Raises Exports of High Technology to Pace Third World;" "Brazil's Liberalization Survives a Scare;" or "Brazil Stresses Farming and Enrolls Its 'Miracle' Worker." A great deal of attention is devoted to business success stories Daniel Ludwig, chicken and orange juice export developments, the coming of McDonalds to Brazil and to the trials and tribulations of the elite in combatting traffic conditions and crowded beaches.

The perspective of the majority within the NSSs is not often on display in the western mass media. Consider the almost totally neglected phenomenon of street urchins uncared for vagrant young children, whose numbers in the big cities of Latin America are estimated to reach into the millions. In Colombia, for example, "thousands of street children, so-called gamins, struggle to survive with little or no support from the traditional institutions of family, church, school, or state." Or in Brazil, where the huge numbers of abandoned children are treated as cases for the police.

Abandoned children are officially considered eyesores to be removed from downtown streets, usually by police trucks which round up the unlucky youths and transport them to another state, where they are left with warning never to return. Brazil's 3.5 million abandoned children are not seen as a social ill but as statistics to be eliminated. These roundups are normal procedure, explained Police Investigator William do Amaral, after one such operation came to light in Sao Paulo.

As another example of the different world of the majority, unattended by the western mass media, we read in *Latin America Press*, about "Civil War in Rio De Janeiro," with more than a million citizens in that city robbed in 1979–1980 and its 60,000 soldiers and police unable to stem the tide, which comes from the NSS conditions of staggering inequality and massive dispossession and poverty. The armed forces still try. "*Veja* reported that last year 2,006 bodies were 'planted' by parapolice bands along thoroughfares in the Baixada Fluminense, all with signs of savage torture and abuse. However, this terrible, massive, disguised government repression was not enough to halt the increase in crime." Two million live in the slums of Rio and another 3 million live in "bedroom cities," like Nova Iguazu, where 1.5 million people make do with 290,000 houses, only 30 percent with running water, 8% connected to a sewer system, and with minimal health and educational facilities. This article concludes that Fear is so great that some inhabitants have asked for the region to be occupied by army troops. The commandant of the First Army Corps, Gen. Gentil Marcondes Filho, categorically turned down that possibility because it would be admitting that the country is in a state of civil war. 'I cannot use guns against marginalized people or patrol Cinelandia (a downtown section of Rio) with war tanks,' he said. This is Brazil today.

8. The United States as a disinterested party

This is a principle applied only when convenient. Thus, in the case of El Salvador, it means that the United States is not to be allocated any responsibility for the evolution of the terrorist government that preceded the October, 1979 coup, or Orden; and any arms and training that flow to the El Salvadoran army and death squads directly or via a U.S. client does not count as "intervention." If the Soviet Union or Cuba were to train 1,500 rebels to fight in El Salvador this would be a criminal plot and blatant intervention; whereas the 1,500 El Salvadoran soldiers in training at Fort Benning, Georgia in early 1982 fall into a different class altogether this is "aid," not "intervention," which we disinterestedly extend to our hemispheric cousins. This purely self serving differentiation between their intrusions and our own is rarely stated outright, but it is always implicit in Free Press discussions of these matters, exactly as Pravda starts out on the premise that Soviet "aid" to Czechoslavakia is inherently justified by the fact that its own state (by definition disinterested and serving larger beneficent ends) is the active party. The Free Press may carp at whether our "aid" is effectual, whether we may be getting bogged down in "another Vietnam" but this aid is never called by its right name (i.e., indirect aggression by a long-term subversive arming, training, and other support of rightwing military and paramilitary thugs), or castigated as immoral and illegal at the root, even when the entire enterprise of mass killing originated with us and continues mainly as a function of our ongoing decisions and choices.

The same principle is applicable in Guatemala and Chile. In the former, where the United States organized in detail the overthrow of the last democratic government the last also to show the slightest concern over either civil liberties or the basic needs of the majority and where the U.S. role in creating and training the apparatus of murder was unequivocal, U.S. news reports on the slaughter, and opinion pieces by Flora Lewis, suppress the background and pretend that the struggles and killings are indigenous and inexplicable. But just as the Vietnam war would have been over in 1953 without U.S. intervention, so Guatemalan violence dates from 1954, and Chilean violence dates from 1973 and the U.S. cultivated triumph of the military junta.

In their study of media handling of the Chilean coup, Moraes and Lawton show that, in contrast with the European press, the leading U.S. newspapers took the position that there is not a scintilla of evidence of U.S. participation in the coup. The media achieved this trick by concentrating on the *plans of the last moment,* ignoring the long background of encouragement and support. The evidence that has come to light since 1973 shows that the United States was the *key* factor in the coup as a result of its very extensive destabilization and subversive efforts, which included long-standing incitement of public frenzy through media which it bought and manipulated, training, supply and subversive encouragement of the military, and economic destabilization efforts, that together overwhelmed Chilean democracy.

9. The U.S. natural right to intervene

This patriotic principle' is sometimes in conflict with the preceding and is sometimes a complement to it. Thus, a good propaganda system suppresses inconvenient background facts, like U.S. sponsorship, training and supply of the Guatemalan and El Salvadoran death machines. But these facts, and the large servicing of the El Salvadoran military by ourselves and our clients in the last few years (while we are denouncing alleged Communist supply), rests in part on our natural right to be there. We can ship arms to El Salvador's junta and impose a Vietnam style land reform on that country because this is our backyard, our property. If the peasants of South Vietnam had no right to stand in the way of our choice of their government, certainly the El Salvadoran peasant doesn't. Schumacher says that "the Reagan administration has made Mr. Duarte the symbol and hope of the American policy of *creating* [sic] a centrist, noncommunist government in El Salvador." The "centrist" line has already been shown to be fraudulent, but note how Schumacher admits that the U.S. is completely in charge, molding an image and fixing the de facto government he doesn't have to hide this; he knows we all take for granted our natural right to intervene.

10. Communist Terror as the Pot of Gold at the End of the Rainbow

As indicated earlier, communist or radical terror, retail or wholesale, is really bad, its victims are worthy, and the systematic bias of the western mass media in attaching themselves to such terror is tremendous. The mass media can pursue communist radical terror without offending anybody important, valuable lessons can be drawn concerning the merits of private property and the link between it and "freedom," and it provides a wonderful diversion from the escalating violence within the Free World. Refugees from Cambodia, Vietnam and Cuba are of extreme interest to the western mass media. Victims of NSS terror fleeing from Uruguay are not; and the *internal* refugees of the NSSs, "the greatest migratory movement in all history" in the view of former ECLA economist Ernest Feder, is a non-issue in the west. We have already seen that Lech Walesa is newsworthy, but da Silva in Brazil is not. Another interesting contrast is between Sakharov and José Luis Massera, an eminent mathematician and former member of the Uruguyan parliament, arrested in 1975, and accused of "subversive association," "attacking the constitution," and "attacking the morals of the armed forces" of Uruguay. Subjected to torture, he was tried before a military court and sentenced to 20 years in prison. His wife was arrested, and his son-in-law was arrested, tortured, and sentenced to four and a half years in prison for "assistance to subversive association." The physicist Joel Primack states that Massera is ill; and while he writes in prison his writings are confiscated by the authorities. Massera has been offered positions at more than half a dozen major universities in the United States, Canada, France and elsewhere. Committees of scientists in the United States and elsewhere have been pressing his case. It is obvious that the abuses that he and his family have suffered are outrageous yet the mass media do not give Massera any attention; no campaign emerges; no serious pressures are brought to bear. Massera fails to satisfy this principle.

Table 3.1 provides a graphic display of the fact of systematic mass media bias which consistently leads them away from NSS (constructive and benign) violence and toward communist (nefarious) terror. The table shows, first, the number of times various abused individuals were mentioned in the *New York Times* between January 1, 1976, and June 30, 1981; and, secondly, the number of times these individuals attracted *intense* coverage during that period. These are not randomly selected individuals, but the fact clearly observable from the table that NSS victims are incapable of attracting more than flickering mass media attention in the United States results not from any bias in selection but rather from their "structural unworthiness," as a group. Most of the NSS victims listed here have been quite well-known in their own countries and have demonstrated high nobility of character (as have the Soviet sphere victims) in the face of severe police state abuse. By and large, the NSS victims on this list have been subject to more extreme violence than those in the Soviet sphere six were murdered, and at least two others have been severely tortured. The *New York Times* itself has editorialized on the fact that Luis da Silva "is to Brazil what Lech Walesa is to Poland." But Luis da Silva's arrest and conviction by a military tribunal in Brazil for strike activity was virtually ignored by the *Times*, and by the mass media in general, and da Silva has never generated intense coverage, as Walesa has been able to do on four separate occasions (up to March 31, 1981). The table shows that only one of 22 cases of intense coverage involved a NSS victim; the other 21 of 22 were victims within the Soviet sphere. The one exception followed the cold blooded murder of Archbishop Oscar Romero, the leading Church official in El Salvador; but the coverage here was not only modest in terms of the seriousness of the crime, it petered out quickly, and the connection of Romero's

Table 3.1: Press Coverage of Abused Persons in the Soviet Sphere and in Eight U.S. Client States Frequency of Maximum Times

	Frequency of Mention in the New York Times 1/1/76-6/30/81	Frequency of Intensive Coverage in the New York Times 1/1/76-6/30/81	Maximum Times Mentioned where subject to Intense Coverage
Heri Akhmadi, student leader, Indonesia	0	0	-
Archbishop Dom Heider Camara, Church leader, Brazil	4	0	-
Bishop Dom Pedro Casáldáliga, Church leader, Brazil	0	0	-
Enrique Alvarez Cordova, political leader, El Salvador	2	0	0
Father Luis Espinel, Church leader, Bolivia	0	0	-
Father Carlos Galvez, Church leader, Guatemala	1	0	-
Alexander Ginzburg, writer, Soviet Union	68	2	20
Kim Chi Ha, poet, South Korea		0	-
Muhammed Heikal, journalist, Egypt	8	0	-
Father Francesco Jentel, Church leader, Brazil	0	0	-
José Luis Massera, mathematician, Uruguay	5	0	-

Zelmar Michelini, politician, Uruguay	5	0	-
Yury Orlov, scientist, Soviet Union	70	2	15
Ananta Toer Pramoedya, writer, Indonesia	0	0	-
Archbishop Oscar Romero, Church leader, El Salvador	36	1	8
Father Stanley Rother, Church leader, Guatemala	0	0	-
Andrei Sakharov, scientist, Soviet Union	223	8	19
Anatoly Shcharansky, writer, Soviet Union	138	5	22
Luis Silva, trade union leader, Brazil	3	0	-
Lech Walesa, trade union leader, Poland	81	4	15

murder with the thug-complex long supported by the United States was downplayed. Romero's death was part of a seamless web in which numerous priests have been abused and killed, nuns have been raped and murdered, and many thousands of innocent civilians have been killed and frequently mutilated. But this enormous bloodbath is U.S.-sponsored, and the mass media therefore provide muted coverage, little indignation, and carefully avoid stress on the "linkages" and role of the superpower, such as those noted between the Soviet Union and the earlier abuse of Cardinal Mindzenty in Hungary and the 1981 imposition of martial law in Poland nor has there been any suggestion that the local elite of El Salvador should have to "pay dearly" for the murder of the Archbishop (or any of the thousands of others). The bias displayed by this table is real and massive; its explanation, as I have shown, lies, on the one hand, in the propaganda value of communist terror; on the other hand, in the fact that the NSS is U.S. sponsored and protected, with its terror serving large U.S. interests.

❑❑❑

4

Terror and Terrorism in South Africa

Introduction

Apartheid aspired to create a total pigmentocracy created by, and combined with, massive oppression and exploitation. The tale told here ends in an improvement the death of apartheid but with the majority in South Africa still in poverty. The termination of apartheid was finally achieved through the suffering and deaths of the brave in that country, but without the tragedy of the much predicted racial holocaust. Unfortunately, this last assertion is in need of major qualification. No such holocaust occurred in South Africa itself. But massacres and wholesale starvation did occur in surrounding countries, a result of the "total strategy," a murderous scheme adopted by Pretoria after a coup d'état in Lisbon resulted in the independence of Angola and Mozambique.

The Nationalists came to power in South Africa in 1949 with great expectations to institutionalize white domination of blacks, but without having spelled out just how apartheid was to be achieved. With larger and larger mandates in subsequent (white-only) elections, they pushed through progressively restrictive legislation enforcing racial segregation in white areas for Africans, the colored, and Asians. And they sought to establish separate Bantustans for the separate tribal development of the Africans. Ideally, they would force all Africans into these "homelands," each one restricted to one of the many ethnic groups into which the Africans at one time were divided. The Bantustan was a centerpiece of the apartheid plan to remold and to restructure the racial architecture of South African society. The plan was to pretend that the Bantustans were to become, or at least would seem to become, separate, sovereign nations. But it was too late for this "ideal" solution. The majority of Africans had left the countryside to work in white factories, farms, mines, and homes. Their cheap labor was too valuable to be dispensed with. Regulations formulated in 1967 forcing Africans not born or long domiciled or employed in urban areas to return to rural areas, notably the Bantustans, turned their victims into migratory laborers. Labor officials in the Bantustans sent the worker to a particular job, and normally he was required to return to the Bantustan within a year. Usually, the worker left his family behind to live in an all male dormitory in the city. The African family was thereby victimized as well. Prostitution and homosexuality flourished, and this in a country where the dominant elites were self-proclaimed Christians. Actually the few Bantustans that were created simply became the satellites of the South African government. Racism apart, their development served the white economy and the policy of divide and rule.

Inter-racial marriage, and even inter-racial intercourse were made illegal. The colored who had been allowed to vote in Cape Province were taken off the rolls. The government divided cities into racial areas for ownership, occupancy, and commerce. When outside their homelands, the movement of Africans was tightly controlled. They had to carry passes and receive permission to change jobs. The ultimate goal of the Population Registration Act and the Group Areas Act was to restrict each racial group to specific regions in or near cities for purposes of residence, ownership, and commerce. To accomplish this end, the burden fell on the three dominated racial groups, who were uprooted and made to move to less desirable areas. More than three million were "ethnically cleansed" in this way. Education was put in the hands of the central white-ruled government, and Africans were trained for inferior roles in society. The few non-whites who sought a university education were forced to do so by correspondence or obliged to attend segregated institutions staffed mainly by Afrikaners.

Cooperating with UNICEF to reduce infant mortality or revealing the misconduct of a state official could be construed as "terrorism".

The Terrorism Act was passed in 1967, but was made retroactive to 1962. It viewed this phenomenon so broadly that virtually any political or social act came under its purview. Cooperating with UNICEF to reduce infant mortality or revealing the misconduct of a state official could be construed as "terrorism," indicating again, the flexibility of the term and the political purposes for which it can be used. The act denied the accused the right of habeas corpus, and the accused were guilty until proved innocent beyond reasonable doubt.

The policy of apartheid obviously was propelled by the ideology of racism, but it was prodded on by economic considerations as well. Apartheid maintained low wages for the Africans, low costs for South African industry and agriculture, and also for maid service. It preserved the existing governmental policy that was highly discriminatory against labor. Though they outnumbered other workers, Africans were excluded from the category "employee" as found in the Industrial Conciliation Act. They thus had no right of entree to, and membership in, the industrial councils that worked out the differences between labor and management. Nor could they directly participate in negotiations over wages. Moreover, strikes were forbidden from 1942 until 1973, and were so hedged in with restrictions when they were allowed in that year as in effect to continue the prohibition. Most of the Africans lived in the "white" part of the country, and most of these lived in urban townships on the edges of cities rather than on white farms. Africans outnumbered whites in virtually all urban settings. These townships served as dormitories and warehouses for the black bodies and hands that supported the mines, factories, stores, and kitchens of the whites. Despite the restrictions placed on residence in these townships, their African populations increased. It was the African youth from these townships who since the mid-seventies so persistently demonstrated and rioted.

Although Africans outnumbered whites more than four to one, the Bantustans were to constitute only 13 percent of the land and were to include some of the most arid and infertile land. No major cities or mineral deposits were included. The land set aside for them was scattered and non-contiguous, originally consisting of 110 separate pieces from which the nine homelands were to be patched together. The number of separate pieces would be reduced to 36. One Bantustan thus constructed, KwaZulu, would still feature ten disconnected patches, divided by white-owned farms. To transit these farms, Africans would require special papers. The average density of population in the homelands in 1972 would have been 46 per square kilometer, compared with 13 for white South Africa, which had all the industry, valuable land, and mineral deposits. These rural slums, besides accommodating the white elites' peculiar view of race, were meant to be appendages of the white economy. They were designed as holding tanks to serve the white economy with cheap labor and as breeding grounds to assure the future supply of such labor. They were the rural counterparts of the African-populated townships.

The Truth and Reconciliation Commission report (TRCR) concluded that the policy of establishing homelands "was an extension of a colonially established practice of 'divide and rule'." The report is hereafter referred to as the TRCR. Their establishment was meant to protect the privileges of the whites and to inhibit the attainment of democratic rights by the black majority. The report accused the homeland governments of gross violations of human rights, the subject of the next section. These governments were charged with attempted killings, conspiracies to kill, actual killings, arson, abductions, and the torture of their enemies and opponents as well as covering up the crimes committed by the friends of the homeland governments. The report revealed that the police force in KwaZulu cooperated with the South African police and military intelligence in covert activities and projects aimed at destabilizing popular opposition to the state and homeland governments.

Archbishop Tutu argued that the racist convolutions brought about by the apartheid system would have been utterly ridiculous except that they had ghastly repercussions. Visiting Japanese businessmen were classified "honorary whites." A person of Chinese origin born in South Africa was a non-European. If born in China, he or she was a European. The South Africa racial classification scheme led some South Africans to commit suicide because they had been put on the wrong side of the social divide, since worth and privilege depended so much on one's racial classification. It determined where a person could live, what schools he or she could attend, whom the person could marry, what job the person could have, and finally where he or she could be buried.

No description of apartheid can leave unexplored the terrorism and the gross violations of human rights committed in South Africa in pursuance of this racist policy, as they were inseparable from it. I rely here primarily on the findings of the TRCR for the exposure of those committed from 1960 to 1994 at least. President Mandela appointed 17 members to the commission that wrote the report, and Archbishop Tutu, who won the Nobel Prize for Peace in 1984, served as its chairperson. Both de Klerk and practically all of the notables in the National Party plus those in Inkatha opposed the establishment of the commission. Although it was first proposed by the ANC, this party later tried, unsuccessfully it turned out, to block its publication. The TRCR's investigation was limited to what it called "gross violations of human rights" that occurred during that period. These violations were defined by the TRCR to mean killings, abductions, torture, and severe ill treatment of any person, or any attempt, conspiracy, incitement, or command to commit such acts. Included also is what this volume calls terror.

Exempted from the commission's purview were acts committed in any other period and such terrible abuses as the forcible removal of millions of Africans from their neighborhoods for racial reasons, the arrest of millions of Africans for pass law violations, and the use of detention without trial. Included were violations committed not only by the state and its security forces and any such forces by the homelands, but also those committed by the liberation movements. This was the so-called "two-devil policy," a policy objected to by guerrilla and liberation movements. The African National Congress (ANC) objected to this provision on the grounds that the fight against apartheid by these movements was a just cause and that therefore their violations of human rights were of less moral significance than those committed in support of an unjust system. The commission granted that the ANC and the PAC (Pan African Congress) were internationally recognized liberation movements and that apartheid was a crime against humanity. But it drew a distinction between a just war and the means of fighting such a war. It concluded that liberation movements were not allowed to commit gross violations of human rights in pursuance of their just cause.

Before agreeing to the death of apartheid and the birth of majority rule, de Klerk insisted on amnesty provisions. These were written into the new constitution.

Before agreeing to the death of apartheid and the birth of majority rule, de Klerk insisted on amnesty provisions. These were written into the new constitution. There is doubt that he would have agreed to the new dispensation without these provisions. The political situation of the time as well as the commission that wrote the TRCR were subject to cross pressures, not unlike those existing at the initiation of other truth commissions. The Africans had the votes, but the whites had the guns and the economy. The whites were generally unrepentant, sometimes arrogant, hidden away as they were in their all-white neighborhoods and generally unaware of the plight of the Africans. The possibility of a coup existed. Whites learned from the hearings that were held of what had been done in their name, that is, if they bothered to listen. Samples of the applications for amnesty were televised during the first weeks of the hearings. White viewership increased as the program progressed. Amnesty also became part of the terms of reference of the TRCR. The commission established a special organization to deal with it. Other special features of the commission were its power to subpoena and its holding of public hearings. Only individual applications for amnesty were considered, and then only if the violation had been committed for political reasons, not for personal ones. The panel had to be convinced that the applicant had made a full disclosure. The commission reported that of the 7000 applications that it had received, only some 150 had been granted amnesty with 2000 still to be considered.

Anyone could come to the commission to lodge a complaint, to fill out a statement about gross violations of human rights. During the two years from the time the commission began work until the cut off date in December, 1997, some 21,296 took advantage of this opportunity to file a statement or complaint about what happened to the one making the statement, the deponent, or someone else. The sample that resulted was self-selective, and the commission made no attempt to collect a representative or random sample from which a total of violations could be "scientifically" deduced. Eighty-nine and nine tenths percent of the statements or complaints were made by Africans, with much smaller percentages (in order) by the colored, whites, and Asians. The low percentage for whites (1.1 percent) relative to their percentage of the South African population was explained by the commission in two ways: white hostility to the commission and the fact that the repression during apartheid was not aimed directly at whites. All complaints were investigated, and a finding was made in each case, together with a recommendation for reparations. The commission gathered evidence from other submissions, amnesty applications, and documents to which it had access. The total number of reported violations, whether gross violations or other was 46,696, of which 36, 935 were judged to be gross violations.

The number of victims was found to be 28,750, with the average victim having received 1.6 violations. Of the gross violations, 9,980 were killings. Most of those who suffered gross violations were men, whereas most deponents were women. The commission divided the violations into four periods. The last two from 1983 to 1989 and from 1990 to 1995 experienced many more violations than the previous two periods. The dramatic increases occurred during the administrations of Botha and de Klerk. The commission heard testimony from every part of the political spectrum. It interviewed generals, policemen, murderers, former guerrilla leaders, saboteurs, and torturers, and it searched through government documents. Yet much of the record was denied to it. Apartheid governments shredded tons of documents, and even as the commission investigated, the security establishment continued to shred despite orders to the contrary by the Mandela government. Having noted that the submissions by the officials of the former government were often deliberately intended to be of little assistance, the commission estimated that the destruction of state documents did more to undermine the work of the commission than any other single factor. A large number of investigations of gross human rights violations were hampered by the absence of documentation.

Gross Human Rights Violations: Pretoria and the Inkatha

Nonetheless, the report of the commission was voluminous, consisting of no less than 2,759 pages, distributed in five volumes. Despite the deficiencies noted above, the commission expressed confidence in the validity of its findings. I regard it as a fine basis, the best I have seen, upon which to evaluate the terrorism and the violations of human rights that occurred in South Africa from 1960 to 1995. The commission found that "the predominate portion of gross violations of human rights was committed by the former state through its security and law-enforcement agencies." This is the beginning of an answer to a central question posed by this study: Whether the terrorism committed in South Africa was state terrorism committed by the government or private terrorism committed by the opposition. Moreover, in the period from the late seventies to the early nineties the state "became involved in activities of a criminal nature," including the extra-judicial killing of political opponents. In doing so, the Botha and de Klerk administrations acted in collusion with other political groupings, most notably the Inkatha Freedom Party.

The commission went on to explain that the administrations before Botha killed opponents, but not in the systematic way introduced by his administration. During its first five to seven years in office, the Botha administration implemented its "total strategy" by invading neighboring countries and waging counter-insurgency warfare against them. This strategy led to the deaths of some 1.5 million victims in neighboring countries. The TRCR mentioned this slaughter only in passing. Its estimates were confined to what had happened within the Republic of South Africa itself. When the conflict intensified within South Africa itself in the mid eighties, the tactics that worked abroad were applied domestically. A military style of opposing internal dissent became the hallmark of the State Security Council, whose decisions were almost always accepted by the cabinet. Actually, all of its key members sat on the council as did the leadership of the security forces. The South African military began to play an increasing role in domestic security, and the military way of destroying the enemy was transferred from the external to the internal and became more and more common practice within the country. The public rhetoric of the cabinet and security forces as well as their internal documents mirrored this change as they began to be laced with terms such as "take out", "neutralize," "wipe out," "remove," "eliminate," "cause to disappear," and "destroy terrorists." The word 'terrorist' was used constantly, but never defined. Botha himself called Mandela a "communist terrorist." No distinction was drawn between activists engaged in military operations or acts of terrorism and those who opposed apartheid by lawful and peaceful means. All were lumped together as one target, a single category of persons to be killed. The kill rate perpetrated by the government increased accordingly, as did the use of torture, abduction, arson, and sabotage. The commission alleged that Botha, as head of the state and as chairperson of the State Security Council, contributed to a climate in which gross violations of human rights could and did occur. It concluded that he was responsible for such violations.

Botha was brought to trial, found guilty, and fined 10,000 Rand, the equivalent of $1,320. His sentence was overturned on a technicality.

Archbishop Tutu tried to get Botha to appear before the commission, and the commission subpoenaed him to appear. By then 81 years old with a heart problem and recovering from a hip operation, he steadfastly refused to do so. He maintained that he was a follower of Christ, that he was innocent of any wrong doing, and that the conflicts in which he was involved were directed against Soviet imperialism. He did, however, dispatch a 1,800 page submission to the commission in which he accused it of being involved "in a transparent attempt to finally discredit the Afrikaner and its former leadership corps." He was brought to trial, found guilty, and fined 10,000 Rand, the equivalent of $1,320. His sentence was overturned on a technicality.

One of the witnesses at the trial was Eugene de Kock, a highly decorated police colonel and former commander of the counterinsurgency agency at Vlakplaas, He had worked closely with Botha as a "foot soldier," and was said to be involved in the murder of at least 70 victims. He was sentenced for only six of these murders, but also for conspiracy to murder, attempted murder, culpable homicide, abduction, assault, possession of illegal arms, and sixty-six charges of fraud. He was sentenced to 212 years in prison. Declared sane in a psychiatric examination, he characterized himself as a loyal defender of the white state. "I'm a relentless hunter who stays on the track until the problem is solved." He claimed that he received his orders from police generals, who in turn received their orders from the highest levels of government. De Kock looked straight at Botha at the latter's trial and declared that politicians who refuse to take responsibility for the illegal actions of their followers are cowards. "The politicians wanted lamb, but they didn't want to see the blood and guts."

In the closing pages of his book, de Kock declared that "the person who sticks most in my throat is former State President F.W. de Klerk." This was not because he failed to take responsibility for the death of this person or for that particular raid or even because of the holier-than-thou attitude he assumed before the commission. The former police colonel, now a convicted killer, said that it was because de Klerk did not have the courage to admit that "we at the top levels" condoned what was done on our behalf by the security forces; that if we did not give the orders, we turned a blind eye to what happened; that we did not stop what was happening; and that we did not declare that "the foot soldiers" be excused. De Klerk put in a mixed performance before he appeared before the commission. He earned the respect of much of the world when he released Mandela from prison, lifted the ban on the African National Congress, the Pan African Congress, and the Communist Party, and opened the way for a negotiated settlement. In 1993 he shared the Nobel Prize for peace with Mandela. On the other hand, he had been a stalwart supporter of apartheid and a member of previous racist governments, even before his own government came to power. This government was marked by some of the worst human rights abuses, the realm of criminal misconduct extending into his period of office. But the violence of the period was not a monopoly of the state security apparatus. It was also perpetrated by the ANC and Inkatha.

In his appearance before the commission, de Klerk acknowledged that many "unacceptable things" occurred during the rule of the National Party and that they caused immeasurable pain and suffering to many. But he denied being any part of a decision to commit gross violations of human rights. He granted that things happened that were not authorized, not intended," or of which we were unaware." But he wrote these off as the unauthorized actions of rogue elements. He claimed never to have condoned gross violations of human rights, and he rejected any insinuation that it was ever the policy of his government or his party. He repeatedly proclaimed his innocence and characterized accusations to the contrary as lies. The commission found that de Klerk failed to make a full disclosure of the gross human rights violations committed by the senior members of the government and the police. Therefore, it found him to be an accessory to the commission of gross violations of human rights. The generals and the politicians that had run the security establishment were equally unhelpful in describing their role and unwilling to accept responsibility. Most of them showed hostility to the commission.

The commission returned to its principal charge against the South African state. It used these words: "The state in the form of the South African government, the civil service, and its security forces was, in the period 1960–1994, the primary perpetrator of gross violations of human rights in South Africa, and from 1974, in southern Africa." It reasserted this accusation in its discussion of apartheid, which it characterized as a crime against humanity. The commission found this extreme form of racism, sometimes called "evangelical racism," to be "the motivating core of the South African political order." It was adopted to preserve the power and the privileges of the white minority, and as a consequence of this racism the white citizens in general "adopted a dehumanizing position toward black citizens" to the extent that the state "largely labelled them as the enemy. This created the climate in which gross atrocities committed against them were seen as legitimate." This allowed torture, abduction, killing, and other gross violations of human rights as well as the creation of an authoritarian state. In one of its rare references to the West, the commission charged that the racism that served as the motivating core of the South African political system was in the period 1960 to 1990 "largely endorsed by the investment and other policies of South Africa's major trading partners."

The commission reminded its readers that four former National Party cabinet members agreed before the commission that apartheid had no moral basis and that De Klerk himself admitted that the system brought suffering to millions of its victims. The commission granted, however, that some whites at the time honestly believed that apartheid was an acceptable way to solve difficult racial problems. It conceded that a virulent form of anti-communism had become widespread in South Africa after the National Party's electoral victory in 1948. By the sixties virtually any opposition to the government was labelled communist. Former Minister of Law and Order Adriaan Vlok testified before the commission that the ANC and the PAC were correctly seen as tools and fronts of the Marxist communist threat to the country. He continued: Had the communists taken over, they would have made South Africa a backward country with an atheistic ideology. He saw it as his duty to fight against such thoughts, programs, and initiatives. Craig Williamson, former intelligence officer and bomber, admitted that the members of the South African security system paid little attention to the personal political motivation of the liberation forces beyond regarding them as a part of the Soviet onslaught against the civilized, free, and democratic Western world. This belief made it easier for these forces to take the most violent action against the liberation movement, because the action was seen as being taken against a foreign enemy.

The commission rejected the notion that communism and its opposite, anticommunism, together constituted the central issue in South Africa during the apartheid era.

Archbishop Tutu argued that Soviet communism played a pivotal role in the politics of the apartheid era, with nations defining themselves in terms of their relationship to communism. The communist threat was regarded as being so serious that prominent democracies such as the United States supported the world's worst dictatorships, such as that of Pinochet, rather than countenance social change on the scale that communism promised. Similarly, so the Archbishop charged, the United States had been willing to subvert democratically elected governments merely because the governments were communist-influenced. And the United States did not care much about the human rights records of their surrogates. The Archbishop concluded that the South African government in its own crusade against communism was far from being an exception.

As indicated above, the commission rejected the notion that communism and its opposite, anti-communism, together constituted the central issue in South Africa during the apartheid era. It was rather a Cain-and-Abel dialectic that pitted an oppressive, illegal, and inhuman apartheid system against those struggling for a just cause. For decades the struggle was non-violent, at least on the part of the liberation forces. Only when non-violence failed was armed resistance used. The commission found that the moral position of those who sought to uphold apartheid could not be equated with that of those who sought to undermine it. Nonetheless, the commission argued that a just cause does not exempt the organization from pursuing its goals through just means. It does not legitimize the perpetration of gross violations of human rights. But the commission held the government to a higher moral standard than private organizations, because of its privileges and superior resources.

The commission portrayed the Inkatha (IPF) and its leader Buthelezi as allies of the Botha and de Klerk governments. Posing as a liberation movement, the IPF sought to crush the ANC and to disrupt the elections held in 1993–1994. It received financial and logistical support from these governments. The special forces unit of the South African army in 1986 trained its hit squads in the Caprivi strip under a plan whose code name was Operation Marion. In addition, the South African Army provided financial, logistical, and behind the scenes training. The activities of these hit squads were notorious in KwaZulu and Natal. "The Commission received evidence from thousands of people about attacks and massacres perpetrated by IPF (Inkatha) supporters over the twelve year period after April 1983." It found Buthelezi responsible for making speeches that incited supporters to commit violence, for authorizing paramilitary training intended to disrupt the 1993–1994 elections, and for numerous violations of human rights including murder. As indicated below, the Inkatha was found to be the foremost perpetrator of murder within the country.

Gross Human Rights Violations: The ANC and PAC

The ANC signed the Geneva Convention on the conduct of wars of national liberation and made a conscious effort to conduct its armed struggle within the framework of international humanitarian law.

The commission was critical of some of the violence committed by the ANC. Condemning the atrocities committed by liberation movements is not uncommon for truth commissions. It is in accord with the "two-devil principle" that the activities of liberation movements as well as those of governments must be investigated and judged. But the truth commission for South Africa was appointed by the former head of the ANC who had been sentenced to life imprisonment because of the violence committed by the ANC. The commission first congratulated the ANC for its "openness" to the commission, by providing two full submissions and making available its inquiry reports on alleged violations in exile camps. It noted also that the ANC signed the Geneva Convention on the conduct of wars of national liberation and made a conscious effort to conduct its armed struggle within the framework of international humanitarian law. In general it was not ANC policy to target civilians. The commission observed, however, that ANC guerrillas killed more civilians than security forces. In the period 1985–1987, these guerrillas laid mines in the rural areas of Northern and Eastern Transvaal, designated as "military zones" by the government, where farmers were trained and equipped to operate as an extension of the military. The commission held the ANC responsible for the resulting deaths of civilians killed or injured by these mines, the victims including farm laborers and children this despite the fact that the government had blurred the distinction between military and "soft targets" by establishing these zones and arming the farmers living there. The commission granted that the ANC leadership instructed the guerrillas to abandon the land mining program when it became clear that innocent civilians were being killed and injured by the mines. Nonetheless, the commission held the ANC responsible for the atrocities already committed. Although the commission found that torture was not the general policy of the ANC, it concluded that torture was used against suspected agents and routinely by its security department in its camps. In contrast to the behavior of the government, the leadership of the ANC accepted responsibility for all the actions of its members in the period 1960 to 1994.

The Pan African Congress (PAC) was an all African institution that differed from the ANC in that it refused to accept whites as members. The commission recognized it as a liberation movement, but it proved to be less open to, or cooperative with, the commission than the ANC. It differed with the ANC also when the latter suspended its armed struggle in 1990. It vowed to fight on, to continue with a protracted people's war, and it launched Operation Great Storm that targeted whites at random and white farmers in particular. In a hearing before the commission, Brigadier Mofokeng explained that the enemy of the liberation movement and of the people was always the white settler colonial group. He charged that the pillars of the apartheid state against the "black danger" were not only the military, but also the "arming" of the entire white population. "This militarization, of necessity, made every white citizen a member of the security establishment." Despite this contention, the commission applied to the activities of the PAC the same moral and legal yardstick used in measuring the behavior of the ANC. It charged that the targeting of civilians was a gross violation of human rights and a violation of international humanitarian law. It rejected PAC's claim that its killing of white farmers constituted acts of war. It held the PAC accountable morally and politically for this killing.

In July, 1993 operatives of the PAC struck the St. James Church in Kenilworth. One of them entered the church firing his automatic rifle; the other threw hand grenades coated with nails at the assembled worshipers. After the second assailant ran out of grenades, he fired as well. Eleven were killed and fifty-eight were injured. Ironically, the church was integrated, and Russian sailors were regular visitors. Four Russian sailors were killed. In July, 1997 the two assailants plus their driver asked for amnesty before the TRCR. They claimed that their attack was politically motivated, inspired by PAC's attempt to get the land back from the whites. They charged that whites used churches to oppress the blacks. "They took our country using churches and bibles."

One of the three parishioners who opposed the amnesty was Dawie Ackermann whose wife had been killed in the attack. His lawyer argued that there was no reasonable connection between the slaughter of those assembled in a racially integrated church and any defined political goal. Ackermann told how he had walked to the back of the church searching for his wife Maria who was seated there. He had to step over a dead Russian seaman and pools of blood before he saw her sitting upright. He thought she might have survived the attack, but she was dead. He broke into tears as he pointed to the three assailants and declared that he was not angry with them, but with his own family. He said that it was hard to say, but he wanted the assailants to know that since the death of his wife, he fights more with his children, and over stupid things. He asked if the assailants would turn around and face him. They did. After he observed that this was the first time that they had the opportunity to look each other in the face and talk, he turned to the assailant who had entered the church first and asked him if he had killed his wife. "My wife was sitting right at the door when you came in; she was wearing a long blue coat; can you remember if you shot her?" Ackermann added that he did not know why this was important to him, but it just was. The assailant answered by declaring that he pointed his gun at the congregation, and he fired some shots, but he did not know who he shot and who he did not shoot.

Ackermann accepted this statement. He then observed that the lawyer for the three assailants had said "we apologize," but Ackermann wanted to hear it from each of them. "I would like to hear from each of you, as you look me in the face, that you are sorry for what you have done, that you regret it, and that you want to be personally reconciled." The three complied, but the first qualified his apology by pointing to the situation as it existed in South Africa. "We are asking from you, please do forgive us. All that we did, we can see the effects today." Ackermann responded.

The Guilt of Civil Society

The commission quite wisely concluded that civil society was also guilty, through acts of omission and commission, of supporting an apartheid regime that committed gross violations of human rights. Quite appropriately, the commission introduced this subject with a quote from Major Craig Williamson made at a commission hearing on the armed forces. He was "handled" by General Johan Coetzee, who later became the commissioner of the police. A member of the security forces, the major allowed himself to be recruited by the ANC. He then set up what was ostensibly an ANC cell, but actually it consisted entirely of members of the security forces. A specialty of the major was to provide pamphlet bombs to the ANC. This procedure led to entrapment operations in which ANC operatives were caught and killed. At the hearings the major said:

> *It is therefore not only the task of the security forces to examine themselves and their deeds. It is for every member of the society which we served to do so. Our weapons, ammunition, uniforms, vehicles, radios, and other equipment were all developed and provided by industry. Our finances and banking were done by bankers who even gave us covert credit cards for covert operations. Our chaplains prayed for our victory, and our universities educated us in war. Our propaganda was carried by the media, and our political masters were voted back in power time after time with ever-increasing majorities.*

The commission granted that the sectors of civil society generally were not directly involved in the gross violations, but they were structurally part of a system that was. At the broadest level, the white electorate gave the National Party the mandate to do what it did, and this party's popularity increased after the 1948 elections as it embarked upon its program. Singled out for specific blame and mention were the health sector, organized religion, business, the media, and the judiciary.

Singled out for specific blame and mention were the health sector, organized religion, business, the media, and the judiciary.

The media and organized religion exerted immense influence on the formation of ideas and moral codes, as did professional bodies of doctors and lawyers who were often seen as the custodians of scientific knowledge and impartiality. Although there was little evidence of direct involvement of health professionals in gross violations, they failed, among other things, to provide adequate health care for black South Africans and to draw attention to the negative health effects of apartheid, torture, and solitary confinement. The commission took organized religion to task for promoting the ideology of apartheid in a range of different ways that included biblical and theological teachings. The churches provided chaplains who wore the uniforms of the police and armed forces, enjoyed the ranks of armed personnel, and some even carried side arms. On occasion they accompanied the troops engaged in internal conflicts or invasions of bordering countries.

Having pointed out that South African society was divided not only on racial lines, but on class lines as well, the commission argued that business was central to the economy that sustained apartheid. Most businesses benefited from operating in a racially structured context those especially favored were mining, white agriculture, and the industry that supplied the military. The commission noted in its hearings that the business sector failed to accept responsibility for its involvement in state security initiatives. More than 100 laws were passed to restrict the media, their impact after 1985 amounting to pre-publication censorship of information about state-sanctioned violations. The commission found that the racism that permeated white society permeated the media as well. Moreover, mainstream English-language media adopted "a policy of appeasement towards the state, ensuring a large measure of self-censorship." With rare exceptions, the Afrikaans media provided direct support for apartheid and the activities of the security forces.

The commission criticized the judiciary for its collusion with the police regarding the torture of detainees and its collaboration in producing the highest capital punishment rate in the" Western world," an execution rate that overwhelmingly impacted poor black males. It found both the judiciary and the organized legal profession "locked into an overwhelmingly passive mind set" in the face of the injustices of apartheid. They had a choice of opposing such injustice, or taking the honorable way out by resigning.

Applying Terror

The reader must be warned not to draw the conclusion from the above discussion that the liberation forces or the government featured domestic killing as a principal means of accomplishing its goals. South Africa was not Guatemala or even El Salvador at least the commission did not find it to be. However, the impact of Pretoria's "total strategy" on neighboring countries is an entirely different and more lethal story, one that is recounted below. The commission estimated that in the period from 1960 to 1994, Inkatha was responsible for more than 4,500 deaths, the police for 2,700, and the ANC for 1,300. Expressed in percentages, this comes respectively to 53, 32, and 15 percent. As indicated above, Inkatha was allied with the Botha and de Klerk governments and received financial and logistical support from them. The ANC was its enemy. The conclusion to draw from this is that most of the killing done in the period 1960 to 1994 must be put at the door of the government and its ally, leaving 15 percent for the account of the true opposition, the ANC. This percentage is greater than that found for the opponents of the governments in Guatemala, El Salvador, and Chile. Nonetheless, this kill ratio is further evidence that what happened in South Africa was more government terror than private terror. The relatively small number of killings by the ANC is suggested also by police statistics. They indicated that for the period from 1976 to 1986, 130 people were killed by "terrorists." True, only some thirty were said to be members of security forces and some hundred were said to be civilians, but the total number for the two is low.

An examination of the graphs contained in the TRCR representing the known organizational affiliation of the victims who suffered gross violations of human rights also suggests that what happened in South Africa was more state terrorism committed by the government than private terrorism committed by the guerrillas. This conclusion is again based upon the logical inference that organizations terrorize and violate the human rights of enemy organizations. In this example, most victims were affiliated with the ANC and other liberation organizations, much fewer with government institutions and their ally, the Inkatha Freedom Party (IFP). Therefore, the conclusion is warranted that it was the government and its ally that committed most of the violations. The graphs in the TRCR do not provide exact numbers, but they are sufficient for what is being done here. The one depicting the numbers killed whose known organizational affiliation could be determined indicates that those with an affiliation with the ANC were far and away the greatest number: some 2,900. The IFP placed second, with approximately 750; followed by the United Democratic Front (UDF), a liberation organization, with 550; and non-partisan, non-aligned organizations with perhaps 400. The other four organizations barely made an impression on the graph. Notable among these was the SAP (the South African Police), which placed seventh, second from the bottom. The graph on severe ill treatment tells the same story. ANC affiliates again are in first place (some 5,000 victims), UDF (1,400), IFP (1,200), the non-partisan-non-aligned (700), PAC 300, and unions (200). Again, SAP placed seventh, too small to estimate, followed by another liberation organization. The breakdown of the graph depicting the affiliation of torture victims leads to the same conclusion, with liberation organizations placing first, second, and third, and the SAP not finding a place on the graph.

Detention without Trial

The usual way the government treated dissidents was to imprison them and hold them without trial. The commission found that the period 1960 to 1994 saw "the systematic and extensive use of detention without trial" and that this "frequently led to the gross violation of human rights." Government detention and torture was not confined to any part of the country, and its perpetration was not the work of only one of the security forces. The commission concluded allegations of torture formed a large percentage of the violations reported to it and that most of those who said they had been detained added that they had been subjected in the process to some form of assault or torture. It estimated that from 1960 to 1990, eighty thousand were detained, of whom 10,000 were women and 15,000 were under the age of 15. Detention without trial represented the first line of defense by the security forces, and it was only after it seemed to fail that the tactic of killing increased. A law enacted in 1963 allowed the police to hold detainees in solitary confinement without access to lawyers or family until they answered all questions satisfactorily. Their period of detention was initially set at 30 days, then extended to 180 days, but it could be renewed indefinitely by the police.

Torture

In 83 percent of the cases, the detainee was physically tortured.

According to a study based on fieldwork conducted in 1983 and 1984 by Foster and his associates, in 83 percent of the cases the detainee was physically tortured. The researchers interviewed 158 persons formerly detained by the government from all parts of South Africa who had experienced detention 176 times, some undergoing multiple detentions. The most frequent form of physical torture they endured (75 percent) was beating. This included punching, hitting, kicking, and slapping, sometimes with the help of implements. The second most widespread form of physical torture (50 percent) was forced standing for long periods of time. This meant maintaining abnormal body positions, such as holding a position as though sitting on a chair or standing tiptoe with the arms outstretched. Twenty-five percent reported that they were subjected to electric shock torture, 18 percent to strangulation either by hand, cloth, or towel, and 14 percent to suspension. The commission found that during the period 1960 to 1994 the most common form of torture by the security forces was beating, followed by electric shock treatment, suffocation techniques, and forced standing for long periods of time. According to the study by Foster and his associates, the percentage of females tortured was less than for men and much less for whites than for other races. Whereas only 31 percent of the whites claimed to have been tortured, 93 percent of the blacks and 83 percent of the Indians made the same claim. That racism followed the victims to the torture chamber seems logical in an apartheid society, The study by Foster and his associates provides, in its own words, "clear and definitive evidence that physical torture occurs on a widespread basis and constitutes a systematic and common experience for those detained for interrogation purposes under South African security legislation." The study went on to claim that the frequency and range of torture used contradicted the standard claim of state officials that torture did not occur in South Africa aside from a few isolated cases. The data "show that it is a standard form of treatment during detention, particularly in the case of young black detainees." A study released two years before the one quoted above came to very similar conclusions. It also found that 83 percent of those in its sample were tortured, and many of the forms of torture catalogued in that study were the same as those found in the report of the commission.

The study by Foster and his associates reported that not one of the detainees interviewed reported an entire lack of psychological abuse. Eighty-three percent were subjected to false accusations; 79 percent to solitary confinement; 71 percent to verbal abuse; 64 percent to threats of violence; 41 percent to threats of execution for themselves or their families; 23 percent to constant interrogation; and 15 percent to sleep deprivation. Only four percent of the sample reported that they experienced no health problems during their detention. Examples of these problems were difficulty sleeping (60 percent), headaches (53 percent), weight loss (45 percent), appetite loss (44 percent), and nightmares (41 percent).

On June 14, 1986 three people were killed and some sixty-nine were injured when a car bomb exploded at Magoo's Bar on the Durban beachfront. This attack was carried out by a three-member cell of the Umkhonto We Sizwe (MK), the military wing of the ANC. One member of the cell turned state witness. Another, Ms. Greta Apelgren (later known as Zahrah Narkedien) broke down after being tortured, gave the police the information they wanted, and was acquitted. The third was Robert Mc Bride who was convicted and sentenced to death but later released during negotiations between political parties in the early nineties. In its first submission to the commission, the ANC maintained that the attack was a mistake and that the real target was the nearby Why Not Bar. The latter was often frequented by the security police. Mc Bride maintained that he parked the car with the bomb in it directly opposite the Why Not Bar and that Magoo's was never an intended target.

Before being acquitted, Narkedien was detained, tortured for seven days, and held in solitary confinement. She told the commission that what made her break down and talk was the threat to kidnap her four year old nephew, Christopher, and throw him out the window on the thirteenth floor. She figured that she could risk her own life and "let my body just be handed over to these men to do what they liked, but I couldn't hand over someone else's body so at that point I cooperated." During her detention she was kept in solitary confinement for seven months in a cell the size of a small bathroom with high walls. She described her ordeal this way:

I don't even want to describe psychologically what I had to do to survive down there. It did teach me something and that is that no person can live alone for more than I think a month. I felt as the months went by that I was going deeper and deeper into the ground. I felt so psychologically damaged that I used to feel that all these cells are all like coffins and there were dead people in there, because they were not there, no one was there. It was as if I was alive and all these people were dead. I'm out of prison now for more than seven or ten years but I haven't recovered and I will never recover. I have tried to and the more I struggle to be normal, the more disturbed I become. I had to accept that I was damaged, a part of my soul was eaten away as if by maggots and I will never get it back again.

Haroon Aziz, a local leader of the ANC in Natal was arrested, detained, and given the "invisible chair" treatment. He was made to squat in thin air as though he was sitting on a chair. He had to hold his hands out and click his fingers. He was interrogated as he was forced to assume this position. Directly behind him was the wall, but he was not allowed to touch it. Special branch policemen placed in front of him took turns holding a knife at his navel to prevent him from lunging forward. If his tormenters were not satisfied with his answers, they hit him on the penis or squeezed it. When he did fall forward, they withdrew the knife, but they then kicked him. The kicking went on while he screamed and hollered, and they laughed at him like mad hyenas.

Frank Bennetts, a former member of the Durban Riot Unit, provided the commission with a description of what was alternately called the "helicopter," "boeing" or the "aeroplane." The victim would be handcuffed with his hands behind his back, and his feet would be handcuffed at the ankles. He then would be laid down on his stomach with his feet in the air and a broom or piece of wood would be put between his ankles and pushed through under the handcuffs on his wrists. Each end of the broom or piece of wood would be placed on a desk. He would then dangle between the two desks, the result being similar to crucifixion. His muscles would be pulled taut, his chest closed, with the result that he could not breathe. Mr. Bennetts assured the commission that if left there long enough, the victim would talk.

The commission held Jeffrey Benzien's amnesty hearing in Cape Town in 1997. A former warrant officer, he was still employed by the police air wing. By his own admission, he was Cape Town's most successful torturer. His former commanding officer characterized him as "the best exponent of unconventional methods of extracting information from suspects." His specialty was the wet bag, a technique that he described to the commission at the request of Tony Yengeni. The latter was a former guerrilla commander, and at the time of the hearing, a member of parliament. Benzien had used the wet bag on him, but he was blindfolded at the time. He had never seen it used on anybody else; in fact, he had never seen the wet bag. He requested that Benzien demonstrate its use. Benzien obliged, using a volunteer from the audience to demonstrate how it was done. Benzien explained:

> *... it would be a cloth bag that would be submerged in water to get it completely wet. I get the person to lie down on the ground on his stomach with that person `s hands handcuffed behind his back. Then*

> *I would take up a position in the small of the person `s back, put my feet through between his arms to maintain my balance and then pull the bag over the person `s head and twist it closed around his neck, cutting off the air supply to the person. On occasions people have, I presume, and I say presume, lost consciousness. They would go slack and every time that was done, I would release the bag.*

Asked about the reaction of the victim, Benzien replied:

> *There would be movement, there would be head movement, distress. All the time there would be questions asked 'Do you want to speak?` and as soon as an indication was given that this person wanted to speak, the air would be allowed back the person would moan, cry.*

Benzien assured the commission that, with a few exceptions, there would be results within half an hour.

> *Yengeni pressed him: "And you did this to each and every one of us?" Benzien replied: "To the majority of you, yes..."*

Then Yengeni asked Benzien what was his reaction to the torture, to which Benzien responded that he did not remember except that Yengeni took the police to the house where the guerrillas kept their weapons. Yengeni then asked:

> *What kind of man uses a method like this one of the wet bag, to people, to other human beings, repeatedly and listening to those moans and cries and groans and taking each of those people near to death? What kind of a man are you? I want to understand what happened. I am talking about the man behind the wet bag. When you do these things, what happens to you as a human being? What goes through your head, your mind?*

Benzien did not really confront these questions. He said that he had also asked himself what kind of a man he was and that he had approached a psychiatrist with the same question. He granted that he was raised in a privileged white neighborhood and that he wanted to preserve these privileges. Another former guerrilla commander pressed Benzien to remember the details of his torture, but the former warrant officer remained "the professional," insisting on speaking in the abstract about methods, not remembering specific cases. He refused to remember the details of this man's torture, despite the victim's strong desire to hear Benzien admit and confirm them. This second guerrilla commander had tried to commit suicide rather than face another torture session. He finally did get Benzien to admit that at one torture session Benzien threatened to take him to the verge of death as many times as necessary to get him to talk.

Washington's Policy toward South Africa

Both Republican and Democratic administrations subordinated foreign policy issues to Cold War requirements and to the prevention of social revolution.

Apartheid was a highly imaginative policy, so audacious, thorough, and ruthless as to challenge the human capacity to believe. Although less lethal, it shared this with Hitler's earlier "final solution of the Jewish problem." Another parallel is that between Schmitz's view of Washington's earlier policy in Latin America and Minter's view of its policy toward South Africa between 1960 and the late 1980's. The views of the two scholars are strikingly similar despite differences in time frame and geographical reference. Minter characterized the policy pursued by Washington toward South Africa in the period indicated above as "conservative Realpolitik or pragmatism." He judged that both Republican and Democratic administrations subordinated foreign policy issues to Cold War requirements and to the prevention of social revolution. Like Schmitz for the earlier period, Minter found a continuity in Washington's policy. He argued that the faith that the Reagan administration put in white Pretoria was not an innovation. Indeed, all administrations supported anti-communist allies, even though they were right-wing dictatorships, white settler regimes, or colonial powers. Certain parameters were observed, limits beyond which no policy would be pushed. No administration imposed serious sanctions on Pretoria, nor did any openly proclaim its support for apartheid. Even the arms embargoes adopted in 1963 and 1977 by the Kennedy and Carter administrations due to domestic pressure were largely symbolic and hemmed in with numerous qualifications. Within these limits, certain policy variations did occur, depending upon outside circumstances, the give and take within the administration in question, and private actors.

Minter identified two liberal variations of the central theme, what he calls "interludes". He dates them at the beginning of the Kennedy and Carter administrations. They lasted for brief periods of less than two years. And they "promised far more than they delivered; each time, the image of pro-African liberation dissolved to reveal business-as-usual ties with the white regimes." These symbolic variations did offend Pretoria, but they were intended primarily to ease the discomfort and to attract the votes of African Americans and domestic human rights advocates. Minter concluded that no adjustments to Washington's policy were made out of concern for rising African nationalism, racism, or human rights violations. These would have been considered to be "sentimental distractions from the real business of defending US interests." Later, Washington did switch to embrace these "sentimental distractions." But this became serious policy only after South Africa's racists saw the necessity of doing the same. Minter's reference here seems to be the sanctions imposed by Congress in 1986 that did appear to be serious.

From Truman to Carter

Despite changes in administrations Washington supported a racist Pretoria from 1960 to the late 1980's. In 1950 Washington's delegate opposed a United Nations General Assembly resolution that faulted racial segregation on the grounds that it was discriminatory. The resolution also called upon South Africa not to implement the Group Areas Act, a law that became a centerpiece of its apartheid policy. Given that the American variation of apartheid (segregation) was still in existence at the time, opposition to the resolution seems logical. It is true that President Truman integrated the armed forces. But it is also true that in private conversation he used the word "nigger" to describe African Americans. He held to the racial stereotypes and categories that he had learned as a youth. In 1950 Secretary of State Acheson gave a short lecture in world politics to a gathering at the White House. He chided those "democratic purists who were repelled by some of the practices reported in Greece, Turkey, and North and South Africa." Such a posture he labeled "escapism," avoiding building foreign policy with the materials at hand. Later, as elder statesman, he opposed criticism of apartheid and Portuguese colonial policy and supported the white minority government in Rhodesia. He denounced the United Nations for interfering in the internal affairs of weak white nations.

In 1952 the United States delegate in the General Assembly proclaimed his government's respect for the sovereignty of "the great Union of South Africa" with which it had long been associated in friendly relations. He declared his delegation's determination not to criticize it. The same year Asian and Arab members of the world institution proposed the creation of a commission to study the question of race conflict in South Africa resulting from the policy of apartheid. The United States plus all other Western states abstained on the enabling resolution. The resolution passed because of third world and communist bloc support. Through 1958 U.S. delegations continued to abstain on anti-apartheid resolutions on the grounds that the world institution lacked the legal competence to make such judgments. The conclusion from this is obvious. Both the Truman and the Eisenhower administrations rendered diplomatic support to Pretoria in this early part of the cold war period.

Washington provided military support as well. In this period, the South African military bought arms in the United States as a matter of course. Such a deal in October, 1952 provided for a purchase of $112 million in weapons, and the contract specifically noted that the weapons could be used for internal security. In a visit to the United States in 1950, the South African finance minister failed to get the full amount of a projected $70 million loan he sought. But after the two countries and Britain agreed to the development of South African uranium production, the financing was forthcoming from the World Bank and other sources. The 1950 agreement on the development of South African uranium was followed by years of nuclear cooperation between the African country and the West. In 1976 Dr. Roux, President of the South African Atomic Energy Board, ascribed "our" degree of nuclear advancement "in large measure to the training and assistance so willingly provided by the USA during the earlier years of our nuclear programme." With help from the West, Pretoria did develop a nuclear bomb, a subject discussed below.

In his study of Washington's policy toward South Africa in the Truman years, Borstelmann argues that Cold War concerns led that administration "into a close embrace of the imperial authorities in southern Africa, and the outbreak of war in Korea resulted in a series of agreements with Pretoria that bound the United States government to the apartheid regime." It was the period of the emergence of the Cold War and "the tendency of Americans to view it as a struggle of transcendent good and evil guaranteed all opponents of the Soviet Union a warm welcome in Washington." Despite this bonding with South Africa, the Truman administration and its successors attempted to distance themselves from the extreme forms of racism practiced there. This was crucial, given the racial discrimination and segregation that existed in the United States itself. White rule in South Africa was preferred not only because it was adamantly anti-communist, but also because it brought stability to the country. This was good for business and trade, and investments in South Africa grew apace. Moreover, South Africa was strategically located, and had sizeable uranium deposits. In an address to a branch of the African National Congress in 1953, Nelson Mandela reminded his fellow party members that "there is no easy walk to freedom anywhere." Borstelmann concludes that for most people in southern Africa, the Truman administration "had proven itself willing only to increase, not lighten, the load to be carried."

In 1955 Washington's delegate to the United Nations warned against what it termed were "ringing resolutions to correct overnight situations which have existed for generations." The reference was to racial conditions in South Africa, and the delegate was part of, and spokesperson for, the Eisenhower administration. He expressed the hope that the General Assembly would not bring up the question again, because South Africa seemed "deeply aggrieved" by the proceedings. He proposed that the world institution focus its attention on human rights violations in the communist world. "South Africa continued as a military ally of the West during these years, although neither Britain nor the United States acceded to South African proposals for a formal defense pact." South Africa's friendship was of more concern than the policy of apartheid. To Eisenhower and to his secretary of state, John Foster Dulles, "South Africa was one more ally in the struggle against international communism."

In August, 1963 the Security Council passed a resolution that called for a voluntary arms embargo on Pretoria. It called upon the members not to sell and ship arms, ammunition, and military vehicles to South Africa. The embargo was voluntary, allowing those nations not so inclined to ignore it. Not so obvious was Washington's successful insistence that the resolution not refer to a "threat to the peace," an assertion that could logically lead the Security Council to impose compulsory sanctions. This protected governments such as those of Britain and France that refused to accept the embargo. Adlai Stevenson, the Kennedy administration's ambassador to the United Nation at the time, observed that existing contracts for defense against external threats would be honored. He added that if it should prove necessary for the common defense the United States would feel free to provide equipment to South Africa. Washington voted in favor of a Security Council resolution in March, 1961 that called for an inquiry into the Angolan situation. The resolution was introduced immediately after the guerrillas began their uprising. The resolution did not pass because it lacked the votes, including those of France and Britain. But the Portuguese were furious. Of course, none of this stopped Lisbon from using its U.S. supplied weaponry from responding to the uprising. Washington approved of two other resolutions of similar caliber in April and June of the same year. In the first the General Assembly called upon Portugal "urgently" to consider reforms in Angola. The second was a Security Council instrument that deplored "the severely repressive measures" used in Angola. While deliveries of weapons under the Mutual Security Program were cut from $25 million to $3 million in 1961, official aid figures indicate that Portugal received $39.1 million in military aid from 1962 to 1968. Washington never used the leverage of cutting off spare parts, despite the fact that the Portuguese air force in 1961 depended primarily upon United States equipment. In an internal memorandum in April, 1964, G. Mennen Williams, head of the Africa Bureau of the State Department, referred to "Portugal's diversion and continued use of vast amounts of U.S. MAP (Mutual Assistance Program) equipment in Portuguese Africa." Two months earlier in a letter to a critical Methodist minister in Oregon he asserted that charges of such use "were completely unfounded." This occurred during the Johnson administration.

Criticism of Portugal did not lead to an attempt to cripple the colonialist counter-insurgency war that it launched to contain the African guerrillas. In fact, the Kennedy administration retreated from its early policy of strongly criticizing Portuguese policy. The acceptance of the critical resolutions in the first half of 1961 led to a policy review. Officials dealing with Africa and the United Nations came out in favor of a continuation of the policy. This was opposed by the Defense Department and the National Security Council, both of which argued that criticism should be muted. This view prevailed, and it was expressed in National Security Action Memorandum 60 of July 14, 1961. Washington did give material aid to the guerrilla movements, but it was minuscule compared with that delivered to Portugal. The purpose of the aid was to buy influence with the guerrillas, not to tip the balance of forces in their favor. The fact was that a guerrilla victory was not thought possible. Washington preached reform to both sides, and deplored violence. It looked to Portugal to help bring stability to southern Africa.

Toward South Africa, the Kennedy team followed a policy that it chose to call "bifurcated." It distinguished between non-cooperation in matters directly or indirectly related to apartheid and cooperation in all other matters. "Other matters" turned out to be a spacious category. In June, 1962 an agreement between the two countries allowed NASA to set up a tracking station in the African country. It also allowed South Africa to purchase American arms "for use against communist aggression," but not to enforce apartheid. This distinction did result in the denial of sale of police and infantry type weapons, but not in the rejection for export of air to-air sidewinder missiles and anti-submarine weapons. However, Washington continued to buy uranium from South Africa and to provide aid for its nuclear program. In 1961 Allis-Chalmers sold its first nuclear reactor to Pretoria. South African scientists came to study nuclear physics in the United States, and American warships continued their visits to ports in South Africa. In 1961 and 1963 American warships joined with the British in participating in joint naval exercises with the African country. American private investments grew apace, and the International Monetary Fund and the World Bank provided additional funds to South Africa.

That the Kennedy policy toward Portugal was adopted by the Johnson administration is suggested by the contents of an African Bureau Action Memorandum of April 29, 1964. The memorandum assumed that a stalemate existed in the fighting and that the Portuguese would eventually have to negotiate a solution. The immediate problem was to prevent the nationalists from mortgaging their future to the communists and from reaching a stage "where they no longer will be disposed to negotiate a moderate and evolutionary settlement when Portugal comes around to offering one." The memorandum concluded that the United States should encourage the guerrillas to turn to non-violence. This would in turn encourage Portugal to offer the moderate and evolutionary settlement referred to above.

An immediate issue the Johnson administration faced was the independence of Namibia (then called South-west Africa). What should be done to procure its independence in the face of a hostile Pretoria? Minter reveals that sanctions were ruled out in favor of encouragement of South Africa to modify its policy toward the former mandate that, according to the United Nations, Pretoria was occupying illegally. Washington did not challenge the legitimacy of South African control. It abstained on a resolution to establish a council to rule Namibia. This was after the General Assembly had, on paper, removed the colony from South African control. In 1968, the Security Council passed by a unanimous vote a resolution that condemned the guerrillas as terrorists. But no sanctions were imposed. Sanctions were also ruled out when Pretoria issued the report of the Odendaal commission that sought to promote the establishment of Bantustans. President Johnson signed option three of National Security Council Action Memorandum No. 295. It authorized diplomatic activity and pressure designed to prevent the implementation of the plan. Washington continued on with most routine measures of cooperation with South Africa, including the shipping of nuclear fuel. Coker describes the policy of the Johnson administration as one of marking time, occupied as it was with Vietnam.

In February, 1970 President Nixon accepted as official American policy the creation of closer ties with the white regimes in southern Africa. This policy was based on what by then was the time-honored assumption that constructive change could come about only through cooperation with the white regimes in control in South Africa, Namibia, Southern Rhodesia, and Portuguese Angola and Mozambique. No hope was seen for the attempts of Africans to gain political rights through violence. Such attempts would lead only to chaos and increase the opportunities for the communists. The policy was expressed in National Security Council Memorandum 39 (NSCM 39). It served as the inspiration for the policy of the Nixon administration toward the region, but previous policy had been similarly inspired. The memorandum was nicknamed with the racist epithet "tar baby".

The Nixon administration openly and illegally violated the sanctions imposed upon Northern Rhodesia by the Security Council.

Washington continued to export dual-use equipment to South Africa. The agreement with Portugal that extended Washington's base rights in the Azores provided for, in addition to other benefits, $400 million in export-import credits. Washington provided civilian aircraft used by Portugal in Africa to transport its troops, and Germany and France provided weapons to use against the guerrillas. The Nixon administration openly and illegally violated the sanctions imposed upon Northern Rhodesia by the Security Council. Washington did vote to affirm the non-recognition of South Africa's mandate in Namibia. It abstained, however, on a resolution that recognized "the legitimacy of the struggle of the people of Namibia against the illegal presence of the South African authorities in the territory." In December, 1973 Kissinger offered Portugal new military equipment to fight its wars in Africa. With strong backing from the Ford and Carter administrations, the International Monetary Fund made substantial loans to South Africa. This backing came on the heels of the Soweto uprising, an explosion that was sparked by an incident involving the killing of a student demonstrator on June 16, 1976. The uprising featured African youth in confrontation with the police. Six months into the uprising, one thousand demonstrators lay dead, half shot in the back.

The Carter people adopted a policy that combined a symbolic disassociation from Pretoria with the same basic contention that no reforms were possible in southern Africa without the consent and cooperation of the controlling white rulers. If the Nixon and Ford people had Kissinger to advise them, Carter had the counsel of Brzezinski. Both were European born, but more importantly, both were cold warriors and realists in the strongest sense of the term. Economic sanctions for Pretoria were ruled out for the purported reason that reforms were expected to come through greater economic ties with the outside capitalist world. U.S. exports to South Africa jumped from one billion dollars in 1977 to $2.5 billion in 1980. Aircraft and computers led the list of export categories.

The symbolic disassociation of the Kennedy administration was continued by the Carter team, but at a higher decibel level. The "preaching" was provided by Carter himself, Vice-President Mondale, and Andrew Young. In his inaugural address the president made human rights the cornerstone of American policy. He affirmed, "Because we are free, we can never be indifferent to the fate of freedom elsewhere." In his first years in office he looked to revolutionary changes in the third world as not favoring Soviet interests. But by 1979 the goal of containing the Soviet Union, particularly in Africa, re-emerged as the priority. Once again, the emphasis was not on sanctions, but on the supposed beneficent effects of enlightened capitalism. Not coincidently, the president, the vice-president, the United States ambassador to the United Nations, and others in the administration were members of the business-oriented Trilateral Commission. Young advised Africans to use the non-violent methods of the U.S. civil rights movement and to abjure armed struggle and demands for international economic sanctions.

The Carter administration, however, did approve the Security Council resolution which in 1977 imposed compulsory military sanctions on the errant country. Minter is not impressed with this action, characterizing the sanctions as being "blatantly porous." Their enforcement contrasted with the strict system set up by Washington for the Soviet bloc. Minter exemplifies the porous nature of the sanctions with the example of the export of long range 155 millimeter shells by the Space Research Corporation, a Canadian-American company. Pretoria made contact with this company through a CIA source. From 1976 through 1978 the company exported 6,000 shells to South Africa and provided technical assistance as well. Reporters who investigated the case affirmed that these exports could not have happened without U.S. officials being aware of them. Yet no action was taken until after the clandestine operation began unraveling when dock-workers in Antigua reported the transshipment of the shells in October, 1977. No shipments were blocked until the next year. The Stockholm International Peace Research Institute revealed that a large number of military items were sold by the United States to South Africa in the early seventies, including tanks, armed personnel carriers, 155 millimeter self-propelled guns, and helicopters. The Justice Department disclosed in 1978 that at least 178 of South Africa's 578 military aircraft had been purchased from the United States since 1963 and that of those purchased since 1972 some were clearly military aircraft. The above information indicates that all of the administrations from Truman to and including that of Carter provided support for a racist Pretoria and for other racist and colonial regimes in southern Africa. This support increased during the Reagan years.

Reagan and Botha: "From Repression to Criminal Activity"

Soon after taking office, President Reagan strongly endorsed friendship with South Africa on nationwide TV. He initiated a policy that his administration called "constructive engagement." He asked rhetorically, "Can we abandon a country that has stood by us in every war that we have ever fought, a country that is strategically essential to the free world"? The South African Broadcasting Company praised these remarks, adding that they cleared up the ambiguity and veiled hostility that had characterized Washington's attitude in recent years. The broadcast was followed by an unofficial visit to the United States of five high-ranking South African military officers. They conferred with the National Security Council, Pentagon officials, and Kirkpatrick, the U.S. Ambassador to the United Nations. Reagan's remarks were similar to those of his Under-Secretary of State William Clark. Clark raised his glass to Foreign Minister Pik Botha at a reception in Washington in May, 1981 with these hopeful and generous words: "Let this be the new beginning of trust and confidence between the United States and South Africa, old friends, like minister Botha, who are getting together again." The reference was to the hopes for a new policy between two countries, but it also took account of the fact that Botha had been South African ambassador to the United States from 1975 to 1977. Chester Crocker, Assistant Secretary of State for Africa, provided the rationale for establishing more friendly relations with Pretoria. In a scope paper for internal consumption, Crocker affirmed that U.S. policy in Africa was designed above everything else to stop Soviet encroachment. The paper went on to say that Pretoria shared this priority, and that a new U.S. policy toward South Africa should be based upon this common objective. The new relationship with South Africa "should be based upon our shared hopes for the future prosperity, security, and stability of southern Africa, constructive internal change within South Africa and our shared perceptions of the role of the Soviet Union and its surrogates in thwarting those goals."

Archbishop Tutu declared that this was a period in which Washington enthusiastically supported any government however shabby its human rights record was so long as it declared itself to be anti-communist. "Thus the apartheid government benefited hugely from President Ronald Reagan's notorious 'constructive engagement' policy." While paying lip service to anti-apartheid sentiment, the Reagan administration said that it could more likely bring about change by maintaining relations with Pretoria than by isolating it. After receiving the Nobel Prize for peace in 1984, the archbishop engaged in some private diplomacy in Washington and London. He tried to get both Reagan and Thatcher to impose economic sanctions on South Africa. He met with Reagan and his cabinet, but to no avail. The president was a bit shocked when the archbishop showed him his travel document. He was not allowed a regular South African passport. The shock was caused by the entry in the space for nationality. The entry read "Undeterminable at present." He had an hour-long tea with Prime Minster Thatcher. Although she "oozed oodles of charm," the archbishop failed again. He added that "the people in both countries eventually heeded our pleas, some sanctions were imposed, especially by the United States, and they contributed very substantially to the demise of apartheid." This development is recounted below.

South Africa's "total strategy" for preserving apartheid at all costs was a total, holistic strategy that brought together the internal and the external, as well as the economic, military, political, and diplomatic institutions of the country.

Some two and a third years before Reagan was sworn in as president, P. W. Botha on September 29, 1978 became the Prime Minister of South Africa. He remained in that office until 1989, when he was replaced by de Klerk. As indicated above, the Truth and Reconciliation Commission charged that with Botha's ascendancy to power, Pretoria left behind government repression and entered "the realm of criminal misconduct." The new government adopted a policy called "total strategy," a cruel policy that resulted in the widespread use of torture, abduction, arson, sabotage, and the killing of its opponents. The terror committed by Pretoria before was dramatically increased, and the Reagan administration reacted by offering its friendship and support. "Total strategy" was laid out in a defense white paper in 1977 and adopted as official policy after Botha became prime minister. It was a strategy for preserving apartheid at all costs, and its application was accompanied by an effort to gain legitimacy for a cosmetic version of this extreme type of racism. It was a total, holistic strategy that brought together the internal and the external, as well as the economic, military, political, and diplomatic institutions of the country. To assure the coordination of the strategy, the government created the Joint Security Management System with a military structure, and put it directly under the powerful State Security Council.

Total strategy was adopted in the wake of the independence of Angola and Mozambique, two colonies originally envisaged as part of the group of political entities necessary for the protection of the apartheid state. After independence, these former colonies, now states, were seen as the enemy. The original group of political entities so considered included Namibia and Southern Rhodesia. In 1980 Southern Rhodesia, now renamed Zimbabwe, elected an African government. It was then switched to the list of enemies. The dominoes were falling, and the arrival of the Reaganites in Washington was welcomed as good news by the white elites in Pretoria. Their total strategy was many-sided, however, and it made provision for such unwelcome contingencies as falling and fallen dominoes. Better to have friendly white neighboring governments, but if they are or they turn black, make them dependent surrogates, politically submissive, through trade or other economic means. Failing this, reduce them to impotent enemies.

Botha at first called for the formation of a southern African "constellation of states," one dominated by Pretoria. The dark side of the strategy was the one implemented at tremendous cost to the Africans in neighboring countries. Pretoria thus was engaged in a war on two fronts, an internal war with the domestic majority and a more lethal external one with neighboring countries. South African forces and their surrogates invaded and/or committed acts of sabotage, terror, and destruction against South Africa's neighbors Angola, Mozambique, Botswana, Lesotho, Swaziland, Zambia, and Zimbabwe. They assassinated political opponents and sought to destabilize regimes. Favorite targets were transportation systems, but other economic assets were destroyed, including food supplies. The destruction of transportation facilities in Angola and Mozambique forced other surrounding land locked states to use South African ports. The transit states lost revenue, Pretoria gained revenue. The total strategy of horror and terror continued to be implemented until 1988, with a tremendous cost in wealth, human life, and misery.

The CIA gave the government information that led to capture of Nelson Mandela.

Botha did not have to build his total strategy from scratch. In fact, throughout the seventies the South African army taught courses and gave lectures in counter-insurgency to the security and non-security forces of the nation. It was during this period that General Jannie Geldenhuys introduced the South African military to the ideas of the American security theorist J. J. McCuen. Even before this in 1962–1963, General Magnus Malan was exposed to counter-insurgency theory in the United States where he completed the regular command and general staff officer's course. He became chief of the South African Army and from 1980, Minister of Defense. As the officer in charge of the South West Africa Command from 1966 to 1968 he conducted a war largely on the principles of counter-insurgency. Some suggestion of the brutality of that campaign is recorded in a different part of this chapter. During his tour of duty as chief of the army from 1973 to 1976, he established a series of joint inter-agency counterinsurgency agencies. Counter-insurgency thinking had an impact on the patterns and modes of human rights violations by South Africa. It introduced a regional component to the government's struggle and became important domestically as an inspiration for devising new and more repressive measures for domestic crowd control. Moreover, this manner of thinking legitimized the establishment of covert governmental units and inspired the abduction and killing of political activists. "Further U.S. influence was evident in the co-operation between the security forces and the Central Intelligence Agency (CIA) which considered South Africa a local ally against the Soviet Union." The commission gave as examples the information the CIA gave the government that led to capture of Nelson Mandela and the training given to General Van den Bergh prior to the creation of BOSS, the national intelligence agency of South Africa. The general became its first head.

A prime component in total strategy was the strengthening and expansion of the military and the police. The military budget showed dramatic expansion even before Pretoria adopted this strategy. This resulted in great part from the impact of counter-insurgency thought. The budget continued its upward thrust after the acceptance of total strategy as well. It jumped from 44 million Rand in 1960 to 1.3 billion Rand in 1977. The budget was estimated at 4.274 billion Rand for fiscal 1984–1985. The budget thus increased over three times during the period of the new strategy. In 1985 the government announced that it was going to expand its police force from 45,000 by 11,000 during the next 17 months. South Africa developed the world's tenth largest arms industry, with sufficient capacity to manufacture for export.

Just days after President Reagan was inaugurated, Pretoria launched an attack on Maputo, the capital of

Mozambique. It appeared as though the South African elites were testing the validity of the friendlier attitude expressed by Washington. The operation was a small part of the implementation of the total strategy of the apartheid regime. Twelve people in the capital city were killed. The incursion followed a speech in which the new Secretary of State Haig condemned rampant international terrorism and promised that a priority of the new administration was to fight it. Pretoria justified the attack as an attempt to root out the terrorist bases of the African National Congress located in the Mozambican capital. When the Security Council attempted to condemn the attack, the American delegate vetoed the draft resolution. Even before the advent of the Reagan administration, Washington had crafted a definition of "terrorism" such that attacks like these by allies and friendly states were exempt from criticism by definition.

Two months later Mozambique expelled several U.S. diplomats on the grounds that they were part of a CIA network that was targeting the government as well as South African exiles. Washington retaliated by cutting off food assistance. Later in August, 1981 Pretoria sent a force of 11,000 to occupy the southern part of Angola. Secretary of State Haig justified this invasion and occupation as a defensive maneuver intended to protect against the threat of Cuban forces and Soviet weapons and advisers. Washington broke with its allies to veto a Security Council resolution that would have condemned this invasion and occupation of Angola. This operation was also part of the implementation of total strategy. In a major foreign policy speech two days before the veto, Under-Secretary of State Crocker argued that the United States should sustain those who "would resist the siren call of violence and the blandishments of Moscow and its clients." He went on to imply that South Africa's actions were defensive and blamed the Warsaw Pact for supporting the guerrillas in Namibia and South Africa. He noted that Pretoria "clearly signaled its determination to resist guerrilla encroachments and strike at countries giving sanctuary." Export controls on security items and on nuclear related items were loosened despite the fact that Pretoria refused to sign the Nuclear Non-Proliferation Treaty. In November, 1982 Washington used its influence and its vote in the International Monetary Fund to help improve the economic situation in South Africa. The year before the General Assembly had deplored the increased political, economic, and military assistance rendered South Africa by "certain Western countries." It demanded that this assistance be terminated as well as aid from the International Monetary Fund.

The Reaganites provided diplomatic, military, and economic support for a terrorist Pretoria.

Clearly, the Reagan administration gave its blessing to the Pretoria regime, to its continuing nuclear program, and to the way the "total strategy" first unfolded. Minter observed "the signals from Washington shone brightly green." The Reaganites provided diplomatic, military, and economic support for a terrorist Pretoria. Minter also accused Haig of "racial insensitivity" the Secretary of State playfully beat the table like a jungle drum whenever African topics were discussed at meetings of the National Security Council. The Reagan administration continued the policy of granting scholarships for South African blacks to study in the United States. It offered this aid as an alternative to sanctions. The president demonstrated that he did not always keep up with things when he declared in a radio interview on August, 24, 1985 that South Africa had "eliminated the segregation that we once had in our own country." Violent demonstrations in South Africa escalated to the level of civil war. Human rights groups estimated that between September, 1984 and mid 1986, 2,500 were killed, nearly all Africans. At least 30,000 were detained, including 300 youngsters under eighteen. These demonstrations were triggered by a new constitution that provided for Indian and colored representation, but not for African representation and by a defiant speech delivered by Botha. The violent street reaction in South Africa was matched in the United States by peaceful demonstrations instigated by African-Americans, students, churches, and others. Some six thousand protestors were arrested picketing the South African embassy and its consulates, including eighteen members of congress, one being a Senator (Senator Weicker). Pressure was put on universities, local government, and businesses resulting in divestiture and the refusal of banks to role over loans for South Africa. More than half of the American firms with direct investments in South Africa withdrew them between 1984 and the end of 1986. The value of the rand plunged. A declining economy and a volatile political situation induced South African business to pressure the government for change.

Washington finally imposed sanctions on South Africa in 1985 and 1986. The first imposition was by the Reagan administration, intended to ward off more serious action by Congress. It banned the sale of Kuggerrands in the United States, incorporated the Sullivan principles into law, and restricted bank loans and technological exports. The sanctions were subject to discretionary reversal by the president. The Reagan administration showed its limited commitment to the new dispensation when in November of the same year it vetoed a Security Council resolution that mandated compulsory sanctions for South Africa because of its continuing occupation of Namibia. On October 2, 1986 Congress overrode a presidential veto to impose the first substantive, albeit not comprehensive, sanctions of the United States on South Africa. This did not occur before the administration vetoed another attempt by the Security Council to impose sanctions. The sanctions imposed by Congress banned new investments and loans as well as imports of coal, iron, steel, uranium, agricultural products, and textiles. They also prohibited the right of South African Airways to land in the United States. The legislation threatened to cut off military aid to those countries that breached the international arms embargo against Pretoria.

This could have been a warning to Israel because that country had become an important source of arms and military expertise for South Africa. The sanctions legislation did not confine its criticism to the government that had instituted apartheid, but included the two African parties, the African National Congress and the Pan African Congress as well. The Inkatha Freedom Party, responsible for much of the ongoing violence within South Africa, was not mentioned. The Reagan administration showed its disagreement again by vetoing a sanctions resolution in the Security Council and by its lax enforcement of the sanctions legislation passed by Congress. The resolution it vetoed was almost identical to the legislation passed by Congress. The administration continued to provide aid to UNITA and did not criticize Pretoria as the latter repeatedly attacked neighboring countries and implemented other aspects of its total strategy.

In 1987 for the first time the U.S. representative to the United Nations Human Rights Commission submitted a resolution that criticized Pretoria's policies. It called for the release from prison of Mandela and other political prisoners and condemned the widespread incarceration of children under the apartheid system. Human rights groups in South Africa estimated over 25,000 people had been incarcerated since June, 1986 under the State of Emergency Act. Ten thousand of these were children. Finally, Reagan's ambassador to South Africa "was activated." At first, Edward Perkins, the first African-American ambassador to Pretoria, kept a low profile. As his tenure progressed, he became more visible, attending the treason trials, protesting the jailing of dissidents, and authoring an article in a local journal that seemed to call for majority rule. He went so far as to be labeled "too outspoken" by Pretoria. Washington's conversion to a new policy toward apartheid had been long in coming and was shaky at best. Moreover, it seemed to be driven by the realization that apartheid was being killed at the local level and that realism dictated that its death be accepted at other levels as well.

The Republican platform for 1988 opposed sanctions; the Democratic platform called for comprehensive sanctions and named South Africa a "terrorist state."

The Republican platform for the 1988 election reaffirmed its support for the Reagan administration's policies in South Africa and opposed sanctions. In contrast to this, the Democratic platform called for comprehensive sanctions and named South Africa a "terrorist state."

In 1989 T.W. de Klerk replaced P.W. Botha as head of the ruling party in South Africa and as head of the government. The Botha government had waged a war on the home front and one abroad as well. It invaded neighboring countries, pillaging and terrorizing their civilian populations. On the home front, Africans had become more and more militant, and were in open rebellion. The government declared martial law and states of emergency, detained prisoners without trial and tortured them, censored the press, banned political meetings, committed political murders, and organized death squads. Domestic support for apartheid was dwindling, and the Reagan administration, despite its own feelings and policies, was forced by Congress to impose meaningful economic sanctions. One of the last straws occurred when the Dutch Reformed Church, a beacon of moral leadership for most Afrikaners, switched theological positions on apartheid. Whereas before the church argued that apartheid had been mandated by the Bible, after the switch the church declared apartheid to be immoral. It was in this context that apartheid legislation was repealed and Africans and other non-whites were allowed to vote.

De Klerk released top African leaders from prison, including Nelson Mandela, the head of the African National Congress. He then initiated negotiations with the former "saboteur," "terrorist," and prison inmate, to lay the groundwork for a democratic regime. Mandela had served some 28 years of a life sentence under the Suppression of Communism Act for involvement in sabotage. Just four years and two months after his release from jail, he became the president of South Africa. This turnabout was accomplished without the usually predicted racial war. True, an estimated 15,000 were killed in the violence that pitted supporters of the African National Congress against those of the Inkatha Freedom Party. This latter party was a surrogate of Pretoria, and it drew its support from the Zulu living in the "homeland" Kwa Zulwi. But apartheid was scrapped without the usually predicted white-on-black/black-on-white holocaust. This heartening conclusion drawn by the media and others did not take into account the massacres and terror that Pretoria inflicted on its neighbors as it implemented its total strategy on them. Nor did it expose the recklessness of the West in helping a desperate Pretoria succeed in developing weapons of mass destruction.

Impact of Pretoria's Total Strategy on Neighboring Countries

The commission reminded its readers that while its focus was understandably on what happened inside South Africa, this represented somewhat of an historical distortion because most of the violations had occurred outside, in neighboring countries. These countries, some of the poorest nations in the world, "bore the brunt of the South African conflict and suffered the greatest number of individual casualties and the greatest damage to their countries' economies and infrastructure." Again, the commission charged that it was the state that was primarily responsible. "The state in the form of the South African government, the civil service, and its security forces was, in the period 1960–1994, the primary perpetrator of gross violations of human rights in South Africa, and from 1974, in southern Africa." It re-asserted the gravity of what Pretoria did to its neighbors when in another context it charged that a majority of the victims of the South African government's attempt to stay in power were outside of that country. "Tens of thousands of people in the region died as a direct or indirect result of the South African government's aggressive intent toward its neighbors." One of its conclusions was that the South African government's military in Angola between 1977 and 1988 led to gross violations of human rights "on a vast scale." As though to confirm this, it quoted an estimate of UNICEF that at least 100,000 Angolans died between 1980 and 1985 mainly as a result of war-related famine. The cumulative effect of the devastation of the economy and the infrastructure in that period produced an even greater escalation of the death rate. Between 1981 and 1988, again according to UNICEF, 333,000 Angolan children died of unnatural causes.

A 1982 visit by Archbishop Hurley from the Southern African Catholic Bishops Conference resulted in a detailed study of torture based on interviews with 180 South West Africans (Namibians). The Archbishop was charged under the Police Act for making the study, and newspapers in South Africa and South West Africa were threatened with prosecution if they published its findings. The charges against the Archbishop were dropped because of international protests. The Bishops Conference reported in 1982:

> The Security Forces will stop at nothing to force information out of people. They break into homes, beat up residents, shoot people, steal cattle and often pillage stores and tea rooms. When the tracks of SWAPO guerrillas are discovered by the Security Forces, the local people are in danger. Harsh measures are intensified. People are blindfolded, taken from their homes and left beaten up or even dead by the roadside. Women are often raped. There is no redress because reporting irregularities or atrocities to commanders is considered a dangerous or fruitless exercise.

When Pretoria failed to create a guerrilla group in Namibia that would do its bidding, it decided in 1978 to establish Koevoet (Special Operations K Unit of the South African Security police). Koevoet patterned itself after the Rhodesian Selous Scotts, the organization that taught most of its original organizers their counter-insurgency skills.

Louis le Grange, the Minister of Law and Order, described the organization as: "The crowbar which prises terrorists out of the bushveld like nails from rotten wood." John Deegan, one of its members, described its activities this way: "We were basically automatons. We would just kill. That's how we got our kicks. We were adrenaline junkies."

At peak strength, the unit numbered one thousand 250 white officers and the remainder local Africans from South West Africa. Broken down into mobile units of ten to fifteen locals and one white officer, it roamed the bush in Casspirs (specially designed armored personnel carriers) to gather intelligence, track guerrillas, and kill them. Koevoet borrowed the practice of "turning" from the Rhodesian Selous Scotts. Captured guerrillas (members of SWAPO) were offered the choice of joining with them or summary execution.

Captured SWAPO guerrillas were offered the choice of joining with Koevet or summary execution. Those who joined often committed atrocities that were then blamed on SWAPO.

The commission revealed that there existed extensive documentation that confirmed the activities of Koevoet. These activities included the destruction of property, sexual assault, solitary confinement, hooding, electric shock, submersion in water, mock burials, roasting over fire, and sleep, food, and water deprivation. Rape was common, and women and girls of all ages were its victims. The records indicated that the unit's personnel raped an eighty year-old woman and a four-year-old girl. The authorities devised a unique method of rewarding the members of the unit, and the method bore bitter fruit. They were rewarded on a sliding scale for discovering caches of arms, capturing guerrillas, or killing them with the largest reward going for killing. In the mid-eighties Koevoet killed from 300 to 500 per year. "Corpses were used for purposes of spreading terror and intimidating villagers." Rough body counts were issued by military headquarters, but there never was independent confirmation to determine how accurate the figures were or whether the corpses were those of SWAPO members or civilians. A document obtained by the commission suggested that the bounty for killing achieved its apparent purpose. In the engagements listed, 3,323 "insurgents" were killed, but only 104 were taken prisoner the ratio of those taken prisoner to those killed being about one to thirty-two.

Two main sources are used here in an attempt to assess the general impact of Pretoria's total strategy upon neighboring countries. Both were commissioned by United Nations agencies. The first is named *South African Destabilization: The Economic Cost of the Frontline Resistance to Apartheid.* Initiated by an economic task force appointed by the Secretary General, its purpose was to determine the impact of South Africa's total strategy on the prospects for development of the region. The second source is entitled *Children on the Frontline: the Impact of Apartheid, Destabilization and Warfare on the Children of Southern Africa.* It was commissioned by the United Nations Children's Fund (UNICEF). Its publication resulted from a decision made by UNICEF's executive board in 1986 to assess the impact of military and political activities in the region upon women and children. It has four authors. They are Reg Green, a fellow at the Institute of Development Studies of the University of Sussex; a UNICEF staff member; a UNICEF project officer; and the UNICEF representative for Mozambique and Swaziland. The preface to the report enlarged upon the reason for the initiation and publishing of the report. It alleged that apartheid itself and South Africa's incursions into surrounding countries have been universally condemned. But it went on to say:

> *But the extent to which South Africa`s policies of apartheid, economic disruption and de-stabilization have seriously affected the lives, health, and welfare of children in other countries of southern Africa has been hardly reported upon, and almost certainly too little appreciated. To help remedy this situation, UNICEF has commissioned this paper.*

The above quote singles out children as the victims of these massacres since UNICEF's mandate is with these innocents. Obviously, the massacres affected adults as well, and their fate was not widely advertised either. The ignoring and minimizing of the massacres and terror committed by Pretoria against neighboring African populations is an extremely significant point. Despite my longstanding interest in Africa, I was unaware of its extent. But these phenomena of minimizing and being ignorant of abuse have come up again and again in connection with other massacres and terror described in this volume. The report returned to this subject a few pages later, but from a new angle. Its reference shifted from the exclusive concern with the welfare of children, the chief human victims of the total strategy, to reflect on the general situation in Angola and Mozambique, the chief territorial victims of the strategy. The report declared:

> *Since independence Angola and Mozambique have been beset by internal fighting and external attacks from South Africa. Hardly a week has been passed in peace.*

The widespread and continuing conflict in these two countries has been virtually ignored as most of the world has concentrated its attention on events within South Africa and Namibia. It is necessary to outline here its instruments, its economic and social costs to the region and, above all, the human costs in the lives of the region's children.

Tom Brennan, a consultant to the U.S. Committee for Refugees, complained of the lack of coverage of the violence in the American media. He registered this complaint in a publication written in 1986, affirming that the crisis had been ongoing for eleven years and had steadily grown more violent. He asserted that human suffering and human displacements were truly massive in scale in the entire southern third of the African continent and that there existed a potential for catastrophe. He continued:

> *Until very recently, however, little has appeared in the American media regarding the domestic situations in Mozambique or of the other nations in southern Africa, or regarding their relationships*

> *with each other and with the South African government. Even less has appeared on the impact that the existing and potential armed conflicts in the region stemming from ideological as well as ethnic and racial differences are likely to have on the civilian populations of the area as the struggle to eliminate apartheid gains momentum.*

The UNICEF report indicated that Mozambique and Angola had the highest infant and children mortality rates in the world. This is ironic since these two countries gave priority in the post independence period to public health measures designed to improve the health of the population, especially infants and children. Their governments created networks of health centers and posts, thousands of health workers were trained, and mass vaccination programs were implemented. The groundwork for this ambitious public health program was laid in the immediate post colonial period. It took root and blossomed in 1979 and 1980, only to be poisoned after that. It is no accident that this setback occurred at the very time that Pretoria started seriously to apply its total strategy. The UNICEF report charged that the war and the destabilization campaign (total strategy) chose health and educational facilities as targets. It offered as examples the 718 health posts and centers destroyed in Mozambique since 1981 and the schools for 300,000 primary school children. The destruction of the health posts and centers deprived two million people of health care. In areas of southern Angola and in much of rural Mozambique vaccinations were no longer given because of lack of security. Many health workers were maimed, wounded, kidnapped, or killed. The result was that easily preventable diseases and curable illnesses "are now taking a hideous and rising toll on the vulnerable age group of infants and children under five."

In 1986 one hundred and forty thousand children under the age of five in these two countries lost their lives because of South Africa's "war and destabilization" campaign, what we refer to as its "total strategy." The number of deaths was expected to increase in 1987. But it was not merely the state of the children in these countries that "is grave and getting worse." All fifteen million children in the region whose countries border South Africa were considered to be in the same perilous situation. They were caught up in the throes of an external civil conflict and an economic de-stabilization campaign (total strategy). While the report set forth a number of conditions responsible for undermining the health of children in these two countries and the others in southern Africa, war and de-stabilization were identified as the major causes. And the report concluded that all countries in the region suffered economic losses either directly from South African aggression or from its de-stabilization campaign or indirectly by having to spend more on defense. Mozambique spent 42 percent of its budget on defense, one of the highest percentages in the world. This diminished the revenue left over for social services, for example, for children. The dislocation of the population also contributed to malnutrition and starvation. This was particularly evident in the case of Angola and Mozambique where 9 million people became refugees at one time or another. After 1981 sabotage units were particularly active. The principal targets were transportation and power infrastructure, but major production units came under the gun as well, especially those earning foreign exchange. The destruction of the transportation systems of neighboring countries made these countries more dependent on South Africa's system for the export of their commodities.

UNICEF: Pretoria's "total strategy" went beyond seeking merely to destroy military and economic targets to include those that sustain the very social fabric of nations.

The UNICEF report argued that what is called here Pretoria's "total strategy" went beyond seeking merely to destroy military and economic targets to include those that sustain the very social fabric of nations. The report gave as examples of the fruit of this objective the destruction of health and educational facilities, the dislocation of communities, the loss of food production, and the reduction of the health and water budgets because of expenditures for defense. In another section, some of this type of destruction appeared again, but as the result of mass terrorism.

One of the deadliest weapons of the war is the mass terrorism carried out by forces which have burned crops and farm houses, pillaged and destroyed schools, clinics, churches, mosques, stores and villages, poisoned wells by throwing bodies down them, and attacked the transport system which is a vital part of rural life. Members of religious orders, mainly Catholics, have been murdered and kidnapped. So too have foreign aid workers from both West and East. In Angola and Mozambique teachers, nurses, agricultural technicians, engineers, and geologists have also been killed and kidnapped, maimed and mutilated.

The carnage has been indiscriminate, with infants and children not exempted. The results are clear and tragic: death for many, and for the survivors fear and flight, destruction and displacement. About 8.5 million Angolans and Mozambicans—roughly half the rural population of the two countries have been displaced or are internal refugees in their own countries.

The costs of the war are cumulative, have been escalating since 1981, and are likely to continue to do so.

South African De-stabilization, a report initiated by a task force appointed by the Secretary General of the United Nations, provides an estimate of the total economic and demographic cost to the victims in neighboring countries of the implementation of South Africa's total strategy. Its purpose was to provide a synthesis of the impact of South Africa's total strategy upon neighboring countries. It concluded that the cost to these countries from 1980 to 1988 was over $60 billion at 1988 prices, reflecting the loss in gross domestic product attributed to the implementation of this strategy by South Africa and its accomplices. The report added that the losses promise to extend beyond 1988. The report indicated that Pretoria's strategy killed the inhabitants of neighboring countries in three ways. The first was directly by war or terrorism, the victims being military personnel or civilians. The second was through a combination of malnutrition, disease, and the destruction of rural health networks. Those killed by this method were usually infants and young children. The third consisted of famine-related deaths as a result of the lack of food caused by drought in combination with general insecurity. The report concluded that by the end of 1988, 1.5 million had been killed in these three ways. Over half of the fatalities were infants or children under five. The report estimated that almost half of the populations of Angola and Mozambique had been driven from their homes at least once, usually with the loss of possessions. It calculated that at the time of the writing, 1.5 million were refugees abroad and 6.1 million were displaced internally.

The estimate of the task force that 1.5 million were killed can be compared with a 1988 study commissioned by the U.S. State Department that concluded that the guerrilla group, the Mozambican National Resistance (RENAMO), alone killed 100,000 civilians in Mozambique. By the time of the study Washington was supportive of the Mozambican government, rather than opposing it as before. This guerrilla group was established by Southern Rhodesia's intelligence organization around 1975, and after that colony became African-governing in 1980, the South African Army adopted it. Until the middle of 1979, it had little more than nuisance value. But with South African supplies and support it witnessed a marked improvement in its destructive power. It became active in all parts of Mozambique and, besides its propensity to kill, it was responsible for much of the damage to the country's transportation system. RENAMO carried on guerrilla operations differently from the way the Front for the Liberation of Mozambique (FRELIMO) did when it was leading the fight against Portuguese rule. FRELIMO sought only to disrupt economic activity and used a selective targeting system for civilians. In contrast, RENAMO "has often completely destroyed economic infrastructure and has been generally indiscriminate in its attacks on the civilian population."

WASHINGTON, SOUTH AFRICA AND WEAPONS OF MASS DESTRUCTION

Chemical and Bacteriological Weapons

The apartheid governments developed a chemical and bacteriological warfare (CBW) capability; the security forces used these toxins against anti-apartheid activists.

The commission discovered that the apartheid governments developed a chemical and bacteriological warfare (CBW) capability. The TRCR based its investigation of the CBW program on more than 150 documents, affidavits, amnesty applications, and interviews. Given the code name Project Coast, this program was under the general management of the chief of staff of the defense force, the chief of staff of intelligence, the surgeon general of the army, and Dr. Wouter Basson, the project director. Its goals included the manufacture of cholera, botulism, anthrax, chemical poisoning, drugs of abuse allegedly for crowd control, lethal microorganisms for use against individuals, and "applicators" (murder weapons) developed for their administration. As examples, anthrax was "applied" in cigarettes, botulism in milk, and paraoxon in whiskey. A company was enlisted secretly to act as a front for the project. The commission concluded that toxins had been used by the security forces against anti-apartheid activists. Although the production of a thousand kilograms of methaqualone (mandrax) was started, its production was stopped in 1988, because its ability to incapacitate was found to be too slow to act as an efficient agent for crowd control. Work on its analogues continued. A British scientist alleged that South African troops used a chemical agent against guerrillas from Mozambique in a military encounter along the South African-Mozambican border in January, 1992. Other investigators, including the United Nations, could not verify the charge. The commission concluded that the matter remained unresolved.

The commission concluded that "without some level of foreign assistance, the (CBW) programme would not have been possible." The assistance was forthcoming from Belgium, Israel, the United Kingdom, and the United States. In the early eighties, Dr. Basson attended a conference on the subject held in San Antonio. "Other documents reveal links between the surgeon general (of the South African army) and Americans who were part of the United States CBW programme, and demonstrate their willingness to assist South Africans." Dr. Basson visited the United States in 1981, and later Dr. Knobel, the surgeon general, had contact with scientists who were part of the American CBW program. As 1993 drew to a close and the ANC seemed closer to taking over the government, both the Unites States and the British governments expressed concern lest a government under the control of the African National Congress take over the program. At a hearing of the commission both Dr. Basson and Dr. Knobel testified that these governments told them that they did not want this to happen.

Nuclear Weapons

Much earlier Washington helped Pretoria develop a nuclear capability. In 1957 Washington signed a 50-year agreement for nuclear cooperation with Pretoria, and the latter has received "extensive assistance in the nuclear field" from the United States. In 1961 South Africa purchased a Safari 1 research reactor from the United States. There has been some variation between administrations in the intensity of the collaboration. The Carter administration sought to impose more restrictive parameters on the sale of nuclear technology than the Reaganites. They approved the sale of vital equipment that could be used, for example, to simulate nuclear explosions and to test warheads and re-entry equipment. A study by the General Accounting Office found that in 1981 South Africa was the second leading country purchasing "dual-purpose, nuclear related" equipment from the United States. In 1984 a substantial number of the licenses issued by the Commerce Department for export to South Africa were for material that could be used in producing or testing nuclear weapons despite the fact that Pretoria had refused to sign the Nuclear Non-proliferation Treaty. Britain, West Germany, France, and more recently Israel were heavily involved in assisting as well. When challenged, the political elites of each country insisted that their collaboration was for peaceful purposes only. The General Assembly of the United Nations on numerous occasions called for a stop to such collaboration, but it continued. Efforts to exclude South Africa from the International Atomic Energy Agency failed, because of the opposition to exclusion by the Western nations. There was evidence that Pretoria conducted nuclear tests in 1979, 1981, and 1987. Despite strong evidence to the contrary, Washington claimed that there was no "corroborating evidence" for the first test or that the evidence was "inconclusive". In like manner, it shrugged off the other reported tests as well.

The nuclear collaboration of the Western powers in the last days of apartheid was "a dangerous and puzzling policy given the instability and desperation of the apartheid regime."

Western collaboration with South Africa continued, and "it paid off." In August 1988 Foreign Minister Pik Botha announced that South Africa had a nuclear capability, and in March 1993 President de Klerk acknowledged that the apartheid state had produced six nuclear bombs in 1989. He asserted that the bombs had been dismantled by the time of his announcement and that the pilot enrichment plant necessary for their production had been decommissioned. The white government seemed determined not to see this nuclear prize fall into the hands of a black government. And so with the aid and silence of Washington and its Western allies, white Pretoria went nuclear, but only temporarily. The silence was deafening, in view of Washington's continuous warnings and condemnations of the efforts of states such as Iraq and Iran to go nuclear. Minty finds the nuclear collaboration of the Western powers in the last days of apartheid to be "a dangerous and puzzling policy given the instability and desperation of the apartheid regime." They certainly knew of the nuclear capability of Pretoria, and of the testing as well. In particular, he indicts the Reagan administration, because it increased nuclear collaboration during the last days of apartheid, the most sensitive period. As they must have been aware, some desperate racist could have unleashed a nuclear holocaust to accompany the non-nuclear one that had already been unleashed by the apartheid state in its neighboring countries. Fortunately, by the time the white elites in South Africa had developed an atomic bomb they decided not to use it. They should be congratulated for this. Unfortunately, by then the holocaust unleashed by their total strategy had already cost the lives of a reported 1.5 million inhabitants of neighboring countries.

5

Settler Terrorism and its Global Impact

Introduction

It is tempting to reduce these complexities to terms that are not specific to history and globally founded relationships. It is appealing to cast issues in the language of anti-Semitism, culture-clash, religious intolerance, superpower rivalry, or a Semitic blood feud. It is seductive to speak in terms of moderates and extremists on both sides, and to identify personalities, parties, and factions who either advance or retard the quest for peace. It is even attractive to throw up one's hands and argue that the grievances are so deep that no *rapprochement* is possible (a position that implicitly leaves the field to military and other forms of deadly force). But to yield to such temptations is to obscure the more transcendent forces of order and change.

In the pages to come, the question of terrorism and the state will be placed in the context of the Israeli-Palestinian conflict. Once again, there are larger relationships here, historically grounded relationships that embody the dialectic of transnational and internal colonialism. These dynamics will be specified, not only with respect to the major parties, but as they reflect factional interests within Israeli economy and polity. That the power of the Israeli state has been used to control the Palestinian population is self-evident. However, not all colonizers are created equal. All Jews in the state of Israel, as well as Jewish settlers in the occupied territories, may enjoy certain caste-like advantages that come from living in a Jewish nation. But the claim to political rights should not be confused with claims to wealth and privilege for all.

It was the descendants of the Ashkenazim Jews, who settled in middle and northern Europe after the Jewish Diaspora, who waged a violent struggle to form and defend/ expand the new state of Israel. However, it is the descendants of the Sephardim, who lived originally in Spain and Portugal before the Inquisition, and many of whom entered Israel from Morocco, that now represent a demographic majority in the Jewish state. Although both groups have been served by the state, it is the poorer, more recently arrived Sephardim who now seek to use its power to redress their categorical position as economic marginals. Thus to the internal colonial dyad of Jew and Palestinian, must be added the class divisions within the chosen; divisions that have both preserved yet altered the nature of colonial settlement.

Maxime Rodinson's analysis of the founding of Israel as a variation of European colonialism is useful, as it specifies the institutional ties between Israel and the West. However, to his portrayal of transnational settlement must be added the compounding dilemma of new waves of Jewish settlers seeking land and sustenance. Thus the dynamics implicit in the term "settler" must be explored on two levels. Consistent with Rodinson's thesis, the founding of a Western state in the Middle East embodied European colonial processes. This is not to equate the early adherents of political Zionism with the organized programs of empire building of Britain and other imperial powers. The oppression suffered by Jews in Eastern Europe and Tsarist Russia, and the systematic genocide at the hands of the Nazis, were terrifying and real. Such conditions represented fertile ground for an ideology of deliverance; one that merged the messianic promise of religion with a secular political vision. However, the historical point should not be obscured. The ideology and objectives of the Zionist movement merged quite easily with larger imperial forces, with routine disregard for the pattern of successive victimization directed at Palestinian Arabs.

At the second level, the settling of Israel is not confined to earlier transnational history. The support of settlers and settlements in economic, ideological and military forms has become fully institutionalized at the level of the Israeli state. That such patterns can only evoke resistance at the hands of the dispossessed should be clear to all, unless the structures and processes of internal settlement are obscured by ideological forces. And it is to these forces that we now turn.

In an edited book entitled *Terrorism: How the West Can Win,* Benjamin Netanyahu, then Israeli Ambassador to the United Nations concluded: "The terrorist challenge must be answered. The choice is between a free society based on law and compassion and a rampant barbarism in the service of brute force and tyranny. Confusion and vacillation facilitated the rise of terrorism. Clarity and courage will ensure its defeat". Reasonable people would agree that there is indeed confusion on the question of terrorism. However, it is appropriate to inquire into the nature and source of such confusion.

The contributors to Netanyahu's book stand as a "who's who" of political leaders and journalists for the 1980s. They included leading members of the Reagan administration: U.S. Secretary of State George Shultz, U.S. Ambassador to the U.N. Jeanne Kirkpatrick, U.S. Attorney General Edwin Mccsc, and F.B.I. Director William H. Webster. There are articles by U.S. Senators Cranston, Laxalt, and Moynahan, journalists George Will, Paul Johnson, and Claire Sterling, Israeli ministers Moshe Arens and Yitzhak Rabin, and Israeli Chief Justice Meir Shamgar, among others. The contributors were participants in a second international conference on terrorism, organized by the Jonathan Institute, named for Jonathan Netanyahu, brother of Benjamin, who was killed in the raid on Entebbe. The Second Jonathan Conference and Netanyahu's book drawn from presentations by the participants can be said to represent an exemplar of longstanding and official U.S./ Israeli views on the question of terrorism. Accordingly, it deserves careful study by those interested in the ideological problematique of terrorism.

Those whose pronouncements on terrorism were delivered in the Second Jonathan Conference offered concrete identities to Ambassador Natanyahu's "forces of barbarism." As might be expected by now, those movements, states and ideologies that have historically opposed Western world interests were labeled as "terrorist." For example, Israeli ambassador Netanyahu refers to the P.L.O. as the most perfect form of a modern terrorist movement. Paul Johnson alleged that: "Modern terrorism dates from the middle 1960's when the P.L.O. adopted terror and mass murder as its primary policy". To be sure, the *enemies to democracy thesis* did not stop with the P.L.O.

George Shultz discerned a "league of terror" including Libya, Syria, North Korea, and Iran, while arguing that "The Soviets use terrorist groups for their own purposes, and their goal is always the same: to weaken liberal democracy and undermine world stability". In a similar vein, another contributor argued that the use of terror is legitimated both by Marxism and the Soviet constitution. According to Wolfgang Fikentscher, Article 28 of the U.S.S.R. constitution, which calls for the "assistance of the peoples in their fight for national liberation and social progress," is actually a mandate for terrorism. Hence, in the Western view, Marxism and terrorism are wedded into a monolithic evil.

There is more than a permutation of anticommunism here. Three participants in the Second Jonathan Conference found that the political nature of the Muslim faith offered a justification for "Islamic Terrorism". Another argued that terrorism drew "on the immense financial resources of the Arab oil states"; another added Iraq and South Yemen to Schultz's "league of terror"; and still others identified Cuba and Nicaragua. In sum then, the socialist world, the Islamic world, and the Arab world are portrayed, along with national liberation movements that seek independence from the West, as terrorist. There is no troubling ambiguity here, no weighing of complexities, no recognition of the relations of domination and subjugation. The ideological world of terrorism is clearly cast, its characters act out a morality play of good and evil, righteousness and corruption, guardians and false pretenders.

Historically, those responsible for constructing and disseminating the dominant view give little thought to the proxy forms of terror that implicate Western states. Schultz declared: "The resistance fighters in Afghanistan do not destroy villages or kill the helpless. The Contras in Nicaragua do not blow up school buses or hold mass executions of civilians." At a higher level, Israeli ambassador Netanyahu employed the example of a R.A.F. raid on Gestapo headquarters in Copenhagen in 1944, where bombs hit a children's hospital. But this deed by a Western state, he declared, was only an accident of war. By inference, when it is the state that strikes down the innocent, then the raiders are not responsible because they did not willfully and in premeditated fashion take the lives of specific victims. It is once again, the impersonal deadly force of the state that is held up to a different standard.

The ideological construction of terrorism also impinges on interpretations of international law. Yehuda Blum, former Israeli ambassador to the United Nations, declared:

> *Armed reprisals have been repeatedly condemned by states and international organizations as a violation of international law. Let us examine, therefore, the alternative recourse, namely, self-defense. Admittedly, shifting emphasis from reprisals to self-defense may be considered by some as an exercise in semantics, which it probably is: yet given the indisputable potency of language symbols, there is no reason to disregard this aspect of international law.*

Having declared an intent to redefine reprisal as defense, Blum proceeds to discuss the conditions under which a state may exercise armed attack and label it as self-defense. Under Article 51 of the U.N. charter, the right of self-defense may be exercised "if an armed attack occurs". Blum cites the *Nadelstichtaktik* ("tactics of the needle prick") argument, which holds that if a pattern of needle pricks occurs, then the injured state has the right to take military action, in his words as a "legitimate response in anticipation of the next terrorist attack. There are two implications in this argument. The first is that the state or its agents not only have the right to self-defense (clearly recognized by the charter), but that the state can defend itself on anticipatory grounds. Second, Blum seeks to defuse the question of disproportionate use of deadly force on the part of a state by noting a pattern of provocation.

Moving on to the question of civilian casualties, Blum argues that a sanctuary state *whether acting willingly or unwillingly* is responsible for harboring "terrorists". In effect then, civilian casualties in such a sanctuary state are the responsibility of that state, an interpretation that transfers blame from the state whose forces actually inflict the casualties. And finally, Blum argues that "self-defense" (as he has now defined it) takes precedence over the right of "self-determination" calling "self-determination" in effect a legitimating guise of terrorists. This official view of state power is quite revealing. As "self-defense" is a right of states, and "self-determination" refers only to those movements that do not hold the power of the state, the legitimacy of the state is assumed to be pre-eminent. This ideology of statism also brands national liberation movements (whose Utopian ideology routinely includes the language of self-determination) as "terrorist."

Of course, such expressions of *raison d'état* are not confined to Israel. The Reagan State Department also warned of "preemptive strikes" as a legitimate response in anticipation of terrorist acts, while asserting the unavoidability of civilian casualties. After the bombing of Tripoli and Benghazi, the official U.S. view included the "self-defense" and "proportionality" arguments that the Israelis developed in defense of the "iron fist". On this point, Prime Minister Thatcher of Great Britain had a precondition for her political and military support for the raid on Libya: justification under the self-defense provision of Article 51. That Blum's position "fits" the nature of relations between the United States and its antagonist in North Africa is not accidental. Nor is this a case of the Israeli tail wagging the American dog. There is an ideological convergence here born of Western state policy, strategic considerations of Mediterranean hegemony, the future control of Middle Eastern petroleum, and the potential of authentic liberation movements to alter global relations. It is within this more general milieu that the real nature of the conflict between the state of Israel and its primary antagonist must be assessed.

The Question of Terrorism

With the Palestinian cause virtually unknown in the West, the Popular Front for the Liberation of Palestine (a P.L.O. affiliate) devised and implemented a strategy for high visibility hijackings of international flights between 1968 and 1970. In September of 1970, three airliners were hijacked and their 276 passengers held at an abandoned airfield in Jordan. (One jumbo jet was too large to land and was taken to Cairo.) Ultimately the hostages were bussed to Amman, but the aircraft (valued at 30 million dollars) were blown up. After a subsequent conflict with the Jordanian army, the hostages were released. Other episodes of political violence did not end as well. Selecting a global showcase, the renegade Black September group took 11 Israelis hostage at the 1972 Olympic games in Munich. An attempt was made to trade these hostages for 200 Arab prisoners held in Israeli jails. However, a botched assault at the Furstenfeldbruck airport resulted in the deaths of all eleven Israeli hostages and five members of the Black September group. Other examples might be cited, including perhaps the most notorious of recent episodes: the aforementioned attacks on El Al in the Rome and Vienna airports in December of 1985 by the Abu-Nidal faction.

In reviewing these and other episodes of conventionally defined terrorism, certain distinctions are often lost. To begin, the P.L.O. has broadly based support that one would not expect to be accorded to a "terrorist organization." That support is not confined to the Palestinians or the larger Arab world. The P.L.O. has been recognized by more than 130 countries around the world, and has observer status at the United Nations where it is also recognized as the sole legitimate representative of the Palestinian people. The isolation of Israel inside the U.N. and its continued reliance on the U.S. veto in the Security Council is well known. In part, the support enjoyed by the P.L.O. inside the United Nations reflects the changing composition of the member states of that organization. The U.N. began as something of a Western-dominated international club in the post-World War II era. Its General Assembly, however, has provided a forum for many nations that have emerged from a colonial past. It is within this context that the support of the P.L.O., and the opposition to Israel, must be judged.

All of this is not to imply that the U.N., the Arab world and the Palestinian people have sanctioned political violence of the Abu-Nidal type described above. Neither is it possible to somehow attribute these and similar acts to some omnipresent P.L.O. The P.L.O. is not a monolith that embodies the organization and efficiency of the modern state. It consists of a coalition of nine fronts that are united strongly on the question of the establishment of a Palestinian state, and differ widely in ideology and tactics. The largest and better-known Al Fatah organization of Yasir Arafat features a nationalist ideology, in which political independence is central. The P.L.A. (Palestine Liberation Army) is a standing army, consisting of perhaps 15,000 fighters, under the command of Al Fatah. A clear ideological contrast is found in the Popular Front for the Liberation of Palestine (P.F.L.P.) of George Habash. The P.F.L.P. rejects the existence of a state of Israel as historically bound to Western interests, and destined to reproduce the class formations of a capitalist global order. In contrast to the political solution of independence common to many liberation movements historically, the ideology of the P.F.L.P. is informed by an analysis of political economy and features a call for the social transformation of Palestine.

"Splinter" groups that have evolved from the P.F.L.P. include the Popular Front for the Liberation of Palestine-General Command (P.F.L.P.-G.C.), whose most widely recognized leader has been Ahmed Jibril; and the Popular Democratic Front for the Liberation of Palestine (P.D.F.L.P.) formed by Nayaf Hawatmeh. The Palestine Liberation Front (P.L.F.) emerged from the P.F.L.P.-G.C., to seek an alliance with Iraq. These offshoots have retained the P.F.L.P.'s insistence that armed struggle cannot be confined to Israeli soil. Ideologically, it may be true that they are less sanquine about the prospects of a class-based revolution. Another P.L.O. affiliate is the Syrian-aligned Al Saiqa, second in size to the Fatah group, which emerged in the aftermath of the 1967 war. The Palestine National Front (P.N.F.), formed after the 1973 war to carry out operations inside the occupied territories (primarily the West Bank), and the Iraqi-aligned Arab Liberation Front (A.L.F.) conclude the list.

Certain of the more spectacular acts of conventionally defined terror attributed to the P.L.O. have been actually carried out by renegade groups. For example, it was Black September (an organization named for the month during which the Jordanian army drove the Palestinian people from Jordan in 1970) that carried out the Munich operation. This faction split off from the P.F.L.P. in 1970. Other P.L.O. fringe groups have broken with Al Fatah. In 1985, it was the faction lead by Abul Abbas that carried out the sea jacking of the *Achille Lauro*. However, in the murky world of conventional terrorism, where the state is a key player through its intelligence and special forces units, responsibility for random acts of repugnant violence is not easily assigned.

It is more than ironic that Yasir Arafat has come to personify terrorism in the U.S. media. It was at his initiative that the P.L.O. National Council decided in 1974 to seek a political solution to the question of a Palestinian homeland through negotiation and diplomacy, while not abandoning the right to armed struggle. Specifically, this strategy assumed that the new state would be formed from the West Bank and Gaza territories occupied (and increasingly settled) since 1967 by the Israelis. This decision led to the international recognition of the P.L.O., while the P.F.L.P., the P.L.F., and the A.L.F. withdrew from the P.L.O. executive committee in protest. Further, in the Cairo Declaration of 1985 Arafat renounced "armed struggle" outside Israel and the occupied territories. Given such events, the political consequences of applying the terrorist label to the major leader and front within the P.L.O. are clear. Such labels represent a rejection, not merely of vendetta violence; nor of the employment of armed struggle on the part of a resistance movement; but of diplomacy and negotiation. Further, given the international recognition of the P.L.O., the refusal to bargain with this organization is tantamount to a refusal to negotiate in any substantive fashion on the question of a Palestinian homeland. The ultimate result is to keep the conflict on a military plane.

It is not possible to understand the emergence of the Palestinian nationalist movement in isolation. From the Utopian view, the drama of non-state terror is a theatrical production staged for the benefit of an international audience of the deaf. Almost a generation passed from the establishment of the enlarged boundaries of the state of Israel in 1948 until the founding of the P.L.O. in 1964. During that period, and for four years or so later, the Palestinian struggle had been largely political. It had also been ignored. The formation of the P.L.O. confirmed that the Palestinians must have independent political institutions that would represent them as a people. Although the question of a Palestinian entity *al-kiyan al-filastini* was formerly raised by the United Arab Republic in the context of Nasser's dream of Pan-Arabism, it was clear that the Arab states could not take the lead in a Palestinian struggle for self-determination. It was also clear that this movement and its political wing would not be content with refugee doles and U.N. resolutions.

Political violence, even employed circumspectly when all other methods fail, can be a two-edged sword. In the words of Eqbal Ahmad, "today, no one denies that there is a question of Palestine." However, the resort to random violence, no matter how provoked, may retard the development and use of creative tactics of non-violence, while discrediting commando attacks directed at military targets. At a quite different level, the misdirected rage of vendetta terrorism signifies the absence of a mature revolutionary ideology. To point out that the rage is a consequence of victimization; that oppression is an incubator of vengeance would be termed mitigating factors by those trained in law. However, vendetta terror against targets of convenience can only bring scorn to a movement and raise questions about the ability of a people to form a new society.

Still, it can be argued that between 1968 and 1972 the P.L.O. made the deaf to hear again. P.L.O. hijackings ended when the organization gained a base in Lebanon and world recognition. But the *symbolism* of Palestinian skyjackings, seajackings, and international operations against Israeli, U.S., or other Western targets, no matter how repugnant and whether or not they involve disciplined forces or renegades, cannot be ignored. On the one hand, these are tactics without boundaries employed by a people without land. On the other, the targets signify the connection of the Israeli-Palestinian conflict to wider global patterns. And it is to these global patterns that we now turn.

The Jewish State

Although Jewish nationalism has older roots, its emergence in more formalized ideological and political forms took shape in the late nineteenth century. The 1881 wave of eastern European anti-Semitism directed toward Jews was a precipitating factor. However, it is also true that the formation of this ideology borrowed liberally from the broader context of an age of Imperialism. Leo Pinsker (1831–91) in *Auto-Emancipation* questioned the practicality of restoring ancient Judea, calling instead for establishing Jewish self-rule wherever a suitable territory could be found. North America, Palestine, or Syria were offered as possible sites for what Pinsker called a "colonial community."

Theodor Herzl, in the Zionist manifesto *The Jewish State*, noted that Jewish colonization had some roots by late century in Palestine and Argentina. He also held that the latter country was rich in resources, but that Palestine by its very name would offer a unifying symbol to would be settlers. Thus the Zionist Organization, founded at the Congress of Basel, settled on Palestine as the place for a Jewish "homeland." The selection of the term "homeland" is a revealing exercise in political symbolism. Although state sovereignty was the ultimate objective, it could threaten the support of powerful nations with other clients. And too, the vision of a homeland could be expected to neutralize opposition by the religious interested only in a spiritual center, and assimilationists who held fast to their existing national identities.

For his part, Herzl depended less on the will of God and more on temporal power to secure eventual sovereign rule. That early Zionists sought to negotiate the fate of Palestinian Arabs first with Turkey, and later with Britain and other Western powers was simply an extension of the objective conditions of imperialism. Moreover, Herzl understood that Jewish colonization was bound to take a different form that other patterns of European expansion. Unlike settlers attached to a specific nation-state, Jewish settlers were imagined to someday come from all over the continent. The colony they would establish must then be fashioned from other than national-imperial cloth. Instead, a Zionist state would serve more global and transnational interests. More specifically, Herzl argued that such a state would "constitute a bulwark against Asia, " and "the advance post of civilization against barbarism," with its existence guaranteed by "all of Europe."

It is clear that the appeal of Palestine would be founded for some in messianic visions of return granted by God to the chosen. But the broader and sustaining ideology of imperialism conferred upon European powers and their populations a conviction of selection not limited to orthodox Judaism. Thus it is common to find in the specific ambiguities of faith, *rapprochement* with specific ideologies of domination and resistance. Religion, in dialectic relation with the more mundane processes of secular expediency, may be refined to offer sacred legitimations for the material forces of this world. Clearly, the form of the message varies with the social position of its makers and believers. Zionism in its European context offered pride and deliverance to an often victimized population. Transferred and reconstructed to fit the objective conditions of a new settler state, it was to offer legitimation for the reproduction of the colonial relations that build and maintain permanent marginalization for an indigenous population.

It was 20 years after the establishment of the Zionist Organization in Basel, in the context of world war, that Lord

Arthur Balfour offered a declaration pledging support for a "Jewish national home" in Palestine. In 1919, the same Balfour noted in a memorandum that the four great powers were "committed to Zionism and Zionism, be it right or wrong, good or bad, is rooted in age-long tradition, in present needs, in future hopes, of far profounder import than the desires and prejudices of the 700,000 Arabs who now inhabit that ancient land".

Rodinson argues that the League of Nations granted the postwar mandate to Britain in part because of an agreement negotiated at the Peace Conference in Paris between the Zionist leader Chaim Weizman and Emir Faisal, the son of Sharif Hussein (and thus a representative of the Hashemite dynasty). Despite the value of Rodinson's detailed account, there were broader forces at work in these negotiations. Britain at the time was not only an imperial nation state, but a *systemic exemplar* of the global market order. Its national interests cannot be isolated from its core role in the maintenance of that system. It was within the context of this higher role that the British assumed dual responsibility, first for the oversight of Jewish immigration into Palestine, but also for supporting a particular form of Arab nationalism.

What the British recognized was the political independence of monarchal governments and feudal systems; systems that represented continuing dependency on the economic side and potential allies against the forces being unleashed in the Russian Revolution. Moreover, Arab nationalism was historically destined to proceed in accordance with the *territorial* restrictions of colonial lines drawn on maps. Thus the dream of ONE Arab nation would be thwarted in the future by the enduring legacy of colonialism: the geographical, political, and administrative factionalism of the Western model of the nation-state.

At the same time, Jews bringing capital, technical skills, and a European conception of the world could be expected to serve as a colonial outpost, or in Herzl's words as a buffer. But the real buffer, paradoxically, consisted of both Jewish settlers and Arab monarchs. The buffer was to be less a shield against specific nations, and more a force of negation directed against the uncertain future of the Arab masses in particular and the vital Middle Eastern region in general. Thus the Peace Conference of 1919 represented a convergence of systemic interests mediated through Western core states, indigenous feudal orders, and an outpost colony. This alliance of historical roles, sometimes with a changing cast of national players, has proven remarkably durable over time.

By the beginning of the mandate, and after almost three decades of independent Zionist effort, the Jewish population of Palestine in 1922 stood at only 11.1 percent of the total. Under the mandate, the percentage grew to 17.7 percent in 1931 and 28 percent in 1936. As the terrifying specter of the Third Reich grew in Germany, additional immigration pressure brought the Jewish population by 1943 to some 539,000 of 1,676,571, some 31.5 percent of the total. Despite the "push" factors behind the immigration, this dramatic reconstitution of the population could only have occurred under the mandate, with British support expressed not only through the acceptance of settlers, but through its *de facto* intimidation of Palestinians and other Arabs preoccupied with their own national independence. However, as the immigration of Jews accelerated between wars so did the opposition from Palestinian Arabs.

With the failure of the Munich agreement becoming ever clearer, it was evident that Britain would not have the military force to continue to police Palestine. In May of 1939, the British Government issued a White Paper seeking to limit its problems by restricting Jewish immigration and declaring its belated opposition to the goal of a Jewish state. However, this course came too late. Under the mandate, the Zionists had gained sufficient strength and numbers inside Palestine to mount their own campaign. Nazi terror and postwar displacement meant more people would seek to flee from Europe, while Zionists inside Israel and the

United States worked hard to direct the flow of that immigration toward Palestine.

Thus, by the beginning of the postwar period in Palestine, the historical stage was set for the emergence of two inter-related processes. The first was the super-session of British-style colonialism through a pattern of revolt by strongly established Zionist settlers eager to set their own agenda. The second was the fashioning of a protectorate alliance with the new core state in a postwar transnational capitalist system. Each of these processes has implications for the question of terrorism and the state. But it is their inter-dependence that must be kept foremost in mind, even when *intra-system* revolt emerges.

Whatever the British may have come to hope for in the way of a bicultural, Western-oriented state in Palestine, the Zionist leadership viewed the mandate as a framework to guarantee the settlement that would lead to a Jewish state. Thus the execution by the British of their global role, until the eve of the Second World War, proved consistent with the specific objective of Jewish statehood. When the British sought to limit settler immigration, there were consequences. What was tacitly understood within the Zionist movement became real. David Ben-Gurion (president of the Executive Committee of the Jewish Agency and later first prime minister of Israel) recanted his earlier "objections" to acknowledge the goal of statehood. A far greater consequence came in the form of a revolt by Zionist settlers against the British. However, the British role was to be assumed by a new core.

The United States survived World War II with its industrial infrastructure intact, and (paradoxically) without the stress on its resources represented by national liberation movements in the colonial world. It also emerged as the key player in a design for the postwar international economy that began with a meeting of the allies in 1944 at Bretton Woods, New Hampshire. The United States (and its currency) came to play a central role in the modernization of market relations, which took the form of new institutions of global reach such as the International Monetary Fund, the World Bank, and the General Agreement on Tariffs and Trades. It also acted to restore the European economies through the Marshall Plan and nurtured during the occupation period the rebirth of Japanese production. But in this epoch of postwar modernization, complete with new and more sophisticated relations of power and forms of dependency, the defense of the West still meant the defense of resources and influence in regions of *le tiers monde.*

Although much has been made of the role of supporters of Jewish nationalism inside the United States, their program cannot be isolated from this larger historical role of the new core. Despite the considerable influence of American groups committed to "Israeli interests,"-the success of such lobbying is a super structural phenomenon. There is, as many Israeli supporters have argued, a commonality of interests that joins the two states. But the nature of that commonality is secondarily one of politics and culture. The underlying base on which the Israeli-U.S. connection was to be built is that of *world-system convergence,*

> *The nature of that convergence is one of guardian and outpost. The nature of the relationship between the United States as the successor core and Israel as an outpost in the periphery is evidenced in a number of particulars. Through FY87, total U.S. aid to Israel since statehood amounted to more than $38 billion. Much aid has been directed toward the Israeli military-industrial complex, the exports of which grew from a value of $10 million in 1972 and to $1.8 billion in 1985. The United States funded virtually all of the 1.5 billion dollar Lavi fighter, finally urging Israel to give up the project because of escalating costs. In a familiar replay, workers and managers at the Israel Aircraft Industries strongly reacted to the potential loss of thousands of jobs. The cultivation by the United States of the Israeli arms industry has had several manifestations in the international arena.*

Israeli arms deals in Latin America are a case in point. In Central America, Israel has supplied military hardware, technology, and other counter-insurgency aid to "anti-Communist" Central American regimes and movements. During its era of the Generals and the "disappeared," Argentina became one of Israel's major arms customers. Other arms clients and vendors for Israel have been Khomeini's Iran and the Union of South Africa. An arms for export economy is an expected consequence of the Israeli outpost role. That the overall economy will feature stagnation, inflation, uneven development, and dependency on external aid (both public and private) are costs paid by settlers, who in the history of colonialism have often found themselves to be expendable.

Sacred Terrorism

The diary of former Israeli Prime Minister Moshe Sharett describes the military force of that state as "Israel's Sacred Terrorism". The process by which the practices and ideology of sacred terrorism have been institutionalized in modern Israel begins with the revolt of Jewish colonists against the British. Although the guerilla tactics of resisters are routinely termed "terrorist" by representatives of a threatened system of rule, two Zionist groups were noteworthy for their attacks on civilian populations. One of these was the Irgun and the other was its off-shoot Lehi, commonly known as the Stern gang.

The Irgun Tsvai Leumi, one of whose leaders was Menachem Begin, blew up the King David Hotel in Jerusalem with a loss of over 90 lives. Lehi was willing to collaborate with the Nazis against the British, and in the winter of 1941 drafted a proposal calling for the establishment of a Jewish totalitarian state that would seek relations with the Reich. The chief of operations for Lehi, who was later an official in Israeli Intelligence (Mossad) was Yitzhak Shamir. Of course, both Begin and Shamir went on to become prime ministers of the state of Israel.

The United Nations General Assembly (in its early years a Western-dominated organization) voted to partition Palestine into an Arab and a Jewish state in November 29 of 1947. At the time, some 1.3 million Arabs owned 90 percent of the land, and 600,000 Jews owned 7 percent. After partition, 53 percent of the land was given to the Jewish state (with some 590,000 Jews and 497,000 Arab inhabitants), and the remainder to the Palestinian Arab state (Curtiss, 1987:3). Violence intensified, some of it designed as a symbolic eviction notice. On April 9 and 10 in 1948, Irgun-Lehi carried out a well-organized and systematic massacre in the village of Deir Yassin. The death count was 254 persons with some 40 percent of the casualties women and children. The Irgun-Lehi lost four members in the attack. The flight of the already terrified Arab population from land to become the state of Israel was accelerated by this deed. In the ideological tradition of "sacred terrorism" old and new, the Irgun command offered a message of congratulation. "As in Deir Yassin, so everywhere. Oh Lord, Oh Lord, you have chosen us for conquest". Such conceptions of sacred terror both reflect and interact with the objective conditions of domination, offering flexible legitimations that grow stronger in the face of resistance.

The weary British withdrew in May of 1948 as the state of Israel was declared independent on May 14. In the context of massive population transfer (already amounting to some 300,000 persons, which could only mean trouble for Arab states) and the presence of a European outpost at Palestinian expense, a poorly integrated Arab military force, outnumbered and divided, attacked. The Israelis easily defeated the volunteers from Egypt, Jordan, Syria, Lebanon, Iraq, and Saudi Arabia. In the 1948 war another 700,000 Palestinians took flight from terror, some helped along by Israeli programmatic expulsion. At the end of the war, half of the territory designated as a Palestinian state by the U.N. had become part of Israel. The West Bank of the Jordan River was annexed by Jordan, while Egypt and Israel took control of the Gaza Strip. Nineteen years later, Israel in another war of "national survival" took the West Bank, Gaza, and Sinai from Egypt, and the Golan Heights from Syria. (Egypt was to recover the Sinai "wilderness" as a consequence of the Camp David accords brokered by President Carter of the United States. The treaty agreed to by Anwar Sadat for Egypt and Menachim Begin for Israel split Egypt from the Arab League but led to increased aid from the United States, for this most populous of Arab states, as well as to development loans and a staggering 32.5-billion-dollar debt in 1985.

Israeli journalist Tom Segev, in a 1986 book based on Israeli declassified official documents and other archival material, argues that during the first year of Israel's existence, the leadership of the new state decided to expel Arab residents (as at Haifa) and to destroy villages (such as Ikrit and Bir'em). Those who had fled were denied return, as new Jewish refugees from both Europe and now the Arab world left the squalor of detention centers to seize Arab homes and property. Armed Israeli forces, described by Segev as lacking in military discipline, were also clearly responsible for rapes, murder, and massacres of unarmed Arab villagers.

Of course, to place the blame for violence on refugees and the ill-trained and undisciplined military in 1949 may offer back-handed support for a recurring theme emanating from Israeli higher circles. The official story on state violence has routinely denied any *systemic* and *programmatic* attempt to intimidate Palestinians, and to force their expulsion from their lands. Argued thusly, military violence directed toward a civilian population is depicted as an isolated and unofficial response on the part of beleagured forces who suffer periodic lapses in discipline under stress.

The ideological norm for military conduct is *tohor haneshek,* or "purity of arms." This is an extension of the legitimation constructed by Israeli leaders from Ben-Gurion to Peres that Israel's survival was dependent not merely on strength but on *righteousness.* The claim of moral authority for the appealingly named Israeli *Defense* Forces, of course offers legitimation for the state, whose leaders decide the conditions under which military force can be used. Further, if holy warriors are required to eschew violence directed toward civilians and the innocent, then new legitimations may be required to account for such un-righteous terror when it occurs. It is within this context that the responsibility for violence may be expected to pass from inherent structural forces to other factions that do not so centrally implicate the state.

A case study in terrorism and its ideological reformulation is evidenced in the assault by paratroopers of Ariel Sharon's Unit 101 on the Jordanian village of Qibya, mounted in October of 1953. The occasion for the attack was the murder of three Israeli settlers (a mother and two children), although there was no known relationship between the killers and Qibya. U.N. military observers described the scene.

Bullet-riddled bodies near the door-ways and multiple bullet hits on the doors of the demolished houses indicated that the inhabitants had been forced to remain inside until their homes were blown up over them. Witnesses were uniform in describing their experience as a night of horror, during which Israeli soldiers moved about in their village blowing up buildings, firing into doorways and windows with automatic weapons and throwing hand grenades.

The massacre at Qibya claimed 70 lives, including dozens of women and children. However, Prime Minister Ben-Gurion (remaining consistent with the righteousness theme) disavowed official military involvement. Instead, he blamed Israeli settlers consisting of refugees from Arab countries and Nazi concentration camps. The material facts of Qibya are clear, as evidenced in the subsequent condemnation of the raid by the U.N. Security Council. However, Qibya also starkly reveals something of two recurring ideological themes that legitimate Israeli policy on the use of deadly force. The first theme is that of *reprisal,* which can be considered the ideological genesis for what in the Likud era came to be known as the "iron fist." The second addresses the ideological transformation of terrorism, by which zealots and extremists (in this case, settlers on the border), motivated by vendatta, are portrayed as independent of the state.

With the coming to power of Likud in 1977, under the real and ideological leadership of Begin, Shamir, and Sharon, official Israeli pronouncements began to feature an escalation of the language of grandeur and force. The new symbols were those of nationalism, complete with eschatological pronouncements on Judea, Samaria, and the Greater Israel. Some saw in this rhetoric a substantive political realliance inside Israel, a realliance that marked a drastic departure from Israel's civilized and civilizing role in the Middle East. However, this *departure from righteousness* thesis, by which forces of moderation inside the Israeli state (notably the Labor Party) are seen as pitched in battle with terrorists who have simply moved up in life, is misleading. Stated simply, the shift from "righteousness" to "iron fist" represents no great ideological shift. Taken together, these are the components of *sacred terrorism* alluded to earlier.

Thus argued, it should come as no surprise to find the forces of righteousness clearly aware of the power of state terror. It was none other than David Ben-Gurion, often remembered as a proponent of Israeli purity of arms, who in a January 1, 1948, entry in his Independence War Diary wrote: "Blowing up a house is not enough. What is necessary is cruel and strong reactions. We need precision in time, place and casualties. If we know the family we must strike mercilessly, women and children included. Otherwise the reaction is inefficient. At the place of action there is no need to distinguish between guilty and innocent". As documented in the diaries of former Israeli Prime Minister Moshe Sharett, in the 1950s Ben-Gurion and Moshe Dayan (another moderate voice) were clear concerning a vision of the "Greater Israel." Such would involve the seizure of additional lands in Jerusalem, the West Bank, Lebanon, and Syria. The institutional point, of course has little to do with personalities.

The ideology of righteousness implicitly condemns the behavior of the "Israeli Caesar," Ariel Sharon. It was Sharon who led Unit 101 in the destruction of Qibya. It was Sharon who moved his "war on terror" to the Gaza in the early 1970s, where the houses of suspected enemies of the State were blown up, where bulldozers were driven through the camp to divide it into more easily controllable sectors, where "terrorists" were methodically killed. It was Sharon who, as agriculture minister from 1977 to 1981, presided over the settlement of the West Bank. It was Sharon who, as defense minister, commanded the 1982 invasion of Lebanon, ostensibly designed to wipe out P.L.O. terrorism. And it was Sharon who, as reported by the Associated Press on January 29, 1989, called for the death of Yasir Arafat.

In the course of this invasion, according to the Lebanese police, the Israeli Defense Forces (I.D.F.) killed over 19,000 people, including 6,775 in Beirut alone where some 84 percent of the casualties were civilian. However, the invasion of Lebanon was directed at something greater than the guerilla capabilities of the P.L.O. Between 1968 and 1982, some 300,000 Palestinians in Lebanon had developed powerful political and economic institutions and a resurging cultural identity (Rubenberg, 1983). Some Lebanese saw that presence as a threat, but others discerned a potential ally. It was against the larger threat of the P.L.O. mini state; its achievements and its potential for a growing Lebanese alliance that the I.D.F. struck.

It is of course within this wider theater of total war that the real terrorism lies, for Israel as for all states. But the most dramatized event of this invasion occurred in Sabra and Shatila, undefended Palestinian camps under the absolute control of the I.D.F. Here, in September of 1982, 700 to 800 persons were brutally killed by a force of 100 to 150 members of the Israeli allied Phalange and Haddad militia, given entrance into the camps by the Israeli forces who stood idly by. These Lebanese Christian units had a history of atrocities directed against Palestinians; a history well known to all parties in the region. When the predictable happened, it could not be kept secret except, somehow, from the Israeli military.

Despite the presence of Israeli tanks standing guard outside the camps when the militia entered; despite the presence of a main observation post providing a clear view of one killing ground with its mass grave; despite the hysteria of Palestinian women who escaped the camps and begged the soldiers to stop the killing; despite the knowledge of the international press (claimed by the I.D.F. to be the source of their knowledge on the massacre), the Israeli army claimed not to know. The U.N. General Assembly voted 147 to 2 to condemn the atrocity. Those opposed were Israel and the United States.

The fact that Sharon and his allies have continued to enjoy power confirms that what they symbolize is an enduring force. Moreover, the coexistence of the bold use of state violence, with its condemnation by more "rational" voices inside the government may have allowed Israel to have it both ways. On the one side is the terrible expediency of the "iron fist." On the other is the criticism of that use of force (which is no doubt comforting to believers in righteousness.) Whether such a symbiotic arrangement is consciously understood by actors is beside the point. The consequence of this political symmetry is to place the iron fist inside a velvet glove.

For those who respond to the near conspiratorial drama of special forces and "low intensity conflict" (L.I.C.) there is the organizational and tactical descendent of Unit 101 known as Sayaret Matkal. In the plentiful L.I.C. literature from U.S. military sources, the elite 200-member Sayaret Matkal is presented as a "counter-terrorist" organization.

They use the Uzzi, the Israeli invented machine pistol. They also use the Kalashnikov. They are trained on the

Galil, another Israeli-made automatic weapon. Pistol shooting ranks high in the curriculum and here the Israelis use an unusual weapon, the 22 Beretta pistol. They train with this pistol because some of them move on to become members of the hit teams which eliminate Israel's enemies abroad and the '007' squad who fly with El Al. The technique when used by the hitmen is for them to get as close as possible to their victim and then pump a full magazine into him at the closest possible range.

It was the Sayaret Matkal that struck deep into Egyptian territory twice in 1968; that in the same year blew up 13 Arab aircraft in a raid on the Beirut airport; and that attacked a hijacked passenger plane in Lod (while Israeli negotiators were supposedly cooperating with the Red Cross to bring a peaceful solution to the crisis). It was Sayaret Matkal that struck Beirut in 1973 killing scores of Fatah leaders, Lebanese police, and bystanders. And it was Sayaret Matkal that precipitated a slaughter by attacking the Palestinians holding hostages in the cadet school at Ma'alot when the Israelis refused to release 26 prisoners. It is at the least ironic that a leader of the Sayaret Matkal, virtually from its inception until his death at Entebbe was none other than Jonathan Netanyahu, brother of Israeli ambassador Benjamin Netanyahu, in whose name the Jonathan Institute on anti-terrorism was established.

In a more recent scenario, Israeli special forces have responded to the rising that began in the occupied territories in December of 1987. In February of 1988, the P.L.O. sought to sponsor the sailing of their own "ship of return" from Limassol, Cyprus, as a nonviolent demonstration of the plight of exiles. The ship was crippled by an explosion while still in port, and a few hours later Israeli Defense Minister Yitzhak Rabin declared in Tel Aviv that "The State of Israel decided it was compelled not to let them achieve their purpose, and we will do that in whatever ways we find. The following April, a commando team assassinated high-ranking P.L.O. deputy Khalil Wazir at his home in Tunis in front of his wife and child. The U.N. Security Council adopted a resolution on April 25 implicitly condemning Israel for the killing. These events cannot be isolated from the immediate question of revolt and the larger objective conditions of settler terrorism and internal colonialism. It is to these conditions that we now turn.

Settler Terrorism

For Israel, settlement is an ongoing process now rooted in the structural and ideological formations of the society. The welcoming of Jewish in-migration, expressed ideologically and politically in the *law of return* and *dual nationalism,* goes beyond the portrayal of Israel as a safe haven. On the one hand, such conceptions seek to strengthen the state by creating transcendent ties with a globally dispersed population. On the other, the process of settlement has meaning both for population increase and the continuing economic, political and social integration of newcomers into the social order. Given the material need for land and other resources, and the ideological message of the "Greater Israel" (by which the West Bank is redefined as Judea and Samaria and thus belongs to the Jews), the implications for conflict are clear.

If the settlement process has been the means by which the state of Israel was born, then it is also the means by which its frontiers have been expanded. Settlers are routinely described as "extremists" and it is certainly true that these 70,000 Jewish occupiers are among the most nationalistic of Israelis. The Gush Emunim (Block of the Faithful), for example, represent one of several Jewish sects who have sworn to keep the West Bank under Israeli control. Devoutly committed to the concept of a chosen people on a promised land, the Gush envision the expulsion of all Arabs from the West Bank. However, to dwell too long on the fanaticism dimension of the settler phenomenon is to miss the larger context. The settlements in the occupied territories, whether paramilitary outposts or extensive residential and agricultural complexes, did not emerge *ex nihilo*. The Israeli state has provided the planning, the resources, the subsidies, the low mortgages, and the military support (including army-issued Uzi sub-machine guns) for its heavily armed settlers. And it is those Israelis who are subject to unemployment and relative poverty who are most susceptible to such inducements.

One of the ideological meanings of settlement is pacification. This reflects the long-standing colonial assumption that the land is wild and its occupants are savage. Thus the role of settlers is not merely to establish permanent homes but to advance "civilization." As settlers come to define the land as their property, it is clear that others with claims must be increasingly dehumanized. Settlement then, wherever practiced, implies a process of expulsion, whether legitimated by claims of God's favor for the powerful or by complementary visions of the less-than-human standing of the indigenous inhabitants. Expulsion need not be achieved through force and confiscation, although the symbolism of state violence should not be overlooked. The long standing tactic of blowing up the houses of Palestinians suspected of rebellion is a metaphor of negation. It signifies the destruction of home and abode, but more than that—it is an eviction notice served by a would-be landlord.

More sophisticated forms of expulsion involve the imposition of conceptions of law and private property on a traditional culture where such have little meaning. It was by these methods that much "Indian land" fell into the hands of whites who "settled" North America. So it was with Palestine, with even Palestinian citizens of Israel (15 percent of the total population) occupying an inferior social, economic, and political status, often victimized by discriminatory land legislation such as the Absentee Property Law. It is expulsion, whether by force or "market forces," coexisting with the attempts by the expelled to acquire the political or armed strength to take back some of what they have lost, that is at the root of much state and commando terrorism.

Although the terrorism of armed Israeli settlers is well-documented, the theoretical point of isomorphic interests should not be obscured. Certain tactics may be officially condemned, but the ends to which those tactics are directed may be structurally consistent with those of the state. Violence and counter violence in the occupied territories are logical consequences of a state-driven settlement imperative. Thus vigilante methods are to be understood as a continuation of the politics of state expansion by other means.

Other dimensions of the relationship between settlers and state remain instructive. In April of 1988, a group of hikers from the ultranationalist settlement of Elon Moreh, went to the outskirts of the Palestinian village of Beita for a picnic. In a confrontation, a 15-year-old Israeli girl was killed and the story spread throughout Israel that she died from Palestinian stones. After much of Beita had been destroyed by the Israeli military, an army autopsy revealed that Tirza Poret had been killed by an armed settler guard who accompanied the group, a guard who had been involved only six months earlier in a vigilante shooting in Nablus. The other guard had been convicted in 1984 of the destruction of evidence in the killing of an 11-year-old Palestinian girl by a settler. Despite this, both were allowed to play their paramilitary role.

This "picnic," like the 48 other outings mounted by settlers on the same day, can only be described as expulsion theater staged to assert Israeli proprietorship. Had the Israeli army not released the results of the autopsy, the result might well have been to unleash uncontrollable forms of reprisal, leaving the state of Israel on the sharpened horns of its continuing dilemma: how to use the settler vanguard while reigning in excesses that threaten the claims of democracy. To sum up this and earlier points, the relation between the military and settler/vigilantes encapsulates the dialectic of convenience between the forces of occupation and the forces of annexation. Thus understood, the settlers on the frontiers of the "Greater Israel" serve to expand the limits of state power.

Intifadah: The Revolution of Stones

On December 8, 1987, a sustained revolt began in the occupied territories that provides the clearest evidence to date of the "permanent" nature of the settlement crisis. Just as Israeli settlement must be considered a process, so to is the Palestinian movement. Over a generation after the founding of the P.L.O., a new stage in the resistance appears to have taken form. A broadly based pattern of revolt emerged from inside the West Bank, Gaza, and Jerusalem and gained support from within Israel's Arab population. As of winter 1989, the uprising showed no signs of abatement, but should the violence subside, enduring ideological and structural changes in the resistance movement would continue to have sociological implications for the future of Israeli-Palestinian relations.

This new stage offers a change in the roles played by Palestinian nationalists inside the occupied territories, from that of political support and/or sympathy for the P.L.O. to active demonstration and rebellion. This means a new definitional stage for self-determination, in which responsibility is no longer solely vested in the political, economic, social, and guerilla forces of the P.L.O. located in other lands. The development of indigenous forces of resistance from within the 1.5 million Palestinians living under conditions of military rule means increased potential for a sustained rebellion. As the meaning of self-determination is reformulated in ideological institutions (specifically in the mosques and schools) and as new cadres emerge (as with the clandestine Unified National Command), new and more generally based tactics of resistance can be expected to strain the resources of state control.

Further, as resistance escalates, an increased level of state violence can be expected to spur Palestinian solidarity at various levels. The sense of family and tribe, which facilitates a "divide and conquer" strategy of rule, may be expected to give ground to other collective identities embodied in such terms as "nation" or "people." The unexpected support for the resistance from the Israeli Arab population represents another level of solidarity, underscoring the dilemma implicit in reconciling the tenets of democracy with the more exclusionary assumptions of a Jewish state. At the tactical level, in 1988 more sophisticated forms of non-violent civil disobedience emerged to buttress mass demonstrations, with strikes, shop closings, boycotts, the refusal to pay taxes, and other means of supporting the rising.

In keeping with the mandate of the "iron fist," as the Palestinian revolt escalated arithmetically, the Israeli response escalated geometrically. Military authorities halted the education of almost a half-million Palestinians in February, when some 1,200 schools in the West Bank and Gaza Strip were closed for three months, reopened, and then closed early for the year. Jerusalem born Mubarak E. Awad, a Palestinian who took American citizenship before returning to establish a Center for the Study of Non-Violence was ordered deported by Prime Minister Yitzhak Shamir in May. As reported by the Associated Press on January 29, 1989, 370 Palestinians and 15 Israelis had died in the 14 month period. On October 9, 1988, the Associated Press reported that 7,000 Palestinians had been wounded and 18,000 detained, with some 5,600 still jailed and 2,000 serving sentences of up to 6 months without benefit of trial. Al Haq put the Palestinian death toll at 400 with an estimated 20,000 injured.

In the context of the "revolution of stones," the Palestine National Council (the P.L.O.'s parliament in exile) met in

Algiers on November 12-15, 1988. The P.N.C. endorsed U.N. Security Council resolutions 242 and 338 (implicitly recognizing the right of Israel to exist) as the basis for convening an international conference on the question of Palestine. The conference would be organized under U.N. auspices, with the five permanent members of the Security Council and all parties in conflict (including the P.L.O.) participating. It further declared the establishment of the state of Palestine with its capital in Jerusalem (P.N.C. documents in Curtiss, 1988:6). Subsequently, the United States triggered a firestorm of international protest by refusing to grant Yasir Arafat a visa to address the United Nations on the familiar grounds of P.L.O. terrorism. In spite of a 121 to 2 General Assembly vote calling for the granting of the visa (with only Israel and the United States opposed), the U.S. State Department refused. The General Assembly then shifted its session to Geneva in protest, underscoring that global isolation had become one of the costs of the core-client form of imperial formations mystified by the ideology of terrorism. Driven by events having their genesis in the intifadah, on December 14, 1988 the United States agreed to enter into cosmetic low-level talks with the P.L.O.

As demonstrated, this is only the most recent chapter in an historical record of state violence. On the other side, documentation assembled by the Israel Defense Forces (1985 and 1986) (and made available through the Israeli embassy in the United States) details the attacks on Israeli targets both internal and external. One summary covers the period June, 1967 to October, 1985, and the other July, 1968 to July, 1986. A careful reading of these accounts makes it clear that the I.D.F. has included attacks on military personnel as well as civilian; makes no distinction as to whether the "civilian" targets were armed; includes the attack by Japanese terrorists at Ben-Gurion airport in May of 1972 that took 26 lives (claiming they were working "on behalf of" the P.F.L.P.); and takes no responsibility for deaths pursuant to its iron fist policy of no negotiation. [Recall that the death toll of 24 civilians and one soldier at Ma'alot in 1974 followed a rescue attack by Sayaret Matkal. According to Said (1979:172), the Ma'alot incident followed weeks of Israeli napalming of Palestinian camps in southern Lebanon.] All this aside, the total Israeli death toll owing to terrorism (as defined by the I.D.F.) in these two surveys covering almost two decades appears to be fewer than 400 persons.

Maximal Zionism and Apartheid

An increasing number of authors, some already cited in this inquiry, have sought to identify cultural, political, and economic similarities between South Africa and Israel. Such attempts are necessarily limited when they remain at the level of analogies. What is necessary is the construction of a conceptual framework that addresses the *parallel development* of settler economies. By this I mean to identify a set of structural and ideological forces common to the internal relations between settlers and their descendants on the one side and indigenous peoples with prior claim on the other. Such relations defy simple conceptions of ethnicity, faith, or forms of national identity; nor do they coincide with lines drawn on maps.

Internally, the conflict in ancient Palestine is not a simple matter of Jews and Arabs. The objective conditions of Arab citizens of Israel differ from those of Palestinians living in the occupied territories, which differ in turn from those of Palestinians dispersed in other lands. So it is within the Jewish caste inside Israel. It is the Sephardim, and other newly arrived settlers and marginals, who have sought to rectify their material disadvantage through the Likud bloc. The connection with the Afrikaners in South Africa in this respect is not circumstantial. The state has also been the vehicle for the less-favored members of South Africa's white caste to alleviate their standing as marginal. That the most adamant supporters of apartheid have the most to lose from surrendering the patronage and labor advantages offered by the state is axiomatic.

Yet to hold the more recently arrived Sephardim responsible for the Palestinian dilemma is to ignore the total history of the Zionist movement. More important, it is to ignore two theoretical aspects of the settler economy common to both Israel and South Africa. First, the existence of caste conditions may *alter,* but does not *negate,* class formations within a dominant caste. However, those conscious of their intracaste marginality may seek to rectify their disadvantage through seeking state influence. It is their marginality, not their ethnicity that is at issue, although demographic and organizational factors are relevant for electoral success. This form of *caste consciousness* can only retard the formation of a class consciousness that must necessarily transcend the boundaries of birth, faith, and culture.

Once institutionalized in the laws and policies of the state, this consciousness of caste becomes a real force. The emptying of that population's land, labor value, and other resources serves the immediate interests of caste marginal (whether Afrikaner, Sephardim, or their functional equivalent), without severely disrupting existing patterns of privilege. In the process, the system as a whole is maintained. It is at this theoretical level of system-maintenance, with its dialectic reproduction of societal and global relations, that the larger questions of internal colonialism must be joined.

It comes as no surprise to find state representatives in both South Africa and Israel asserting that the indigenous populations they control are materially "better off" than their counterparts in Black African or Arab societies in general. Such claims were not invented by these states of course but are common to imperial ideology whether expressed in the "white man's burden" of Kipling or the *mission civilisée* of the French colonialists. It is clear that such legitimations completely miss the point of self-determination. However, on a less philosophical plane, they also fail to address the material dynamics of internal colonialism. For example, the occupation of Gaza by Israel is not confined to a military presence. It represents instead a process of economic absorption and reverse development that benefits the more privileged.

Palestinians in Gaza do not control their land, labor, technology, or consumption. At least one-third of the strip has been *de facto* confiscated by Israel with most of this designated for settlement. Israel controls not only land allocation but access to water, agricultural production, and trade. Given military restrictions on planting and replacing trees, land loss and water diversion to settlers, Gazan citrus production declined from 243,700 tons in 1975 to 175,000 tons in 1984. The pattern of reverse development is also evidenced in the Israeli imposition of land taxes, value-added taxes, and taxes on exports, which in concert with restrictions on trade thwart authentic economic development. Bans on exports to Western markets, and on exports to Israel of products that compete with Israeli goods coexist with virtually unlimited access to Gazan markets for Israeli producers. On the industrial side, Palestinian manufacturers endure the restriction of credit, the denial by Israel of export subsidies and tax breaks, as well as restrictions on markets.

The uneven exchange that marks the dependency of the periphery in general is evidenced in the Gaza in particular with its trade deficit in 1985 of some $164.5 million, most of that owing to the dumping of Israeli products. On the side of labor dependency, Gaza residents officially registered with the Israeli Employment Service as working inside Israel grew from some 5,900 workers in 1970 to 41,700 in 1985, a number that does not include the illegals in the labor reserve. What is interpreted by Israel as job creation for Palestinians may better be interpreted as labor dependency. Claims of job growth are further suspect as the consumption made possible by the wages paid this absentee work force is channeled toward Israeli markets. The structural parallels with South Africa are clear, and they are more than analogies.

On the administrative side, social control necessitates the cultivation of an indigenous elite that in turn legitimates the claim of self-rule, while representing a counter-insurgency agenda. Israel (as South Africa) has appointed "moderate" Palestinian leaders, who (as their bantustan and township counterparts) have enjoyed power, privilege, and systems of local patronage. In the context of the December, 1987 rising, these appointees came under increasing threats and pressure from Palestinians who accused them of collaboration. In Beit Sahur (a largely Christian village on the Israeli-occupied West Bank), Bicharra Qumsaya resigned as the head of the Village League for the entire West Bank in March of 1988. The league had been created by the Israelis in the hope of offering an alternative to the P.L.O. In the same month, the Israeli-appointed mayor of Gaza City, Hanza Turkamni, stepped down. The rising also saw the resignation of hundreds of Palestinian tax collectors and police.

When the institutions of indigenous control fail, more direct forms of population control will be placed in force. Certain of these have already been discussed, but again the theoretical construct of structural parallelism is apropos. These involve restrictions on the press, mass detention, curfews, and the ready resort to deadly force or highly dangerous riot-control technology (including the introduction of plastic bullets by the I.D.F.). The consequences of the iron fist, as the parallel ideology *of collective responsibility* used by the French in Algeria, can only be to build national solidarity among resisters.

If the exponential recourse to force is insufficient to prevent the emergence of a "permanent" state of revolt against the formations of internal colonialism; and if settlement is in fact *institutionalized;* what may then be predicted for the future of the Israeli-Palestinian conflict? To begin, if settlement is institutionalized within the Israeli state, it follows that the popular liberal solution in the West (and within the Israeli Peace Now movement) is suspect. That solution, which is to trade land for peace, is contrary to the material forces of open immigration and natural increase by which the Jewish population has grown from some 600,000 at the point of statehood, to 3.2 million today. It is contrary to the history of Israel's geographic expansion, ever spurred by the need for new lands for new settlers. It is contrary to the ideological forces that take religious form in the conception of chosenness, and politically in the conception of dual nationalism. It is contrary to the more social-psychological forces by which a people, well-conscious of their historical victimization, are imbued with the imagery of the warrior and the purging process it symbolizes.

Viewed structurally and historically then, the Palestinian question is less about the Palestinian problem than about the nature of a maximal Zionist state. The extension into the future of past and existing forces and counter forces is at best an imprecise exercise. However, the forces of maximal Zionism ascendant in Israel have not emerged in a vacuum. Rather they are consistent with and build upon a history of settlement. Should internal Palestinian resistance to this process intensify and grow more effective, the resort of the state to repression will increase and, in keeping with the legitimations of the iron fist, increase exponentially. In this context, extremism may well be redefined, and the forces of absolutism come to dominate the state.

The settlement imperative aside, some consideration must be briefly given to the militarization of Israeli society. The establishment of a permanent warfare state, engaged in a permanent state of war has already been alluded to. That Israel spent 29 percent of its G.N.P. on "national defense" in 1983 (compared to less than 7 percent for the United States, and the constitutional limit of 1 percent in Japan) cannot be dissociated from the development of its arms industry and its role as an arms exporter. Thus in objective terms the Israeli version of a military-industrial complex has been taking form. This traditional alliance of the military bureaucracy, job-holders, international arms dealers, and politicians seeking to please constituents both reflects and reproduces the higher-level material and ideological forces described above.

On the international scene, future relations with the United States may grow strained as the Israelis pursue interests not precisely coincidental with those of the Western world system or its core. If Palestinian revolt and the specter of intensified Israeli state repression do not undermine U.S. support, then it is altogether possible that the now paranoid fear of waves of conventional terrorism both inside and outside Israel may acquire a real basis in fact. Essentially nonviolent tactics among Palestinians in the occupied territories may develop mass support, but should patterns of brutal state repression continue this can be transformed into more active support for armed insurrection.

At the very least, the 1.2 billion Israeli tourism industry will continue to be disrupted and P.L.O. proscriptions on striking targets outside Israel may be rescinded. As the British four decades ago, the United States may find its burden an increasingly heavy one, with its Middle Eastern policy increasingly mired in strategies of "low-intensity conflict". And remembering the history of the British imperial role may serve notice inside Israel that even the United States is not to be trusted to stay the course. It is within this context that the Jonathan Pollard scandal, in which Israel engaged in espionage against its patron state, must be understood.

Given such conditions, relations between Israel and South Africa will continue to grow in importance, a symbiosis born of common historical forces. The pattern of cooperation in industry, trade, intelligence, and nuclear weapons development is a logical outgrowth of the settler imperative at work in both societies. The racial exclusion grounded in religious fundamentalism has marked both maximal Zionism and apartheid, and attempts to more than cosmetically alter the relations they represent will loosen increasing waves of ultranationalism. Both states must continue to resort to military force and the arming of reactionary states or counter-revolutionary organizations within neighboring states. Such tactics of *regional* destabilization are designed to weaken the forces of insurgency inside Israel and South Africa and to further fragment already-fragmented opposition from without.

Before there is peace in southern Africa or in the Middle East, a transformation of these two surviving settler states appears mandatory a transformation that brings more authentic forms of power sharing, economic rights and reparations, demilitarization, cultural pluralism, and an end to state domination. And as in all such struggles, the lead role will be played by the colonized themselves. Once again however, these flashpoints in history represent the clash between the forces of order and change, the privileged and the dispossessed, the state and mass movements of liberation.

❑❑❑

6

Problems of Clandestine Terrorism

Introduction

The public generally opposes aid to the contras, just as it opposed virtually every major program of the Reagan administration. But central policy issues are largely excluded from the corporate media and barely arise in the political system, one reason why voting continues to decline, to barely 37% in the November, 1986 elections.

Nevertheless, popular dissidence remains significant and cannot be controlled by force. Congress, which is somewhat responsive to the public mood, raised a number of barriers to direct U.S. aggression against Nicaragua. This compelled the Reagan administration to devise a complex array of covert means to maintain its mercenary army attacking Nicaragua. Arms were sent to the contras through a shadowy network of CIA subsidiaries and "private" organizations controlled by U.S. ex-generals in close coordination with the White House. Notorious international terrorists were enlisted in the cause, for example, Luis Posada Carriles, a CIA-trained Cuban exile sprung from a Venezuelan prison where he was charged with planning the

1976 bombing of a Cubana airliner with 73 civilians killed, then taken to El Salvador to help organize the contra supply network from the U.S. controlled Ilopango Air Base. The Reagan administration took over the World Anti-Communist League, a collection of Nazis who had been recruited by the U.S. as part of its global campaign against the anti-fascist resistance in the immediate post-World War II period, fanatic anti-Semites, death squad assassins, torturers and killers from around the world, backed by U.S. client states such as South Korea and Taiwan. This organization was converted into an instrument of international terrorism from Mozambique to Nicaragua. Profits from U.S. arms sales to Iran *via* Israel with Saudi Arabian funding, undertaken for entirely different purposes to which we return, were diverted to the contras through Swiss banks, along with tens of millions of dollars from long-term clients such as Taiwan and Saudi Arabia, and targets of opportunity such as the Sultan of Brunei. In what the *Far Eastern Economic Review* describes as a particularly "remarkable case of arms diplomacy," the U.S. succeeded in arranging a cooperative effort of China and Taiwan "to help the anti-Communist Nicaraguan resistance (sic]," in a November, 1984 deal arranged by Oliver North whereby China shipped arms to the contras through Canadian arms dealers and Portugal, funded by Taiwan. The level of support developed through these state-private networks was so large that when $10 million solicited by the State Department from the Sultan was misplaced, the loss was not even noticed. Such machinations provided the contra armies with an air force and military equipment in violation of explicit congressional legislation and U.S. laws going back to the 18th century Neutrality Act, enabling them to maintain some forces within Nicaragua and to continue the terrorist activities that are generally ignored by the U.S. media and dismissed by apologists as "Sandinista atrocity allegations."

In such ways, the Reagan administration constructed an international terrorist network of impressive sophistication, without parallel in history to my knowledge, and used it for a variety of purposes in conformity with the Reagan Doctrine, as already discussed.

Some eyebrows were raised when it was disclosed, after the public phase of the Iran-contra hearings concluded, that "Senior Reagan administration officials approved a plan in early 1984," with the agreement of Secretary of State George Shultz (as a CIA cable indicated), to enlist South Africa too in contra support operations, and that Eden Pastora's forces in the south received 200,000 pounds of equipment from South Africa, so the CIA reported in February, 1985. But after what Duane Clarridge, the CIA official in charge of the agency's covert support for the contras, called the "hullabaloo" over the CIA mining of the harbors, there were "some second thoughts around town as to the wisdom" of involving South Africa, and the plan was shelved. As the Times puts it, the administration "explicitly ruled out any countries with human rights problems or those dependent on American aid"; the State Department solicited aid only "from countries that had good human rights records," such as "South Korea, Saudi Arabia and Singapore," also Taiwan, China, Israel, all with "good human rights records" by Times standards and "not dependent on American aid."

It is important to bear in mind that the reliance on clandestine terrorism and proxy forces was undertaken to evade public opinion and its weak reflection in congressional legislation. Clandestine operations are not a secret to their victims, or, generally, to foreign powers and other groups, including business interests out to make a buck, foreign states, shady characters of the Manucher Ghorbanifar variety regarded by Oliver North as an Israeli agent as well as a "liar" and a "cheat" while North relied upon his advice as to how to evade congressional legislation, and so on. It is the domestic population which must be protected from knowledge of these operations, because it would not approve them; otherwise, they need not be secret. As we shall see, Congress and the media helped to conceal the operations until the task became virtually impossible, and now seek to limit any significant understanding of them. Such tactics are a natural feature of the "right turn," given its restricted nature as an elite phenomenon.

It is normal for the state to regard the domestic population as a major enemy, which must be excluded, repressed or controlled to serve elite interests. This contempt for the citizenry and for the democratic processes that to some extent reflect their concerns has been a notable feature of the Reagan administration, revealed with some clarity in the congressional hearings despite their narrow focus and evasion of such matters. An intriguing case arose when the questioning of Col. North by Rep. Jack Brooks touched upon his plan to suspend the Constitution and impose martial law in the event of "national crises" such as "violent and widespread internal dissent or national opposition to a U.S. military invasion abroad." In this event, control of the United States was to be turned over to the national crisis-management unit FEMA, directed by Louis Guiffrida. He is a close associate of Reagan and Edwin Meese who, while at the Army War College in 1970, wrote a memorandum recommending internment of all "American Negroes" in "assemble-centers or relocation camps," in the event of civil disorder. Chairman Daniel Inouye quickly intervened to terminate this line of questioning, and these crucial disclosures were also evaded by the national media, unreported in the *New York Times*, for example, apart from the few sentences in the aborted congressional questioning.

The same fear of the domestic population is what lies behind the resort to a clandestine international terrorist network within the framework of the Reagan Doctrine. A central principle of a terrorist culture is that these crucial facts must be obscured, and indeed they are.

In the case of the contra armies, their massive support, supply system, training, access to U.S. intelligence, radio and TV penetration of Nicaragua, and foreign sanctuaries, are far beyond anything available to authentic guerrilla forces; if a real guerrilla movement such as the one in El Salvador had a fraction of the support lavished on the contras, it would have quickly become a major military force and the U.S. imposed regime would have long ago collapsed. Nevertheless, the CIA-directed proxy army proved unable to move beyond random terrorism, so that the CIA was once again compelled as when it carried out the mining of harbors and attacks on oil installations to employ its own commando groups, now parachuted into Nicaragua to conduct sabotage missions from aircraft piloted by mercenaries (including Belgians, former Rhodesian citizens and Americans) working under CIA contract. These operations are conducted from command centers in El Salvador and Honduras and U.S. ships off the Atlantic and Pacific coasts of Nicaragua. The CIA is "choosing precise military targets for the rebels," the *New York Times* reports, providing them "with precise information on dams, bridges, electrical substations, port facilities," etc.; these "precise military targets" were built by the Army Corps of Engineers and other U.S. agencies that supply maps, blueprints and floor plans to facilitate missions by the commandos of the foreign power attacking Nicaragua.

As the Spring Offensive of the refurbished proxy army began, its forces were directed by their U.S. controllers to [go] after soft targets not try to duke it out with the Sandinistas directly," so General John Galvin, commander of the U.S. Southern Command, explained to Congress and the media, adding that with these more sensible tactics, aimed at civilians lacking means of defense against armed terrorist bands, prospects for the contras would improve. Months later, U.S. and Western military observers noted that "the contras have yet to chalk up a major, attention-getting battle success anywhere in Nicaragua. The offensive has not been able to get past Sandinista defenses to move down from the mountains to populous towns, let alone cities, or to strike critical objectives. 'They're still going after small, soft targets' like farmers' cooperatives, the U.S. military analyst says."

Under the Reagan doctrine, the United States has created something new in the annals of international terrorism: a lavishly equipped army organized not for combat but for terror, maintained in the field through an extensive supply system provided and protected by the superpower sponsor, directed to attacking "small, soft targets," to bleeding the victim, which is far too weak to maintain a viable society, let alone persist in social reform, in the face of such a superpower assault. This achievement stands alongside the creation of a terrorist army dedicated to suppressing the population by massive violence in El Salvador, and support for a similar force, in part through the medium of mercenary states, in Guatemala. The program has largely been a success in its basic aims, not very surprisingly, given the balance of force. And there is every reason to expect it to continue, in one or another form, whatever agreements are written down on paper, just as there is little doubt that it will be criticized by responsible opinion only for occasional failings in the pursuit of a noble cause that reveals the benevolence of our intentions.

We should also not overlook the fact that the U.S. strategic weapons system and its intervention forces have constantly been used in the war against Nicaragua. The former serves its traditional function of "deterrence": namely, providing a "nuclear umbrella" to deter any interference with U.S. policies of subversion, aggression and international terrorism—the primary meaning of "deterrence," dismissing here familiar Orwellisms. The threat of overwhelming U.S. force is a crucial factor in maintaining the proxy army attacking Nicaragua. As agreed on all sides, this military force does not remotely resemble guerrillas in any meaningful sense of the term. It has never attempted to formulate a political program or to construct a substantial popular base, even in areas where the government is highly unpopular. The civilian front constructed by the United States to soften the terrorist image for domestic purposes has also lacked the interest or competence to attempt even perfunctory moves in this direction. The U.S. controlled troops can survive in the field only with an extensive supply system, including daily air drops by mid-1987, an elaborate intelligence apparatus also provided by the foreign master, and armaments beyond the dreams of authentic guerrillas. We return to details, but again, the essential facts are not in doubt. It is therefore absolutely necessary to ensure that Nicaragua not be permitted to obtain the means to defend its territory from hostile penetration by a U.S. air supply operation, with an air force of its own, adequate anti-aircraft systems, and so on. That Nicaragua must remain defenseless is accepted across the U.S. political spectrum. Such liberal doves as Senators Paul Tsongas and Christopher Dodd agree that Nicaragua must not be permitted to defend its national territory; Tsongas went so far as to assert that the U.S. would have to bomb Nicaragua should it obtain jet planes, because "they're also capable against the United States," a remark too outlandish to merit comment, except insofar as it illuminates the hysterical intellectual climate in a terrorist superpower. The threat of overwhelming U.S. violence in reserve serves to guarantee that U.S. directives in this regard will not be infringed, a crucial contribution to the survival of the mercenary forces attacking Nicaragua.

U.S. conventional forces are more directly engaged in Central America, not only in such operations as coordinating air strikes in El Salvador but also in the U.S. attack against Nicaragua. The regular maneuvers in Honduras have the dual purpose of creating a U.S. military base in defiance of congressional directives, and compelling Nicaragua to maintain a permanent state of mobilization against the regular threat of invasion. The deployment of 50,000 U.S. forces in maneuvers in May, 1987 served a still more specific function. It was a crucial part of the Spring Offensive of the contra armies; the U.S. maneuvers were designed to draw the Nicaraguan army away from population defense so that the terrorist army could prove to Congress that it could achieve sufficient success in its attacks against "soft targets" so as to merit continued support.

When a U.S. ally is forced to mobilize by threatening actions, we regard this threat as tantamount to aggression, justifying a pre-emptive military strike in self-defense. When Israel was compelled to mobilize in late May, 1967 as Arab armies were deployed in threatening positions, U.S. and Western opinion generally regarded this as intolerable how can Israel be expected to sustain mobilization for more than a few days? so that Israel's attack was therefore justified in self-defense. Israel was not an impoverished country under attack by a terrorist superpower, but when U.S. military threat compels Nicaragua to maintain permanent mobilization, and to remove its forces from defense of the civilian population so as to clear the way for U.S. organized terrorists, there is barely a critical word in the media (or in the West rather generally) except, of course, condemnation of Nicaragua for maintaining defensive military forces, and particularly, for obtaining Soviet arms after the Western allies have refused, under U.S. pressure, to provide them with means to withstand the U.S. terrorist assault, obviously the ultimate proof that they are mere Soviet clients, barely deserving to be called Nicaraguans, a major threat to our security. Putting aside the moral cowardice, the reaction is understandable within a terrorist culture, where it is, furthermore, a crucial obligation to feign ignorance of these obvious facts, systematically suppressed in the media and journals of opinion.

Although the toll of direct murder has been less satisfactory in Nicaragua than in El Salvador and Guatemala, it is a grand success of the Reagan Doctrine, and is no doubt celebrated as such, when thousands of children again die from epidemics that had been eradicated by the early reforms of the Sandinistas. These have been reversed, much to the relief of Washington, along with achievements in literacy and economic development, as a result of U.S. organized terrorism aimed at "soft targets" accompanied with an embargo and pressures on allies and international lending institutions, and the constant threat of invasion. We read an occasional report that "in Nicaragua's remote countryside," the health care programs that had "dramatically lowered" infant mortality and preventable disease are deteriorating, now under funded because the government has been forced to "put more of their meager resources into the war effort" and because the U.S. proxy forces have attacked such "soft targets" as health programs and schools, destroying over 60 health centers and killing or kidnapping large numbers of medical workers. In one village, 150 children died of measles because contras prevented government health workers, regular assassination targets, from reaching them; and tuberculosis and other diseases are again reaching epidemic proportions, while hospitals and health centers lack medicine and equipment and malnutrition is beginning to rise and might even return to its earlier levels if U.S. efforts succeed. Infant mortality, cut in half by Sandinista health reforms, is on the rise, and hospitals that had previously served only the richest 2% of the population but were opened without cost for the general public under the Sandinistas are now unable to function because of the "increasing demand for care" and the lack of supplies, thanks to the U.S. attack and embargo. Similarly, while the number of teachers has almost tripled, supplies are close to nonexistent. "The Contras Have Learned to Hit Where It Hurts," a headline in the *Washington Post* reads, with a report on how the contra army, "reportedly in high spirits and outfitted by the CIA," succeeded in burning down "a church-sponsored health clinic that had been the pride of the community" in the isolated village of Tapalse, proudly reported by the major contra military group (FDN) as "one of its 'most important operations'."

These are among the consequences of the dedication of the United States to reducing Nicaragua to the zero grade of life. In assessing. the crimes of Pol Pot, we rightly count not only those killed outright, but also the victims of disease, malnutrition, and harsh conditions of labor. Those capable of escaping the indoctrination system may recall that the chorus of protest over Khmer Rouge "genocide" or "autogenocide" reached its peak of outrage in early 1977, at a time when State Department intelligence–the only source with substantial information–estimated the toll at "tens if not hundreds of thousands" from all causes, primarily "disease, malnutrition or other factors" rather than outright killing an estimate that stands up rather well in the light of subsequent scholarship. But respectable opinion would never consider an assessment of the Reagan Doctrine or earlier exercises in terms of their actual human costs, and could not comprehend that such an assessment—which would yield a monstrous toll if accurately conducted on a global scale-might perhaps be a proper task in the United States. At the same level of integrity, disciplined Soviet intellectuals are horrified over real or alleged American crimes, but perceive their own only as benevolent intent gone awry, or errors of an earlier day, now overcome; the comparison is inexact and unfair, since Soviet intellectuals can plead fear as an excuse for their services to state violence.

In the real world, the people of Nicaragua must be punished for the criminal effort of the Sandinista government to divert resources to the poor majority. This crime explains "the firm belief' of the Reagan administration that "the Sandinistas must be overthrown or, at least, theirs must become a revolution of misery, a frightful object lesson to the people of the region," Who must be deterred from similar heresies. We may then observe their "miseries" with undisguised pleasure, congratulating ourselves in the *New York Times* that "America's pugnacity" has compelled them to "keep their miseries to themselves."

Much the same thinking lay behind the U.S. resort to large-scale terror against the rural population of South Vietnam. As Kennedy-Johnson adviser General Maxwell Taylor explained to Congress, "We intend to show that the 'war of liberation' is costly, dangerous and doomed to failure," as is any attempt by suffering people to modify the rules of the international order maintained by its powerful beneficiaries, Winston Churchill's "rich men dwelling at peace within their habitations" who are to run the world by virtue of this status. The same reasons explain why this commitment of the Reagan administration represents an elite consensus, and why the plain and simple truth of the matter is barely expressible within the cultural mainstream.

It may also be recalled that the previous state of grim suffering and death in Nicaragua, to which we must again reduce them, elicited scarcely a flicker of interest among the educated classes in the United States, just as the perpetuation of these circumstances in Honduras and elsewhere evokes no concern today. Rather, it was the effort to overcome the grim consequences of a century of U.S. dominance that aroused horror and indignation (concealed in the usual "anti-Communist" disguise), along with a dedicated commitment to restore Nicaragua to the "Central American mode," in the approving words of the editors of the *Washington Post*, to which we return.

Terrorist attacks on "soft targets" such as health clinics and schools serve obvious purposes. The perceived threat of the Sandinistas was that despite their meager resources and the horrifying conditions left by the final phase of the U.S.-backed Somoza terror, they might be able to introduce the kinds of reforms that would have appeal both in neighboring countries, and in regions of Nicaragua where the Somoza regime maintained a degree of popular support within the peasant society and there was antagonism to Sandinista measures, sometimes conducted foolishly and even brutally, particularly in the early period. But the fear of successful reform can be overcome by destroying health services, schools and cooperative farms. It is, therefore, only rational to direct the proxy army to attack such "soft targets," and in the generally remote areas where the terrorist forces can penetrate, these policies have had some success in their aims, so the occasional press reports indicate. Thus in Jinotega province near the Honduran border, Peter Ford reports, contras have succeeded in terrorizing civilians by ambushing trucks with many civilian casualties, killing many doctors, health workers and teachers, forcing the government to close newly opened schools and clinics, and repeatedly burning down houses, educational facilities, cooperative stores, community kitchens and so on, causing such random destruction that cooperative "members barely manage to feed themselves, let alone make a profit from their harvests." The contra leaders also deliver what counts as a "political speech" by U.S. standards: namely, a warning to the cooperative members that if they rebuild their community "100 times, they would destroy it 100 times," so a peasant woman reports. The expectation is that these tactics will abort measures of reform and national integration, fuel discontent, and, ultimately, bring the population to understand that only by a return to "the Central American mode" established by the United States will the terror come to an end.

Partisans of U.S. terror have constructed a special vocabulary to conceal their satisfaction with the achievements of the Reagan Doctrine despite its possible "flaws." Thus, *New Republic* editor Morton Kondracke warns us that failure to stay the course may "jeopardize all that has been achieved for democracy in recent years" in Central America. Meanwhile, at the left-liberal extreme of the expressible spectrum, Charles Lane explains in the same journal, apparently without irony, that the Reagan Doctrine sought "a low-cost way to reconcile America's noble wish for democratic development in the Third World with its muscular desire to overcome the Vietnam syndrome." But while the Doctrine may have succeeded in El Salvador, he continues, it is threatened by American impatience in Nicaragua, where "the United States finds itself faced with a society and a culture that can't be made democratic as quickly as it would like" by "armed rebellion" incidentally, supported by such stellar democracies as Argentina under the rule of the neo-Nazi generals, Taiwan, Saudi Arabia and South Korea, and organized at home by such enthusiasts of democratic processes as William Casey, Edwin Meese, John Poindexter, and the rest of the cabal. Critics of the Reagan Doctrine are concerned that the Reagan administration's active promotion of democracy" may be too "aggressive" (John Rielly), that our efforts "to force the Sandinista revolution into the American democratic mold" may not be worth "the risk" (John Oakes), and that Nicaragua may be "beyond the reach of our good intentions". Lane, Oakes and Morley are at the outer limits of dissent within mainstream journalism.

Beyond this spectrum of respectable opinion, we have only those whom McGeorge Bundy once described as "wild men in the wings," referring to people who dared to question the "first team" that was in charge of our earlier crusade for democracy in Vietnam.

Faith in our "good intentions" remains unimpaired by the historical record in Central America and the Caribbean, not to speak of Southeast Asia, Africa, the Middle East and elsewhere; and properly so, given the irrelevance of the historical and documentary record in a terrorist culture, which carefully avoids any institutional critique and can always appeal to the doctrine of "change of course" if nothing else avails. U. S. sponsorship in Central America of some of the most horrendous atrocities of recent years elicits only the thought that some problems there may be "beyond the reach of our good intentions." The reaction was similar when popular opposition to brutal dictatorship and state terror in South Korea, long supported by the United States, reached a level difficult to ignore by 1987; the resulting outburst of anti-Americanism evoked the reflection that "imposing American morality on other countries' political systems is a ticklish business," nothing more.

The doctrine of "good intentions" is beyond challenge, even beyond awareness at least at home. Others manage a clearer view, even among our allies. As the U.S. was exploiting Britain's travail to take over its traditional domains during World War II, the British foreign services were able to penetrate the ideological mask. In their wartime records, we read that "American imperialism is in the forefront in the conduct of affairs in the Far East," as elsewhere, "attempting to elbow us out." The High Commissioners of the British Dominions warned of "the economic imperialism of American business interests, which is quite active under the cloak of a benevolent and avuncular internationalism." As for the fabled "benevolence" of the United States, a staple of Western ideological systems, the Minister of State at the British Foreign Office, Richard Law, commented to his Cabinet colleagues that Americans believe "that the United States stands for something in the world something of which the world has need, something which the world is going to like, something, in the final analysis, which the world is going to take, whether it likes it or not" a good succinct summary of U.S. foreign policy and its conventional disguise.

Such insights are commonly achieved by the victims: the British displaced by U.S. "economic imperialism"; the peasants subjected to somewhat more rigorous measures of discipline in Central America, Southeast Asia and elsewhere; or the European working classes who were called upon to bear the costs of the reconstruction of capitalism in the interests of U.S. investors and their local associates in the early postwar period. It is the task of the educated classes to conceal these facts as they discourse about the nobility of the "American purpose" and other familiar doctrines, a task that they have conducted with considerable success, and in the United States, with notable uniformity and devotion.

To maintain discipline abroad often proves a harder task. From early on, the Reagan administration has elicited criticism and serious concern, even in conservative circles, for heightening world tension and "debasing the language of international intercourse with feverish rhetoric," creating a "chasm" between "current American perceptions of the world and the world's perception of America". While U.S. terrorism in Nicaragua was still "clandestine" meaning well-known, but kept under cover Canada's leading newspaper, generally restrained and pro-U.S., condemned the Reagan administration for acts of "madness" in organizing a "band of cutthroats" to attack Nicaragua under the direction of its "bizarre cowboy leader" in Washington. As Washington sought to undermine the Central American accords of August, 1987, the centrist British press virtually pleaded with President Reagan to "come to terms with reality in Central America" and allow the peace plan to proceed instead of "financing a murderous and incompetent band of Contra mercenaries" in his "obsession with the overthrow of the elected government of Nicaragua," a crusade that "has brought dishonour to him and his Administration":

> *It also flouts rulings by the International Court of Justice, and parallels the so-called Soviet 'Brezhnev doctrine` as applied in Afghanistan and Eastern Europe. Not least, it has caused the deaths of tens of thousands of men, women and children and million of pounds` worth of destruction in an already wretchedly poor area of the world.*

For all Washington's propaganda efforts, the US is seen internationally as the loser and the Sandinistas as one of the more genuinely popular regimes in Central America. Nicaragua is so weakly aligned to the Soviet Union that Mr. Gorbachov has cut off its oil supplies. Meanwhile, the country that proclaims itself the world's greatest democracy aligns itself with regimes, such as those in Guatemala, Honduras and El Salvador, which are little more than façades for military rule. The symbol of the Republican Party has, of course, always been that of an elephant. It is dismaying to watch it behaving true to form with a gnat.

Such perceptions would be difficult to find in the domestic counterparts of these national journals, though in a few U.S. client states there is a sympathetic popular response to Reaganite "madness."

While exercises of international terrorism cause problems among the allies, there are compensations as well. The state managers are naturally not unaware of the image they present abroad, and they have sought to exploit it for the furtherance of their terrorist operations. A few weeks after its bombing of Libya in April 1986, the Reagan administration sought to line up the Western powers in its anti-Libyan crusade. To this end, it circulated a position paper at the Tokyo summit in May warning of "the need to do something so that the crazy Americans won't take matters into their own hands again." The strategy was successful, and Reagan's aides were quite clear about the reasons:

> *"We've got the madman factor going for us," said one U.S. official, referring not to Kaddafia but to Reagan. "You know, 'Keep me from killing again'."*

Returning to terrorist operations closer to home, the media and other commentators assure us that the Sandinistas merely exploit the pretense that they are under attack and threatened by invasion to justify repression and to explain away the economic catastrophe that has been caused by their incompetence and evil nature. It is unnecessary to provide any factual basis or reasoned argument for these claims, since they are required by the propaganda system and are therefore true by definition. We may therefore cheerfully ignore the record of repression of other states in situations of conflict clearly El Salvador must be avoided because the wrong conclusions will be too obvious, but we must also suppress the record of such states as Israel or the United States itself, in far less onerous circumstances.

The well-behaved commentator must also dismiss the facts about economic performance: for example, the 1983 conclusion of the Inter-American Development Bank, now barred from offering loans to Nicaragua by U.S. pressure, that "Nicaragua has made noteworthy progress in the social sector, which is laying a solid foundation for long-term socio-economic development," a conclusion supported by the charitable development agency Oxfam and numerous others who are not properly disciplined; and the fact that Nicaragua's net increase in Gross Domestic Product "for 1980–1985 was 4.4 percent, almost double the rate of increase of the Latin American GDP as a whole" and well beyond that of any other country in Latin America. We must ignore or disparage the welfare programs, and the substantial increase in capital investment in agriculture, which threatened to allow Nicaragua to become self-sufficient in food while during the same years (early 80s), capital investment in agriculture dropped elsewhere in Central

America, by 57% in Guatemala and 73% in Costa Rica. It would also be inappropriate to consider the figures on export production, increasing by over 11% in Nicaragua from 1979 through 1985 (while the value of these exports declined by almost 25% because of deterioration in terms of trade), in contrast to a 19% decline elsewhere in Central America. We must ignore the general economic crisis throughout Latin America, particularly severe in Central America, or the conclusion of Enrique Bolanos, chairman of the Council of Private Enterprise in Nicaragua and a leading opponent of the Sandinistas (hence a leading democrat in the U.S.), who attributes the economic crisis in Nicaragua to the war (60%), the international economic crisis (10%), the contraction of the Central American Common Market (10%), and decapitalization by the business sector and government errors (20%).

It is also important to forget that the unacceptable achievements after the overthrow of the U.S. backed Somoza regime took place against the background of the devastation it had left, and the final robbery of what remained, leaving the country in such a state that an October, 1980 World Bank mission estimated that "per capita income levels of 1977 will not be attained, in the best of circumstances, until the late 1980s." The actual circumstances were the escalating U.S. war against Nicaragua, requiring mobilization of population and resources at a level that would be unbearable even in a wealthy and well-functioning economy.

All other factors notwithstanding, the problems in Nicaragua must be the responsibility of the official enemy, and nothing more need be said to prove the point. The problems in neighboring countries enjoying bountiful U.S. aid rarely reach the threshold of attention and elicit no impassioned condemnation.

To maintain strict discipline on these matters is no easy task, one of the ancillary ideological problems of clandestine terrorism. But it must be done, and one will find few departures from the doctrinal requirements of the terrorist state.

Closer examination of the charges of Sandinista Marxist Leninist dogmatism and its catastrophic effects helps illuminate the culture of terrorism from another standpoint. The *Wall St. Journal* headlines an article by Clifford Krauss: "Nicaragua is Getting Little Foreign Aid in Righting Economic Mess it Created." Krauss concedes that the war may have "strained" the government budget, but dismisses the effects of the trade embargo and other U.S. measures, though these have plainly been severe in blocking natural markets and sources of supply, even spare parts, and forcing Nicaragua to rely on the Soviet Union in accordance with Reagan administration imperatives. The real problem, he insists, is the "counter-productive government pricing policies," which lead to such "market absurdities" as an artificially low price for bananas, part of the effort to ensure that the urban poor will have access to food. Assume the criticism to be valid. One will search in vain, however, for derisive articles on the pricing policies based on market realities in U.S. domains, for example, Honduras, which exports crops while much of the population literally starves to death. These are simply the natural workings of the market, meriting only approbation for the rational policies that happen to benefit U.S. corporations and their local associates, if not the Honduran peasant.

Condemnation of the Sandinistas for the economic failures resulting from "Marxist-Leninist dogmatism" must also refrain from any comparison with the world's richest and most powerful state, where the brilliant economic management of the Reaganites, largely reflecting an elite consensus, is reviewed in an October, 1986 report of the U.S. Department of Commerce that describes how, "in a few short years, a wealthy creditor nation has become the number one debtor" as "the United States has largely lost its ability to compete successfully in international trade." "The United States required nearly 70 years to attain a creditor position of $150 billion, reached in 1982. As of now, the debtor status is about $250 billion. Some analysts project that the debtor position could approach or exceed $800 billion by 1990." That would constitute a shift of close to a trillion dollars within a decade in the relations of the world-dominant power to its rivals, a remarkable and unprecedented phenomenon in world affairs. The International Monetary Fund warns that the main danger to the world economy "lies in thc huge US budget and trade deficits," which it considers "unsustainable" for the world's economy. Plainly these achievements, only a part of the dismal Reaganite heritage, offer us a proper platform for contemptuous denunciation of the failings of the Sandinistas, in their far more favorable circumstances.

In extenuation of the Reaganite economic managers, one might argue that they have, after all, been dedicated to reducing the gap, or chasm, in living standards that separates the United States from the suffering people of the Third World. Thus we read that "Third world conditions have reached the Middle West," where "We're starting to see goiters and abscessed baby teeth in farm children, which indicates they are not getting adequate nutrition." "Hunger and malnutrition are a new phenomenon among Kansas farm families, experts say," a phenomenon of the 1980s, though not a new phenomenon among the urban power or elsewhere, conditions that have notably worsened during the Reagan years. "Ironically, experts explain, farmers today are suffering more than in the Great Depression" because of "modern practices aimed at increasing efficiency," so that farmers buy their food at supermarkets while producing corn, sorghum and wheat for sale.

We might also take note of another and rather more serious debt crisis, namely, in the Third World. Since 1981, Third World countries have become net capital exporters as debt servicing exceeds new borrowing to which we must add profit repatriations by transnational corporations and massive capital flight, which in Latin America approaches the scale of the debt itself. With non-oil commodity prices declining and the capital outflow rapidly increasing, there is "a historically unprecedented transfer of resources from the poor to the rich countries," a recent analysis observes. This transfer of resources with the predictable human consequences is not regarded by elite opinion as a problem, though inability to pay the banks is a different matter.

The covert activities of the Reagan administration in violation of public opinion and congressional dictates were well-known all along. "Journalists in Central America knew long ago that somebody was flying supplies to the Contras inside Nicaragua," the right-wing correspondent of the London Spectator pointed out after the "scandals" had erupted. "Captain Ricardo Wheelock, the head of the Sandinista military intelligence, was even able to give us fairly precise details of these flights, but nobody bothered to chase the story until Eugene Hasenfus was shot down and captured" in October, 1986. Similarly, reporters failed to follow many leads indicating that "Oliver North was running the Contra operation from his office at the National Security Council." North's role was of course known, and suppressed. Over a year before the scandals broke, the *New York Times* reported that the contras were "receiving direct military advice from White House officials" in an operation run by a military officer on the National Security Council staff who "briefs President Reagan," namely Oliver North, whose name they suppressed for fear of endangering his life, according to the editors. Shortly after, Reagan held a press conference in which the Washington press corps, which has concocted for itself a self-congratulatory image of aggressiveness that is generally laughable, raised 26 questions on 15 different subjects, asking nothing about these reports, which were of no interest because the operations only endanger the lives of people who deserve to suffer for their sins.

It was also apparent that the contras were receiving arms from U.S. clients such as El Salvador, Honduras, and Israel, meaning that in effect they were receiving arms from the United States in violation of congressional directives. Well before the "scandals" had erupted, CIA involvement in contra aid in violation of congressional restrictions was revealed to be at a level that "may astound even the most jaded observer,"

Congressman Sam Gejdenson commented, including funding of military operations and bribing of Honduran and Costa Rican officials. The disclosures attracted little notice.

In general, the facts were known, but suppressible. The same was true of the disclosures concerning Iran, to which we return. In fact, the only really novel insight produced in the 1986-87 exposures is that these two clandestine operations were linked, although the scale and sophistication of the international terrorist network constructed during the Reagan years was not known in detail and is of no little interest. The same was true of the "secret wars" in Laos and Cambodia, known to the media throughout, but suppressible.

Furthermore, it was entirely obvious, even without direct information, that a lawless administration would simply find other ways to pursue its goals if Congress were to bar direct takeover of the war. This is surely understood by the media and Congress as well as it is by the terrorist commanders supported under the Reagan Doctrine, for example, Jonas Savimbi, who remarked to journalists in 1982 that "A great country like the U.S. has other channels. The Clark Amendment barring aid to Savimbi's UNITA means nothing." Those unable to draw the conclusion for themselves could turn to Reagan administration sources for enlightenment. Thus in a front-page story of March 9, 1986, the *Miami Herald* outlined Reagan's request to Congress for aid to the contra armies, quoting its crucial paragraph authorizing the CIA and any other "department or agency in the executive branch" to take over the war effort. "Officials said that if Congress rejects the package, then Reagan may feel free to use other measures to contain Nicaragua" the latter phrase serving as one of the euphemisms for international terrorism. When the "scandals" could no longer be suppressed, the press quoted officials who supervised the secret war as saying that "legality was viewed as an obstacle that had to be gotten around. That was the spirit of the program," then commenting that "the real wonder is that Congress, the Reagan administration and the public took so long to become concerned about the questionable activities and possible violations of law in contra funding that have been evident for several years." A more pertinent question, unasked, is why it took the press so long to report what it had long known. There were numerous other indications of the obvious, but it was more convenient to disregard them, in the usual style of subordination to power.

The supply flights to the contras and other evidence ignored by the media were, of course, known to U.S. intelligence, hence to State Department intelligence; even if the flights had not been arranged by U.S. agencies, it is difficult to imagine that U.S. intelligence is so incompetent that it was unable to detect flights from U.S. supervised military air bases in El Salvador and Honduras to Nicaragua, which is probably under more intense aerial surveillance than any other place in the world, or to learn what was familiar fare to journalists in Managua. All of this was therefore surely known to Elliott Abrams and George Shultz. Their professions of ignorance and the perfunctory inquiry into these matters at the Iran-contra hearings merit no comment, nor need we tarry over "the refreshingly blunt candor of Secretary of State George Shultz, battling for his honor" at the hearings, which so impressed Congress and the media.

But it proved impossible to maintain secrecy after the downing of the contra supply plane in Nicaragua and the revelation by a Beirut journal and by the Iranians of the visit to Teheran by former national security adviser Robert McFarlane. The partial unravelling of the complex web of deceit from October, 1986 became a severe embarrassment to the terrorist commanders in Washington, who were forced to pretend that they knew nothing of the programs carried out under their general orders. These exposures might serve to limit their capacity to conduct the programs of international terrorism to which they are dedicated, at least temporarily.

❐❐❐

7

Racial Terrorism in South Africa

Introduction

Each trade agreement, each bank loan, each new investment is another brick in the wall of our continued existence.

J.B. Vorster, former Prime Minister of South Africa

And what if the Church and the State is the mob that howls at the door?

W.B. Yeats

In the context of the ongoing political violence in South Africa, the nature of the struggle is transformed to fit one of two varieties of the dominant ideology. In the view of the state and those who support it internationally, the violence of resisters is labelled terrorism. In the view of reformers, the regime (as well as the violence of resistance) is condemned. Neither of these addresses the global foundations of *apartheid*. As with other forms of settler terrorism, the roots of S.A. racial separatism are to be found in the historical relations of colonialism; relations that have changed more in form than in substance since the

Dutch established a European outpost in the mid-seventeenth century. The point of departure for this inquiry will be U.S. relations with South Africa in the 1980s. But as always, the forces at play transcend the policies of a particular administration. In this sense, the modern exemplars who speak are locked in the transcendental and dialectical relations of conflict.

The Red Scare in Black Africa

U.S. policy on southern Africa has been driven materially by the forces of capital accumulation (that have taken specific form in South Africa as shall be demonstrated) and ideologically by fervent anti-communism. Alexander Haig, a former officer with general rank, who had served in the Nixon administration before becoming the president and chief executive officer of the United Technologies Corporation, testified before the House of Representatives early in the decade. Citing the importance of South African minerals and the escalation of "Soviet proxy activity in the third world," he argued that "the era of the resource war has arrived". Assistant Secretary of State (for African Affairs) Chester Crocker, in an address to the American Legion in Honolulu on August 29, 1981, had already offered an elaboration of this thesis. He began by noting that U.S. economic interests in that portion of the African continent below the Sahara are heavily concentrated in the south.

This concentration of our interests reflects southern Africa's tremendous mineral wealth and the relative sophistication of the area's economies especially those of South Africa and Zimbabwe. Southern Africa accounts for over 40 percent of sub-Saharan Africa's GNP, 70 percent of its industrial and 60 percent of its mining output, 80 percent of its steel and 85 percent of electricity consumed. The area contains immense deposits of many strategic minerals which are vital to industrial economies like ours.

The specifics of the "economic and national security interests" argument will be addressed in due course. However, from an African perspective, such positions embody the legitimations of imperialism. The concept of a "resource war" between superpowers and their partners bypasses the question of just who it is that resources belong to. When a dominant state enters the global arena on the grounds of what's good for its own economic investment or its own strategic interests, the legitimate rights of indigenous people become secondary. The selective view is that what's good for the interests of dominant states is good for the world. The structural position of less powerful resource states insures an opposing conception.

Crocker also reiterated Haig's insistence on viewing southern Africa as a "contested area" with the U.S.S.R. and its allies seen as major threats in the region. This is a restatement of a longstanding view in the United States (a view that became perhaps more pronounced under the Reagan administration) that the black opposition to white supremacist rule in the Republic of South Africa and Namibia (the colonial name of which is South-West Africa) could be attributed to external Communist intervention.

Faced with large-scale foreign intervention, the pressure of African guerrilla groups, and strains in its relations with its traditional Western partners, South Africa has significantly expanded its defense potential in recent years. The republic, through a sustained self-sufficiency drive, is now an important regional military power. It has clearly signalled its determination to resist guerilla encroachments and strike at countries giving sanctuary.

Once again, a consideration of political language is instructive. Here, the South African military escalation is described in terms of "defense potential" and its political system becomes a "republic." (The country is officially the Republic of South Africa.) If one conventionally defines republic as a state in which the electorate rules directly or indirectly through elected representatives, the problem with the South African republic is that it denies full electoral standing to non-whites. It is by definition a racist republic. Nevertheless, the term republic is a legitimating one that gives credibility to the South African government every time it is used.

Further, Crocker described South African border-crossings into neighboring states as strikes at "sanctuaries" for guerrillas. The guerrillas were in turn defined as allies of the Warsaw pact. This tendency to view the forces of change as/the problem, and the forces of the existing order as defensive has the unsettling effect of placing the United States, its allies, and the international order they represent, on the side of white supremacist rule. In its zeal to identify and oppose the ubiquitous Communist threat, U.S. policy in southern Africa has historically contradicted its own stated purposes and participated dialectically in the ongoing negation, not only of apartheid, but the larger forces that sustain it. For if the system of white supremacist economic and political rule in South Africa is "anti-Communist" and the lead anti-apartheid forces are Soviet proxies, what conclusion is to be drawn by the people of southern Africa, the continent, and the Third World? Once again, it is anti-communism in its material and ideological forms, that helps to build the anticapitalist formations of African socialism as alternatives to modern settler rule.

The U.S. obsession with terrorism in the 1980s was easily transposed to the South African revolutionary context. On this point, in a series of hearings before the Senate Subcommittee on Security and Terrorism, the thesis was developed that the Soviet Union, East Germany, and Cuba were responsible for the "fomenting of terrorism in southern Africa." In the words of that sub-committee's chair, these states "actively and often successfully seek, under the overall control of the Politburo in Moscow, to utilize, infiltrate, and manipulate so-called 'national liberation movements' around the world". From this viewpoint, the Senate sub-committee conceived of terrorism as a political instrument used to reach the alleged goal of "Communist world domination." Specifically, the African National Congress and the South-West African People's Organization, who have resorted to armed struggle, were (and continue to be) portrayed as exponents of Soviet interests.

Such allegations require an inquiry into the history of the resistance movement in southern Africa, and this will follow in due course. However, it is noteworthy that the Senate Sub-committee on Security and Terrorism did not entertain evidence and testimony on the political, economic and social structures of racial domination in southern Africa. This tends to again build the ideological monopoly on terrorism in the United States, marked by a selective perception of only those violent acts that threaten Western states or their allies. Consequently, the role of the West (from its colonial empires to its modern corporations and system of world-market trade) in erecting and supporting the continuing structures of white supremacist rule in South Africa can only be ignored.

The South African National Emergency State

In the late 1980s, the state security system of the R.S.A. remained in the hands of the military and a nationalized police force under the Department of National Security. More specifically, its structure resembled "a military dominated system of secret committees responsible for coordinating the activities of the South African Defence Force (SADF), police intelligence, secret security agencies and other governmental departments.". More formally, this network was known as the National Security Management System (NSMS), established in 1979 to develop a "total strategy" to control and negate the anti-apartheid movement. At the pinnacle of the NSMS stood the State Security Council where the harsh 1985 and 1986 states of emergency appear to have been ordered. Headed by a former head of Military Intelligence, the State Security Council came to effectively supplant the South African cabinet. Under the direct control of the prime minister, the SSC provided the means to take expedient action in the name of national preservation. At a lower, but still national level, it presided over 13 inter-departmental committees.

At the regional level in the late 1980s, the structure of the National Security Management System featured at least ten Joint Management Centres that corresponded with the military command districts into which South African territory is divided. At the grassroots level some 500 local committees were charged to gather intelligence and forward it up the chain of command. Whatever the level, the "total strategy" was to maintain the social, economic, and political institutions of apartheid by breaking the opposition. In August 1986, the Joint Management Centre in Johannesberg sought to end the non-violent resistance of a rent boycott in the townships of the Vaal Triangle. Tactics included the formation of collection action groups, the eviction of tenants, the use of computers to store intelligence information, and the recruitment of the young to reeducation camps where they would be taught to convince their parents to pay rent. The legions of young "detainees" held under the increasingly permanent state of emergency were offered early release contingent upon their agreeing to attend two-week crash courses in political indoctrination.

In the recent history of South Africa, recent emergency restrictions have legitimated the often unrestrained employment of the police power of the state. The South African Police (SAP), the municipal police, the South African Defence Forces, and the homeland (Bantustan) police, aided by part-time Citizen Force army units, have constituted the official enforcement apparatus. The dominant strategy, in a country where whites constitute only one-seventh of the population, is to induce the victims of apartheid to cooperate with the white regime. Thus much of the less savory work of political repression has been carried out by police-recruited vigilantes whose tactics include arson and assassination. Black police have been recruited in increasing numbers, often from the desperately impoverished rural areas, to keep order in the townships. In November of 1986, the *Johannesburg Citizen* reported an announcement from the South African minister of law and order that thc police forces would increase from a level of 56,316 to 96,300. The rationale for the building of a modern police state, which survives in part through nurturing black on black violence, is familiar. The minister of law and order cited the need for maximizing the "ability to control terrorism".

It is clear that the organization of the South African national emergency state raises the question of institutional domination through fear. It is important to remember that the assault is more than the denial of abstract rights; it is more than a case of violation of international law. Certainly laws and rights are involved, but the real terrorism of apartheid has broken bodies as well as statutes and crushes the spirit as well as the ballot box. Under the national security state, police powers are unrestrained resulting in wholesale detention of those suspected of sympathies toward the anti-apartheid movement. In too many instances, detention has meant the brutality of torture.

Over 90 percent of 40 released detainees who were examined by physicians reported details of being hit with a rifle butt, beaten with a whip or heavy stick, or being punched, kicked or slapped. A quarter complained of being stripped and suffering assault to their sexual organs. Eight of the forty former detainees said they were given electric shocks and three that they had a canvas bag or hood pulled over their heads during interrogation.

Apartheid adds literal meaning to the phrase "suffer the children." According to estimates by the opposition Progressive Federal Party of South Africa, the state of emergency that commenced in June of 1986, had resulted by early winter of 1987 in the detention of some 25,000 persons. According to the Detainees' Parents Support Committee that mounted a "free the children campaign," some 10,000 of these detaines were under the age of 18.

Most were in their teens, but a number of ten-year-olds were included. As most of these children were not formally charged, it can be concluded that the random detention of children was designed to provide a lesson in terror. They were held in cells, often overcrowded, cold, and filthy. The allegations of physical torture were commonplace, and the experience of being caged apart from familial and community support represents a clear form of psychological coercion.

Regional Domination

But the terrorism of apartheid is not confined to the internal level. In southern Africa, a wave of national liberation intensifying in the 1970s saw the coming of African rule in Zimbabwe (formally Rhodesia), Mozambique, and Angola, ending the vestiges of settler colonialism in the region. Although the new states represented no direct military threat to the South African regime, they declared early on their solidarity with (while providing some support and sanctuary for) the national liberation forces who have restored to armed struggle against the apartheid regime. Under enormous pressure from the South African military and RSA supported counter-revolutionary forces, these states were forced to enter into agreements with the RSA that have limited their support of the African National Congress (ANC) and the Namibia-based South-West Africa People's Organization (SWAPO).

Perhaps of greater long-term significance, nine states of southern Africa formed the Southern African Development Coordination Conference in an attempt to challenge South African economic domination in the region. In response to the growing threat, South African military spending reached the level of 4 billion rand in the mid-1980s (from 44 million in 1960). According to the United Nations Centre Against

Apartheid, South Africa's fight to maintain white supremacy has featured "direct military invasion and incursions, the use of mercenaries and groups of nationals hostile to the governments of independent states, economic sabotage and pressure, the assassination of individuals, virulent propaganda and, in general, attempts at political and economic destabilisation. These methods have been used in different combinations and to differing degrees against all the African countries that border on South Africa or South African-occupied Namibia". For example, South Africa conducted a massive invasion of Angola in 1981, ostensibly to strike at SWAPO. According to the United Nations Security Council and the U.N.'s International Court of Justice, the South African occupation of Namibia is itself illegal, thus an act of aggression against Angola in the name of the defense of Namibia was, clearly without merit.

South Africa legitimates its war against the ANC as a war against terrorism. This version of history, which renders the apartheid system a victim instead of a perpetrator, found support in the policy of the United States during the 1980s. (As demonstrated earlier, the Reagan administration waged both an ideological and a shooting war against international terrorism, making this the cornerstone of its foreign policy.) Candidate Reagan, prior to his first election, described not only the ANC, but SWAPO of Namibia, and Z.A.N.U. and Z.A.P.U. of Zimbabwe as terrorist organizations. These are mentioned because they are from southern Africa, but the U.S. constructed list of terrorists has been a lengthy one.

It is now true that the ANC in South Africa and SWAPO in Namibia carry on armed struggle. Yet the African National Congress, formed in 1912, is the most senior liberation movement in Africa. And prior to the 1960 massacres at Sharpeville and Langa, it had adopted a position first of negotiating with the white South African government, and then a strategy of nonviolent civil disobedience. Since its founding in 1960, the South-West African People's Organization has opposed the occupation and domination of

Namibia by South Africa. It is recognized by the United Nations as the sole, legitimate representative of the Namibian people. And of course, it was the armed struggle of the Zimbabwe African National Union (Z.A.N.U.) and the Zimbabwe African People's Union (Z.A.P.U.) that brought an end to white rule in what the colonizers called Rhodesia. The Z.A.N.U. Patriotic Front became the ruling party in Zimbabwe with its independence in 1980.

The international community (with the notable exception of some Western states such as the United States and Great Britain) has chosen to focus on the illegitimacy of the apartheid regime, instead of the allegations of terrorism directed toward the African National Conference. It should be understood that South African apartheid, and the institutional structure it symbolizes, stands against the flow of African history. With the coming of continental decolonization, the late twentieth-century white supremacist state stood as an historical anachronism. Given the sounding of the political voices of newly independent states in the international arena, apartheid came to be conceived of as a crime against humanity. This is evidenced in the International Convention on the Suppression and Punishment of the Crime of Apartheid of 1973, and in the declaration by the U.N. General Assembly that the "racist regime of South Africa is illegitimate and has no right to represent the people of South Africa." The General Assembly did more than condemn apartheid. It also declared the "legitimacy of the struggle of the oppressed people of South Africa and their liberation movements" to be considered the "authentic representative of the overwhelming majority of the South African people".

The point is that these movements were and are considered legitimate forces of resistance, certainly by the natives of sub-Saharan Africa. However, they did not conform to the political vision advanced by the U.S. administration in the 1980s. This policy, pleasantly termed "constructive engagement' by its architects, called for the United States to maintain friendly (diplomatic and commercial) relations with the R.S.A. Thus, with the heavy pattern of total investment maintained, it would be possible to influence the peaceful transition from apartheid. In the process, Western-style institutions could be retained, and the role of South Africa in the global market system preserved. This is the crux of a beguilingly palatable conception of social reform in South Africa. It is not merely the resort to armed struggle that is found objectionable, though the hope to improve non-violent methods of conflict resolution is a laudable one. It is the fear that armed struggle may produce new institutions that prove to be independent of undue influence from the Western world.

In assessing the stated objectives of constructive engagement, it is clear that the commitment to "peaceful change" in South Africa was not extended to other regions. Such a critique should not be confined to current events involving the United States. This nation-state was founded in a war of colonial secession. Its expansion came primarily at the expense of the indigenous peoples of North America. Since 1776, the United States has fought eight wars (some undeclared) against foreign powers; a civil war; a century of intermittent conflicts with its natives; and it has intervened repeatedly in Central America, the Caribbean, the Mediterranean, the Western Pacific, and the Persion Gulf. The size of the U.S. nuclear arsenal and its version of the modern warfare state were discussed earlier, as was the militarization of space. One may question whether these are the historical and political credentials of non-violence. This history of armed intervention notwithstanding, the Congress of the United States chose to include language associating the African National Congress with terrorism in its Comprehensive Anti-Apartheid Act passed in October of 1986.

R.S.A. Institutional Terror

The recurring argument then, is the continued predominance of a double standard of terrorism, better fitted for ideological warfare than analysis. The official story denies, ignores, or falsifies the global nature of that form of institutional terrorism embodied in South African internal and international relations. To wit, as of the mid-1980s, South Africa's infant mortality rate was 12 per thousand for the white population, compared with 69 per thousand for urban Africans, and 282 per thousand for rural Africans. The black South African death rate due to malnutrition was estimated at 96 per day, and its rate of illiteracy was 50 percent. The economic terror of apartheid continues to be evidenced in a record of virtually no gains for the African majority after a century of Western-style industrial development.

R.S.A. regime terror is reflected in the industrial world's highest rates of prison population and state execution. It is evidenced in mass detentions, numbering 35,000 in 1984 alone. It is poignantly and personally recorded in the death in 1977 of Black Consciousness leader Steve Biko, who became the forty-fifth known black activist to die in police custody and in the 1964 Rivonia trial where Nelson Mandela and seven other leaders of the ANC were sentenced to life imprisonment. It is etched in the 1960 massacres at Sharpeville and Langa where police fired on unarmed demonstrators killing 67, wounding 186, including many women and children and many shot in the back. It is founded in the Soweto rebellion of 1976, which took 575 lives, and resulted in the wounding of almost 4,000 persons and the arrest of 6,000 more. (The Soweto rising was sparked by police firing on Soweto schoolchildren protesting an education bent on the maintenance of structural inequality.) The historical reliance by this state on deadly force and massive structures of "internal security" to control its own population continue to falsify its claim to legitimacy.

Internal Colonialism

Descriptive accounts of state terrorism, however graphic, only serve to raise the level of abstraction. The emergence, institutionalization, and maintenance of white rule in South Africa is a chapter in the larger history of European conquest. This particular story began in 1652 with the establishment of a colony in Cape Town by the Dutch East India Company. These early colonists brought in slaves from the Dutch East Indies and other parts of Africa, in order to augment thc indigenous labor force made up of the San (Bushmen) and Khoikhoi (Hot-tentot) tribes. Early in the eighteenth century, many of the Dutch, German, and French Huguenot colonists began the "trekking" movement into the north and east. The colonists were known as Boers (Dutch for farmers) and as they sought land they clashed with African Bantu-speaking tribes, which were well-organized and difficult to subdue.

Settler Isolation and the Ideology of the "Chosen"

As the settlers moved inland, they became geographically estranged from the Cape Town colony, and in that context of economic conflict and isolation, began to develop the specific institutional and cultural structures of separatism. On the productive side, the trekkers developed a subsistence-based agricultural economy. Culturally, they took the name *Afrikaner,* which literally means "African," thus asuming a symbolic identity. This identity signalled both a break with Europe, as well as a claim to authentic native standing. However, through adopting the name Afrikaner, the trekkers symbolically transformed the original inhabitants into aliens in their own land. Further marking their geographical and growing cultural isolation, the Boers developed a language called Afrikaans, which became increasingly removed from the original Dutch. But it was on the ideological side that the Afrikaners developed the clearest manifestation of their separatism, thus establishing support for the more sophisticated institutions of racial domination that emerged later.

The trekkers found in the dogma of sixteenth-century Calvinism the legitimation of a chosen people called by God to transform and dominate a wilderness. Calvinism was a harsh protestantism, integrating predestination and total de-pravity. But it also offered the promise of irresistible grace and the certain preservation of the saints. For the early Boers, this faith represented more than a link to tradition. Calvinism was a set of core principles of faith, to which were added the more specific legitimations of racial supremacy. Correctly understood, Calvinism was filtered through the prism of settler life and refitted for the task of ideological domination. Thus, while Calvinism withered elsewhere, it flourished in South Africa. But as with other idea-systems of control, its religious content took political form.

Merged with racism, Calvinist predestination was to be transformed. Not confined to the matter of the elect and damned in the afterlife, it became instead a mandate to establish Afrikaner control of the native population and ultimately Afrikaner nationhood. Depravity became more than a general condition of wretched humanity. It was instead reinterpreted along racial and cultural lines to describe the subject population. And of course, *irresistible grace and the certain perseverance of the saints* conferred upon the Afrikaner a divine mission, well expressed in Psalm 105: "He brought forth his people with joy, and his chosen with gladness, and gave them the lands of the heathen, and they inherited the labor of the people."

But we need not rely on biblical passages or remain in earlier centuries to understand the imperial transformation of theology. D.F. Malan was a minister in the Dutch Reformed Church who became prime minister in 1948 when the Afrikaner Nationalist Party took power. These were his words:

> *It is through the will of God that the Afrikaner People exist at all. In his wisdom He determined that on the southern point of Africa, the dark continent, a People should be born who would be the bearer of Christian culture and civilization. In his wisdom, He surrounded this People by great dangers. He sent the People down upon unfruitful soil so that they had to toil and sweat to exist*

> *upon the soil. From time to time he visited them with droughts and other plagues. But this was only one of the problems. God also willed that the Afrikaans People should be continually threatened by other Peoples. There was the ferocious barbarian who resisted the intruding Christian civilization and caused the Afrikaner`s blood to flow in streams. There were times when as a result of this the Afrikaner was deeply despairing, but God at the same time prevented the swamping of young Afrikaner People in the sea of barbarism.*

Viewed through this particular permutation of settler dogma, the struggle for land, resources, rule, and cultural superiority became a holy war.

Ideological Permutations and Neo-Apartheid

The imploding contradictions of social relations in South Africa in the post-Sharpville era brought a state legitimation crisis. The institutions and ideology of racial domination were not only meeting better organized and mass-oriented internal resistance, the naked use of force increasingly branded the R.S.A. as an international pariah. Western claims that capitalism and authentic democracy were inextricably tied were being falsified beyond denial. U.N. resolutions of condemnation and the 1963 voluntary arms embargo were perhaps symbolic.

More substantive was the flight of foreign capital, and the archaic nature of the South African labor market. Apartheid was poised to assume a new political and ideological dress. Between 1960 and 1970, the ruling Afrikaner Nationalist Party put in place a policy of *separate development,* creating a homeland (bantustan) system for its "African Nations".

The historical consequences of this structure of divide and rule will be examined in due course. For now, it should be noted that the ideology of apartheid in the 1960s was transformed on two levels. First, its legitimation base was to replace God-ordained genetic superiority with new claims of cultural dissimilarity. It was not that God intended domination, but the differences in the customs and lifestyles of peoples that mandated separation. Second, the demand for democratization would be answered through fragmented "citizenship" in the new *tribal-states*. However, the retribalization policy was no more effective in addressing the archaic nature of the R.S.A. labor market than in meeting growing demands for self-determination. It remained rigid and fractured with the state attempting to regulate the flow of workers to mines, towns and farms. The opposing interests of the Afrikaner and British divisions of the R.S.A. white caste, embodied in state bureaucratic controls and patronage on the one side and major private sector domination on the other, will be explored in due course. But the need for skilled black labor, together with the unification of black resistance expressed in both nonviolent and violent forms, led to further permutations in the 1970s. Ideologically, these were expressed in the familiar language of reform, and politically in the form of more cosmetic alterations in petit apartheid. But this reformulation was to resemble more the modernization of apartheid than its negation.

Caste Capitalism

The conflict between Afrikaner and African is only one element of the complex history of South Africa. Perhaps 40 percent of the white population is descended not from the trekkers but from the British. In 1795, the British occupied the Cape as a means of strengthening their colonial possessions elsewhere in the continent. The occupation became permanent in 1806, and sovereignty followed in 1814. Dissatisfied with British rule (and especially afraid that British law would not sanction the slave labor on which the Boers depended), the settlers organized a mass exodus in 1836. The "Great Trek" saw the movement of some 10,000 persons 500 miles inland, where they were to encounter the Zulu nation. There, in December of 1838, they defeated these indigenous tribes people at the battle of Blood River. The trekkers then created independent republics known as the Transvaal and the Orange Free State but were driven out of Natal by the British in 1844. It was the discovery of diamonds and gold in the final three decades of the nineteenth century that signalled the beginning of the end for the independent Boer states.

Cecil Rhodes was at the forefront of the British move north, personifying a pattern of imperialism that, in concrete terms, brought miners, roads, railroads, and military force to southern Africa. Although the British had failed in an earlier attempt at intervention in the Transvaal, the second Anglo-Boer War (1899-1902) proved to be an all-out struggle for domination between the Afrikaners and their more powerful adversaries. The British responded to the Boer guerrilla tactics by torching farms and establishing a system of concentration camps in which 26,000 men, women, and children died. Such tactics brought an end to the war but the cause of Afrikaner nationalism now had its martyrs.

With British rule then assured, a typical pattern of advanced colonialism emerged. The British moved into urban centers, forming the economic apparatus necessary to exploit the land and resource wealth. Despite their position of economic advantage, the British settlers found their position a tenuous one. They were outnumbered by the embittered Afrikaners, and both divisions of the dominant white caste were aware of the threat to white rule represented by native Africans. Driven by a sense of the greater danger, the old European adversaries formed an antagonistic alliance, and the British government responded by recognizing the Union of South Africa in 1910. Comprised of the Transvaal, the Orange Free State, Natal, and the Cape, its all-white parliament was intended to insure that the means of state domination would remain in white hands. Thus there emerged a political alliance between the warring masters of South Africa.

In the first quarter of the twentieth century, the economic centrality of the British in the Union of South Africa was to insure that the Afrikaners lost more ground. With the development of industry, the poorly educated Boers were forced off the land and, without mastery of the English language, thrown into competition with blacks for jobs. They were the beneficiaries of government-sanctioned discrimination, but the once proud trekkers found themselves looking up at the British owners, and living in the growing urban slums. In the meantime, those remaining on their farms were losing much of their black labor to the mines. In response to this growing marginality, there emerged the political arm of the Afrikaner the National Party. Founded by the Boer general J.B.M. Hertzog in 1914, the party came to power first in 1924. But its intensive nationalism had yet to mature.

By the 1930s, the Afrikaner Broederbond ("band of brothers") was becoming a powerful political force. Working underground, it began to recruit not only the disgruntled farmers but the teachers and ministers who would be in a position to promote the new ideology called apartheid. That ideology had been formally developed at the seminary at Stellenbosh, near the Cape of Good Hope, by Boers who had not joined the Great Trek of a century before. Now, aided by the Dutch Reformed Church (which was determined to keep alive the theology and dogma of "chosenness"), apartheid became a purified nationalism founded in religious zeal. However, the new ideal of separation was to become more than an article of faith. In 1938, the Broederbond led a reenactment of the Great Trek of 1836. On a hill outside Pretoria, 100,000 people gathered to demand a monument.

The Voertrekker Monument stands today, a ring of wagons carved in stone. Yet the ideology of apartheid, drawn curiously from the well-springs of a people both despised and despising, dominated and dominating, was to be etched in something other than a monument of stone. When institutionalized, this idea-system came to mean both the state preservation of white supremacy and the repudiation of British imperialism. These dreams of grandeur were only temporarily interrupted by the Second World War. South Africa entered the conflict on the side of the Allies, but that move was bitterly opposed by the Afrikaner nationalists. In the words of Kevin Danaher:

> *Opposed to humanist notions of the state as a device created by humans for their own use, Afrikaner Calvinism viewed the state's monopoly of force and authority over the individual as a divine gift. The emphasis was on discipline and obedience to this higher authority. The parallels to Nazism in Germany and fascism in Italy were direct and explicit.*

It is unnecessary to rely on ideological similarities in the credos of the nation-race that emerged in Nazi Germany and in South Africa. The extremist New Order and Ossewabrandwag factions sought to block South Africa's joining of the allied cause by dynamiting railroads, communications facilities, and some civilian targets. They also engaged in armed assault on the police and military (Bunting, 1964). A commandant of the Ossewabrandwag was B.J. Vorster who declared in 1942 that the National party stood for "Christian Nationalism," which was "an ally of Nazism". Dr. H.F. Verwoerd, a graduate of Stellenbosch, as a wartime editor supported nazism. Both Verwoerd and Vorster, ideological allies of fascism during the war, were later to serve as prime ministers of South Africa under the reign of the National party. But it was to be Hendrik Verwoerd who, as minister of native affairs under the government of D.F. Malan, became responsible for translating the ideology of apartheid into law.

When the National party unified the Afrikaners to win the elections of 1948, the Malan regime moved quickly to use the power of the state to compensate for the economic disadvantage of the lower white caste. This meant that Afrikaners were to be supported in the labor market, with preferential treatment accorded them in both the public and private sectors of the economy. This included, but went beyond, the establishment of state corporations that provided management and employment opportunities for the Afrikaner. Before 1948, some 30 percent of the South African white-collar workforce were Afrikaner. By 1970, that percentage had doubled.

The position of advantage in the labor market did not come at the expense of the British South Africans who were entrenched at the top of industry and commerce. It was paid for instead by the non-white majority, whose position of subordination was further insured by a set of laws establishing the practices of "petit apartheid." Such laws mandated registration by race to insure 'apartness' in the future, and a reconstruction of institutions and living patterns to end the minimal sorts of racial integration that had occurred. Schools, families, unions, political parties, hospitals, neighborhoods all came to embody in material form the ideology of apartheid.

Reference was made earlier to the establishment of a "homelands" policy in the 1960s, the cornerstone of the N.P.'s system of "grand apartheid." Only the R.S.A. recognized some of these "mini-reserves" as independent states. The Bantustans held only 13 percent of the land and were strangely lacking in the lush topsoil and rich mineral reserves South Africa is noted for. In the period between 1960 and 1980, some 3.5 million Africans were forcibly resettled to the reserves. This massive population transfer is best understood as a grand design of labor control, founded in the premise of divide and rule. It makes manifest in stark geographical terms the formation of a cheap labor reserve, while continuing to offer white dominated capitalism the advantage of black disadvantage.

The internal colonialism of these bantustans is best illustrated by the organisation of their economies. In the case of Kwazulu, Ciskei, Bophuthatswana and Lebowa, they are areas which provide cheap and available labour for white industries and domestic service "bussed" to and from their houses by excessively long bus and train journeys up to

140 km each day. For the mines, the immoral system of migrant labour continues, whereby men working on contracts of up to three years are housed in all male compounds. Notwithstanding the abolition of the notorious Pass Laws in 1986 under which up to a quarter of a million Africans were arrested each year, influx control under more sophisticated arrangements ensures that the families of these migrant labourers cannot legally join these male workers.

It is the economic centrality of black labor and the emergence of apartheid as a system of labor discrimination that is at issue in South Africa. This conception includes, but is not restricted to, the point that Afrikaners have compensated through the power of the state for much of their historical economic disadvantage. Nor is it sufficient to argue that the power of the state has denied the black worker "equal opportunity" in the labor market. The Western tendency to see apartheid as only a political problem ignores the broader societal and global forces at play. This is to say that much of the opposition to apartheid in the West is a narrow and selective opposition to the naked racism expressed in both ideology and law. The critique is narrowly focused on the contractual unfairness of this system, marked by the absence of legal entitlements, including the vote. In effect, the Western complaint detaches polity from the base of class relations. However, as the Afrikaners have used their majority to compensate in part for their economic disadvantage vis a vis the British, they are well aware of the power of the state, including the potential to nationalize industries.

It was perhaps with a view toward centralizing power, while offering token representation to potential junior partners in privilege, that a constitutional reform plan was approved by the South African electorate in 1983. This established separate parliamentary chambers for "coloured" and "Indian" segments of the population. However, in the main these chambers legislate separately on the group affairs and have little support from those they are supposed to represent. More important, the new governmental structure served to consolidate the power of the chief executive, now termed the president. This centralization appears to fit well the needs of the S.A. National Emergency State.

Most of the South African symbolic reforms in the 1980s, pushed by the regime headed by Pieter W. Botha, came on the fringes of apartheid in response to fierce black resistance and mounting international pressure. The focus of political change was at the level of petit apartheid under which black trade unions acquired legal standing and the bans on interracial marriage, sporting events, parks and beaches, and other forms of de jure social segregation were lifted or modified. Given the need or skilled black labor, a relative few workers received more training. Such symbolic moves alienated the most reactionary elements of the National Party, and crystalized the opposition on the far right. However, more contemporary reforms must be understood structurally as attempts to make the systems of control more efficient, and as safety valve mechanisms intended to spare the real apartheid. The contradiction in South Africa is that political rights that confer the power of the state will not be peacefully surrendered unless and until new class formations of privilege coopt members of the lesser castes. Otherwise, the power of the state could too easily become a force for nationalization and distribution.

Apartheid is more than a system of racial domination and cultural imperialism; its pre-eminent function has been the control of the labor market. Indeed, the dependence of the white caste on native labor has been a constant in South African economic history. Continued growth and prosperity for labor-dependent sectors thus remains a consequence of relative share of the surplus value of non-white labor. Apartheid may then be shown to differ from earlier colonial patterns of domination, rooted in economic exploitation but expressed in race, in its embodiment in the power of the modern state. Certain of its more outrageous *social and cultural* elements (embodied in petit apartheid) are at least somewhat expendable. However, viewed holistically, the real apartheid is a caste/class system of internal colonialism fully integrated into a global market system. And as apartheid in South Africa both reflects and reproduces that global system, it may not be expected to yield to purely political and social reforms.

Global Apartheid

A more formal expression of the "official story" on the reform of apartheid is that South Africa's homelands (held on the basis of communal tenure) and the control on labor movement represent precapitalist formations. So argued, these are in a state of dysjunction with more contemporary, "rationally-developed" formations, to be spurred on by U.S. and Western assistance. Thus it can be held that to improve the human capital of the working masses is essential to an industrial society, and that improvements in the education, and training of that workforce, as well as growth in unions, and the concomitant growth of political consciousness all mean that irrational apartheid must give way; that a free market produces free people. While such factors may indeed precipitate new class formations, it is unlikely that S.A. caste capitalism can create new privileges and allegiances rapidly enough to negate their revolutionary (as opposed to accommodating) potential. As shown, South Africa's evolving formations of internal colonialism have functioned historically to reconcile the conflicting interests of the class divisions in the white caste. Further, to extend (or surrender) political emancipation to exploited non-whites is to invite the transformation of S.A. capitalism. With such in mind, it is time to raise the theoretical level.

An earlier reference was made to the Reagan administration's policy in southern Africa, formally termed "constructive engagement" by Chester Crocker. Crocker stated its premise succinctly in 1981 arguing that "with the right mix of aid, policy reform, and a strongly reinvigorated role for the private sector, African peoples will opt for the growth and freedom inherent in the free world's international economic system". The thesis is not a novel one. It is the ideological expression of global market imperatives that has historically legitimated (and in some ways driven) U.S. foreign policy in South Africa and elsewhere. Reduced to its essential premise, through multinational business as usual, growth and prosperity will ease the transition from apartheid and all South Africans will benefit. Viewed through an African prism, this may be the logical equivalent of the argument that what benefits the plantation benefits the slaves. However, the claim can be examined more specifically in history.

The base development of the South African economy has followed a distinctive pattern: a minority group of colonizers, both Afrikaner and British, expanded industrially through the domination of a cheap black labor force. This development has historically been facilitated and maintained through the active support of what Chester Crocker referred to as "the free world's international economic system." In point of fact, the Western world's economic system has been in South Africa for a long time, beginning with the ventures of the Dutch in 1652. This may appear to be a sufficient period in which to test the thesis that what's good for the free world's international economy is good for all South Africans. However, if one chooses to ignore most of the history of European conquest, this particular version of trickle down ideology still appears wanting. In the first three decades after World War II, while the R.S.A. gross domestic product increased by over 2,000 percent, little of this reached the black majority.

Based on often sketchy R.S.A. sources (which have often excluded routinely impoverished residents of the Bantustans from official statistics), some portrayal of wage differentials can be attempted. In private manufacturing and construction, the ratio of white to African wages between

1915 and 1982 reached its lowest point in 1944/45 and its high point in 1970 (6.0-1), before retreating to 4.4 in 1982. The pay of African miners, consigned to this most dangerous of occupations and continuing to live for the most part away from their families, improved in the wake of improving gold prices in the 1970s. However, S.A. sources projected the white to African wage ratio at 5.5:1 for 1982. Statistics are notoriously unreliable for agriculture, but some 25 percent of the African workforce were employed in this poorly paying sector in the early 1980s, receiving much of their compensation from payment in kind. Of course, wage analysis alone only obscures the real face of caste capitalism in the R. S.A. where African *ownership* is insignificant. Indeed, the control of African labor pre-supposed their movement (sanctioned in law by the Land Act of 1913) from their own small farms.

The claim of international trickle down can be juxtaposed with the counter argument of global apartheid. The thrust of this argument is with the role of the leading states of the world market system in the emergence, institutionalization, and maintenance of apartheid. The point of departure for modern S.A. Western-style development in the late nineteenth century was its mining industry. It was in fact engineers and managers from the United States who played major roles in the development of that industry. By the end of the century Americans ran approximately 50 percent of South Africa's mines, while American companies became the major source of mining equipment. And it was those who managed the mines, not the National party of the Afrikaners, who established the South African system of labor control. (As one critic was to observe later, "Apartheid has meant an extension to the manufacturing economy of the structure of the gold mining industry".

By the end of the nineteenth century, U.S. firms such as Singer Sewing Machine, Kidder, Peabody Co., Mobil, and General Electric were in South Africa. They were followed after the turn of the century by Ford and Kodak. U.S. companies played critical developmental roles in metals, the motor industry, agricultural equipment, and petrochemicals. Although interrupted from time to time, U.S. corporations have provided computers and other advanced technology which the S.A. police and military have employed in the automating of apartheid. Firms such as General Electric, Honeywell, and Allis-Chalmers assisted in the building of the nuclear industry in this nation, which is widely acknowledged to possess nuclear weapons. A national analysis is insufficient, of course. In 1985, West Germany and Japan along with the United States were S.A.'s leading trading partners. Another major player continues to be Great Britain, which under the Thatcher government steadfastly opposed and minimized economic sanctions against South Africa on the part of the Commonwealth (where on this issue the 48 former British colonies truly remain under the Union Jack). Western transnational corporations are responsible for about 90 percent of the trade in petroleum and petroleum products, a fact of vital importance for South Africa, which has no independent oil supply.

In the past decade, U.S. corporate ties to South Africa came to be the subject of a divestment movement in the United States. As the movement peaked in the mid-1980s, some universities, religious bodies, and branches of local and state government sold or were developing strategies to sell their stock in U.S. corporations dealing with Pretoria. By 1986, some 50 universities and colleges had divested completely and public employee funds had traded stock valued at 3.4 billion. Between January 1, 1986, and October of 1987, 96 U.S. firms severed their direct investment links to South Africa leaving a total of 167 companies so tied. Yet many of the firms who "quit" the country did so in name only. Some firms, like G.M. and I.B.M., sold their subsidiaries to South African groups, which continued to market and service their products. On October 22, 1987, the Investor Responsibility Research Center announced that the curtailment of U.S. investment in South Africa was of little consequence, because many U.S. corporations established licensing and other agreements with former subsidiaries. Thus the economy of South Africa continued to have virtually unrestricted access to U.S. products and technology.

Despite the false front, antiapartheid forces (including the African National Congress) continued to support the divestment movement in the United Sates. This contributed to the symbolic isolation of South Africa, to the provision of moral support for those risking their very lives, and to the raising of consciousness among non-South Africans about the global nature of apartheid. Perhaps it can be argued that the United States and other member states of the "free world international economy" were already isolated, at least in a moral sense because of the commercial support for apartheid. In late 1981, the U.N. General Assembly adopted by large majorities 16 resolutions in condemnation of apartheid, seeking help for its victims and calling for international pressure. The United States voted yes on 2 of the 16, no on 12 and abstained on 2.

There is evidence that Israel has also collaborated in the South African government's policy of regional destabilization. Faced with isolation, South Africa has sought to develop ARMSCOR, its government-owned company that produces and exports weapons. Israel worked openly with South Africa before the U.N. embargo of 1977, and since that time some South African arms look suspiciously like Israeli hardware. For example, the display unit of a computerized firing control system that controls the firing of as many as eight artillery pieces bears a startling resemblance to the Israeli David system. And the Skorpion antiship missile is identical to Israel's Gabriel missile. (Not only Israel, but South Korea and Taiwan appear to be collaborating with South African arms development.) Finally, the S.A. Cheetah fighter aircraft is an upgrade of the French Mirage 3E supplied in the mid-1960s.

The ties between Israel and South Africa are structural and historical. Both reflect the properties of garrison states marked by a blurring of the lines between civilian and military identity and rule, and the ready resort to armed force to control native populations. Former S.A. Prime Minister General J.C. Smuts was a fervent supporter of a separate Jewish state and had an Israeli kibbutz named after him. The name of D.F. Malan is inscribed in Israel's Golden Book of the Jews, and former chief of the Israeli Air Force General Weitzman declared that South African pilots virtually "laid the foundation" of the Israeli Air Force. In the early 1960s, the relationship chilled in the context of Israeli attempts to strengthen relations with African states. However, in the wake of the Arab-Israeli wars of 1967 and 1973, the continuing crisis of the Palestinian Arabs, and in response to initiatives led by Libya and the Organization of African Unity, Israel lost standing in Africa. Tel Aviv then moved to restore the relationship with the R.S.A. Diplomatic relations were elevated to the ambassadorial level in 1974 and Cape Town and Haifa were declared sister cities in 1975.

Conclusion

The first strategy of colonialism, external or internal, is divide and rule. South Africa's strategy of retribalization extends a patronage system to African petit officials who await the withering of apartheid. Some have denounced the design. After five years of independence, Prime Minister George Matanzima of Transkei declared that South Africa viewed the bantustan as a "labor reservoir". Of enduring significance for the factionalization of the resistance movement has been the role of the Zulu tribe, and its political arm, Inkatha. Led by Chief Gatsha Buthelezi of the Kwazulu Bantustan, Inkatha has historically sought co-existence with Pretoria and trumpeted the cause of change through greater foreign investment. Through 1987 and much of 1988, Inkatha and anti-apartheid forces led by the Congress of South African Trade Unions were locked in violent combat.

Official S.A. African surrogates have historically extended Pretoria's regime terror whether as members of the S.A. or the homeland police. Unofficial surrogates, clearly tied to the South African police, include the violent "vigilantes" used in one notorious instance to massively remove people from Crossroads, a black township. Under conditions of omnipresent fear and loathing in the 1980s, youthful resistance assumed a violent turn. Groups calling themselves simply "comrades" turned on collaborators and resorted from time to time to the trade-mark "necklace" execution by which a gasoline soaked tire was tied around the neck and ignited. Any authentic contribution of the comrades will be judged in their ability to retreat from a single-minded punishment of collaborators to form alternative structures of governance in the townships, and to inspire participation on the part of older Africans.

The unitary appeal of the African National Congress can be juxtaposed with the continuing fragmentation in some quarters of the resistance movement. Its original Freedom Charter was adopted in 1955 by 3,000 delegates from all walks of life who met at Kliptown, Johannesburg. In addition to the ANC, the South African Indian Congress, the Coloured People's Organization, the South African Congress of Trade Unions, and the Congress of Democrats participated. The charter and its later amplifications form an ideological link between liberation and a distinctive African socialism intent on economic justice. It is grounded in a condemnation of European colonialism, and the inclusion in the struggle of other ethnic minorities. The ANC charter establishes the premise of non-racial democracy; holding that South Africa belongs to all who live in it with black and white as equals. ANC ideology calls for an Assembly of the People to replace the S.A. parliament, local self-government, and the preservation of the authentic multi-ethnic culture of its diverse national groups.

On the productive side, the ANC has stood for the transfer of mineral wealth, banks, and monopoly industry to the ownership of the people as a whole. In addition to public ownership of the major means of production, ANC ideology has historically favored land reform, equality before the law, human rights (free speech, the right to assemble, to publish, to worship, and to educate) and employment rights (including equal pay for equal work for men and women of all races, unemployment compensation, and the right to form unions, to sick leave, and to maternity leave on full pay). Also embraced have been freedom of movement, decent housing, rent and price controls, and free medical care and hospitalization. On the international side, ANC ideology calls for negotiation to end disputes, and declares that "Democratic South Africa shall take its place as a member of the OAU and work to strengthen Pan-African unity in all fields. Our country will actively support national liberation movements of the peoples of the world against imperialism, colonialism and neo-colonialism".

It is clear that the ANC offers a clear repudiation, not merely of S.A. racial separation and domination but the global design of the apartheid system. Breaking free of the economic domination of the capitalist world market will be extraordinarily difficult and can advance only in stages. However, the authentic development of the devastated African continent is dependent on the establishment of new horizontal relations among its states, in concert with the progressive minimization of the vertical ties between periphery and core that strengthen dependency. A democratic South Africa, with its immense wealth and industrial base can become in the twenty-first century, an engine for new regional and (in concert with progressive sub-Saharan and North African states) a more encompassing continental development. And it is within this higher drama that S.A. state terrorism continues to be played out.

Bibliography

Alibek, K: Biohazard: the chilling true story of the largest covert biological weapons program in the world, told from the inside by the man who ran it. 1st ed. New York : Random House, 1999.

Arquilla, John. *The End of War as We Knew It? Insurgency, Counterinsurgency and Lessons from the Forgotten History of Early Terror Networks.* Third World Quarterly 28:369-386 2007.

Ball K: Biological warfare: what happens if we are attacked? Todays Surg Nurse. 1998 Nov-Dec;20(6):3-6.

Byrnes, Andrew (2002). Apocalyptic Visions and the Law: The Legacy of September 11 A professorial address by Andrew Byrnes at the ANU Law School for the Faculty's 'Inaugural and Valedictory Lecture Series', May 30, 2002.

Canetti-Nisim, Daphna. *Victimization from Terrorist Attacks: Randomness or Routine Activities?* Terrorism and Political Violence 18:485-501 Winter 2006.

Chemical agents. In PDR guide to biological and chemical warfare response. Edited by David W. Sifton and Gwynned L. Kelly. Montvale, N.J., Thomson/ Physicians' Desk Reference, c2002. p. 43-86.

Chemical warfare agents: toxicity at low levels. Satu M. Somani and James A. Romano, Jr., eds. Boca Raton, Fla., CRC Press, c2001. 447 p.

Denton Frank H., and Phillips Warren. "Some Patterns in

the History of Violence." Journal of Conflict Resolution 12 (March 1968): 182-95.

Desouza, Kevin C. and Hensgen, Tobin. *Connectivity among Terrorist Groups: A Two Models Business Maturity Approach.* Studies in Conflict & Terrorism 30:593-613 July 2007.

Effendi, Muhammad Yahya, ' "Pakistan Army Officer Corps: Values in Transition or the Erosion of a Value System"', Pakistan Army Journal (Vol. 34, No. 1, March 1993), pp. 45-58.

Farewell, Byron, Armies of the Raj: From the Mutiny to Independence, 1858-1947. New York: W.W. Norton, 1989.

Feierabend Ivo K., and Feierabend Rosaline L. "Aggressive Bebaviors Within Polities, 1948-1962: A Cross-National Study." Journal of Conflict Resolution 10 (1966): 249-71.

Gardam, Judith Gail (1993). *Non-combatant Immunity as a Norm of International Humanitarian,*Martinus Nijhoff ISBN 0792322452.

Griset, Pamala L. & Mahan, Sue (2003). *Terrorism in perspective*, SAGE, 2003, ISBN 0761924043, 9780761924043

Hutchison, Harold. *Avast! Hold and Deliver — the Modern Version of an Ancient Scourge: Piracy.* Soldier of Fortune 31:52+ August 2006.

Iraq's Deadliest Arms: Puzzles Breed Fears, William Broad and Judith Miller, The New York Times, 26 Feb., 1998, p. A1.

J. Bertranpetit and F. Calafell (1996). Genetic and geographical variability in cystic fibrosis: Evolutionary considerations. In K. M. Weiss, ed., Variation in the Human Genome. Chichester: John Wiley and Sons, pp. 9–118.

Kibble, David G. *Is Democracy a Cure for Terrorism? A Review of Natan Sharansky's The Case for Democracy: The Power of Freedom to Overcome Tyranny and Terror:*

Review Essay. Studies in Conflict and Terrorism 29:383-391 June 2006.

Kydd, Andrew and Walter, Barbara F. *The Strategies of Terrorism.* International Security 31:49-80 Summer 2006.

Laremont, Ricardo and Gregorian, Hrach. *Political Islam in West Africa and the Sahel.* Military Review 86:27-36 January-February 2006.

Lentini, Pete and Bakashmar, Muhammad. *Jihadist Beheading: A Convergence of Technology, Theology, and Teleology?* Studies in Conflict and Terrorism 30:303-325 April 2007.

MacMunn, George F., The Armies of India. London: Adam & Charles Black, 1911.

Magnus, Philip, Kitchener: Portrait of an Imperialist. London: John Murray, 1958.

Mascini, Peter. *Can the Violent Jihad Do Without Sympathizers?* Studies in Conflict and Terrorism 29:343-357 June 2006.

Mauritania's Fractious Future. Jane's Islamic Affairs Analyst, pp 12-13, January 2007. "Mauritania is torn between its Arab and African cultural heritages and between Islam and secularist orientations prevalent in society."

Murphy, Martin. *Maritime Terrorism: The Threat in Context.* Jane's Intelligence Review 18:20-25 February 2006.

Muslim Radicals Enlisting US Inmates. Jane's Islamic Affairs Analyst, pp 14-16, January 2007.

Napoleoni, Loretta. *Terrorist Financing: How the New Generation of Jihadists Funds Its Self.* RUSI Journal 151:60-65 February 2006.

Opall-Rome, Barbara. *Blindsided: Failure to Foresee Hamas Victory Was "a Grave Lapse in Situational Awareness".* C4ISR 5:48 April 2006.

Pargeter, Alison. *Western Converts to Radical Islam: The Global Jihad's New Soldiers?* Jane's Intelligence Review 18:20-26 August 2006.

Peters, Ralph. *Lessons from Lebanon: The New Model Terrorist Army.* Armed Forces Journal 144:38-40+ October 2006.

Peters, Ralph. *Rebels and Religion: How Fighters Become Fanatics.* Armed Forces Journal 144:28-31 January 2007.

Record, Jeffrey (December 2003). Bounding the Global War on Terrorism, December 1, 2003 ISBN 1-58487-146-6.

Rizvi, Hasan-Askari, ' "Civil-Military Relations in Contemporary Pakistan"', Survival (Vol. 40, No. 2, Summer 1998), pp. 96-113.

Rizvi, Hasan-Askari, The Military and Politics in Pakistan. Lahore: Progressive Publishers, 1st edition: 1974, latest edition: 1986.

Salik, Siddiq (Brigadier), Witness to Surrender. Karachi: Oxford University Press, 1979.

Saxena, K. M.L., The Military System of India, 1850-1900. New Delhi: Sterling, 1974.

Smelser, Neil J.; *et al.* (2002). *Terrorism: perspectives from the behavioral and social sciences,* National Academies Press, 2002, ISBN 0309086124, 9780309086127

Ticehurst, Rupert. *The Martens Clause and the Laws of Armed Conflict* 30 April 1997, International Review of the Red Cross no 317, p. 125-134 ISSN 1560-7755

U. S. Army (1975). Field Manual: Military Chemistry and Chemical Compounds (FM3-9). Headquarters, Department of the Army, Washington D. C., October.

World Health Organization. Guide to the laboratory diagnosis of smallpox for smallpox eradication programmes. Geneva,: 1969.

World Health Organization. Health aspects of chemical and biological weapons. Report of a WHO Group of Consultants. Geneva,: 1970.

Wyn Rees and Richard J. Aldrich, "Contending Cultures of Counter-terrorism: Transatlantic Convergence or Divergence?", International Affairs, Vol.81, No.5 (October 2005): 905-23.

Zilinskas, Raymond A. "Rethinking Bioterrorism." Current History 100 (2001): 438–443.

Index

I

J

L

M

N